HARDPRESS.NET
HOME OF HARD-TO-FIND BOOKS

The Lake Regions of Central Africa
by Bayard Taylor

Address:
HardPress
8345 NW 66TH ST #2561
MIAMI FL 33166-2626
USA
Email: info@hardpress.net

The lake regions of Central Africa

Bayard Taylor

Newton Bevan.
East Hampton Ct
Hill, First Ward
J. D. Pike

ILLUSTRATED LIBRARY OF TRAVEL AND ADVENTURE

EDITED BY BAYARD TAYLOR

SCRIBNER, ARMSTRONG, & CO., NEW YORK

*ILLUSTRATED LIBRARY OF TRAVEL,
EXPLORATION, AND ADVENTURE.*

THE LAKE REGIONS

OF

CENTRAL AFRICA.

COMPILED AND ARRANGED BY

BAYARD TAYLOR.

WITH MAP AND NUMEROUS ILLUSTRATIONS.

NEW YORK:
SCRIBNER, ARMSTRONG, AND CO.
1874.

RIVERSIDE, CAMBRIDGE:
PRINTED BY H. O. HOUGHTON AND COMPANY.

CONTENTS.

CONTENTS.

CHAPTER IX.

CONTENTS.

CHAPTER XX.

CHAPTER XXL

CHAPTER XXII.

CHAPTER XXIII.

CHAPTER XXIV.

CHAPTER XXV.

LIST OF ILLUSTRATIONS.

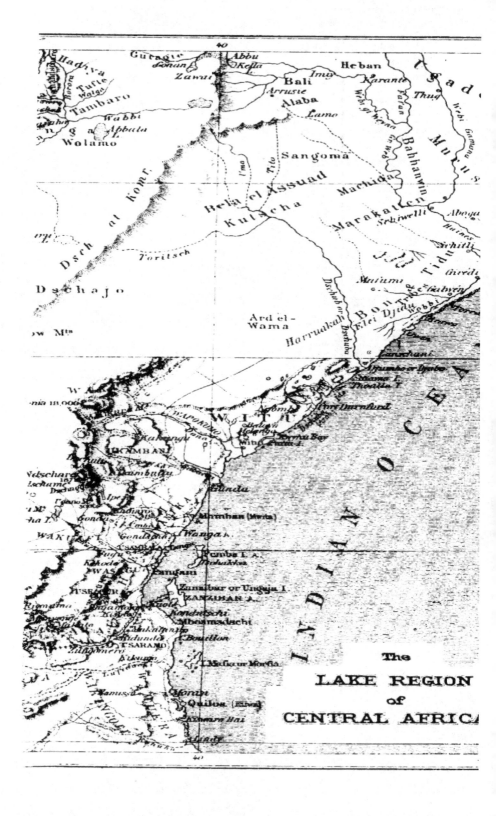

The
LAKE REGION
of
CENTRAL AFRICA

THE LAKE REGIONS

OF

CENTRAL AFRICA.

CHAPTER I.

FIRST ATTEMPTS AT EXPLORATION.

WHAT is now known as the "Lake Regions of Central Africa," appears to have been also known to the ancient Egyptians, though probably rather from report than from actual explorations. The descriptions of the course of the Nile, given both by Herodotus and Eratosthenes, can only be identified as far as the River Sobat, in latitude 9° N., and from the time of the Cæsars until quite recently, the sources of the great African river seemed to be veiled in impenetrable mystery. Yet it is evident, from the ruins at Meroë, and those at Naga, near the modern Khartoum, that Egyptian civilization extended to the junction of the White and Blue Niles, and possibly some distance beyond that point ; while the former branch afforded a direct and easy communication with the regions further south, almost to the equator.

The map of the geographer Ptolemy (in the second century) represents the Nile as flowing from two large lakes, lying on and extending to the southward of the equator. This map, which was published in Rome in 1508, and is partly included in the chart of Africa given in " Purchas's Pilgrims," (1625,) is incorrect in many details, but the correctness of its main features has been verified by the latest discoveries. The Mountains of the Moon, which Ptolemy places between these lakes and the Indian Ocean, were long supposed to be a myth; but the discovery of those mountains, and the tableland of Unia-mezi, (The Land of the Moon,) preceded that of the lakes lying beyond, and the connection of the Nile with the lakes followed, completely verifying the report of the old Egyptian geographer.

Rumors of large lakes, lying in the interior of Equatorial Africa, were first received, in modern times, through the Portuguese. The existence of Lake Nyassa, for instance, was well known long before it had been visited by any European traveller, and many maps of Africa, published in the early part of the present century, contain a conjectured outline of it, (usually much larger than the reality,) under the name of Maravi—a name which really belongs to the tableland to the westward of it.

The Portuguese traveller, Lacerda, who left Tete, on the Zambesi River, in 1797, at the head of an exploring party, and reached the capital of the kingdom of Cazembe the following year, where he died, probably saw Lake Nyassa, and must have heard of the existence of Lake Tanganyika—since the country of Cazembe lies to the westward of the latter lake, between it and the Moluwa country, visited by Magyar and skirted by Livingstone.) The two interior kingdoms, in fact, have been sometimes confounded. Lacerda's manuscripts, until recently, were lying unpublished in the Government archives, at Lisbon ; and at the present time (1872) Captain Burton, the discoverer of Lake Tanganyika, is endeavoring to raise a fund for the purpose of having them translated and published in England.

Two German missionaries, Krapp and Rebmann, who were stationed at Mombas, on the Zanzibar coast, learned, through their intercourse with the natives, of the existence of high mountains, covered with snow, in the interior ; and, in the year 1850, the former succeeded in penetrating far enough to attain a distant view of the great peak of Kilimandjaro, the height of which has since been estimated at 20,000 feet above the sea. Although Dr. Krapp, in subsequent journeys, did not reach the mountain range, he established its existence, with the fact that the peaks of Kilimandjaro and Kenia (the latter supposed to be a volcano) rose above the limit of perpetual snow. He also brought reports of a large lake beyond the mountains, and waters flowing northward, which he conjectured to be the sources of the Nile.

Baron van der Decken, of Holland, devoted himself with singular enthusiasm to the task of reaching Kilimandjaro ; but after spending large sums of money, and giving several years to his repeated efforts, he only succeeded in reaching an elevation of about 13,000 feet, on the slopes of the great mountain, and was soon afterwards murdered by the natives.   The romantic interest which these rediscovered Mountains of the Moon possessed for his mind led him to neglect opportunities of more extensive exploration, which, with the means at his command, he might have attempted with a fairer chance of success.

Lake Tanganyika must have been known, for a long time past, to the Arab traders of Zanzibar. They were not likely, however, to give much voluntary information, and the actual exploration of the region might have been long delayed, but for the interest excited among geographers by the discoveries of Krapp and Rebmann, and the simultaneous attempt to reach the source of the White Nile, which, at that time, had been followed to the parallel of 5° N., where it was still navigable and of such a volume as to suggest that its fountains were south of the Equator.

It is true that the first attempt made to reach the interior from Zanzibar occurred a few years earlier ; but it was so immediately unfortunate as to have deterred all later explorers from venturing on the same ground, without the new stimulus given to them by the reports of the Nile lakes.   M. Maizan, a midshipman in the French navy, conceived the

idea of penetrating into the African continent,
while cruising along the eastern coast, in 1843.
On returning to France, his project was approved
by the Government ; he returned to Zanzibar, where
he spent eight months in studying the language of
the coast tribes. During this time he made preparations, of a somewhat ostentatious character, contrary to the advice of the foreign residents ; and at
last, fearful of being recalled, started on his expedition without waiting for the escort with which
the Sultan had promised to furnish him.

Landing at Bagamoyo, on the mainland, opposite
Zanzibar, in the autumn of 1845, he left there his
private guard of forty armed men, and pressed forward, accompanied by only a few followers, to visit
the chief of the Wákámbá tribe, at a village called
Dega la Mhora, about twenty-seven miles from the
coast. He was received with treacherous cordiality,
and hospitably entertained by the chief for some
days. The latter then suddenly pretended that
M. Maizan had given richer presents to the other
chiefs than to himself, had him seized and bound
by a crowd of natives who were lying in wait, and
then cut him to pieces. The savage was disappointed in his hope of plunder, and the consequences of the murder were felt by him and his
tribe for years afterwards. The French Government sent a frigate to Zanzibar, to demand punish-
ment for the deed, although the native tribe was
not subject to the Sultan. The latter, nevertheless,
was forced to send an armed expedition to the

place; a skirmish ensued, the chief's son was wounded, and one of the natives concerned in the murder was captured and bronght to Zanzibar, where he remained for two years, chained in front of the French consulate.

Moreover, the direct route to the interior through the village of Dega la Mhora was for a long time avoided by the natives, who believed that the ghost of the murdered traveller haunted it in the form a terrible dragon, and the savage chief himself, tormented by the same spirit, withdrew into a kind of exile. Thus the deed gradually avenged itself, and this first sacrifice helped, in the end, to make the route safer for the European explorers who followed.

CHAPTER II.

AFTER Captain Burton's successful journey to
Medina and Mecca,* in 1853, his passion for exploration instigated him to seek new fields in which
his unusual qualifications might be of service.
His military duties in India interfered with his
more ambitious plans, for a time ; but, having obtained a brief leave of absence towards the close of
1854, he landed on the Somali coast of Africa, near
the mouth of the Red Sea, and in his assumed character of an Arab merchant, succeeded in reaching
the independent Mahometan city of Harar, in January, 1855. He was not only the first European who
visited this singular colony, but the first to give an
exact description of its situation and history.

Harar is a petty state, about 175 miles inland
from the port of Zeyla, on the coast. It was founded by Arab invaders, who in the seventh century
conquered and colonized the region lying between
the Gulf of Aden and the Abyssinian mountains.

---

* *Vide* "Travels in Arabia," Vol. III. of the " Illustrated Library of Travel, Exploration and Adventure.''

The state has now shrunk to very small proportions—the greater part of the territory having been re-conquered by the Gallas—and the capital city has a population of about 8,000. It is situated on a table-land, 5,500 feet above the sea, whence the climate is dry, temperate and healthy. The city, which is a mile in length by half a mile in breadth, is inclosed by an irregular wall, built of granite or freestone, with occasional towers for defence, and five large gates. The private residences of the better classes of citizens are of stone, and two stories in height; the poorer people inhabit thatched huts.

Harar has a large mosque, and many smaller ones, and enjoys a high reputation throughout Mahometan Africa, for its sanctity. Its school of Moslem theology is still kept up, though the language spoken by the people is an Arabic much corrupted by native African dialects. It has also some literature of its own, mostly songs and stories. The people show in their bodies the same mixture of descent as in their language : the men are coarse and unprepossessing in their appearance, with a dark, treacherous expression of the face, while the women are more regular in their features and agreeable in their manners. They are yellow in complexion, and fond of brilliant colors in their dress, immoral in their habits, and very fierce, bigoted and suspicious of strangers. Burton's undertaking was one of great hardship and peril, when we consider the limited amount of territory which he traversed.

His narrative of the journey was published in 1856, under the title of "First Footsteps in East Africa."

On reaching England, however, and before the publication of this work, Captain Burton made a proposition to the council of the Royal Geographical Society, to undertake an expedition for the purpose of ascertaining the limits of the "Sea of Ujiji, or Unyamwezi Lake," and secondarily to report upon the exportable produce of the interior and the ethnography of its tribes. At the same time, the missionary Ehrhardt, who had returned from Mombas, applied to the society for an outfit of a few hundred dollars, in order to strike inland from Quiloa, (or Kilwa,) on the coast, and reach the unknown lake, which he evidently confounded with Lake Nyassa, since the latter was afterwards reached from Quiloa by the German traveller, Dr. Roscher.

This conflict of aims and claims caused some delay, but early in 1856 Burton's proposal was accepted by the Society; the Foreign Office granted £1,000 for the expenses of the exploration, and the Directors of the East India Company allowed him two years of absence. The instructions of the Geographical Society, nevertheless, named Quiloa as the starting-point for the expedition. At that time, nothing was known of the interior, beyond the first mountain-range parallel to the coast, except from the reports of the Arab traders. The country of Unia-mezi, (or Unyamwezi, as Burton calls it), the Land of the Moon, was believed to be inhabited by a branch of the Galla race, very fierce and barbarous in character, for which reason a more southern route was considered advisable.

Burton reached Bombay in November, 1856, and was there joined by Captain Speke, also of the Bombay army, who was appointed surveyor to the expedition. Burton seems to have conceived a singular personal dislike to Speke, almost at the start, and the slighting manner in which he invariably mentions the latter, throughout his narrative, impresses the reader, at last, as an annoyance which might better have been spared.

They reached Zanzibar on the 19th of December, 1856, but were unable to set out on the expedition for nearly six months. Burton convinced himself that the most feasible route was not by way of Quiloa, but by crossing directly to the mainland, opposite Zanzibar, and pushing westward into the interior, on the track of the native traders. Having reached the neighborhood of the unknown region, he found that many features of the plan arranged in London were impracticable, and finally determined to organize his expedition without reference to it. As the favor and assistance of the Sultan of Zanzibar was indispensable, he even avoided meeting Mr. Rebmann, of the Mission at Mombas, since the latter had given offence to the Sultan.

While making these preparations, Burton picked up information from the natives which satisfied him that the " Sea of Ujiji " and the Maravi Lake were two distinct bodies of water ; that the former was much the larger of the two ; and that there was no regular caravan route between them. This confirmed him in his determination to make Zanzibar the starting-point, and endeavor to reach the former lake only. Col. Hamerton, the English consul, proposed that he should be escorted through the dangerous coast tribes by a strong guard furnished by the Sultan, and then left to pursue the ordinary caravan route through the Land of the Moon.

Much time was also required to collect donkeys porters, guides, etc., and to procure the great variety of articles, for supplies, presents, and barter with the native tribes, which were prescribed for a journey of unknown length and emergencies. The jealousy of the traders in Zanzibar interposed many annoying obstacles, and the month of June arrived before all the preparations were completed. Indeed, without the favor of the Sultan of Zanzibar, the expedition could not have been successfully set on foot.

About the middle of June, 1857, a part of the supplies were sent to Bagamoyo, on the mainland, to be forwarded thence by porters to the town of Zungomero, at the foot of the mountains, some 145 miles inland ; while Burton and Speke, with their most important outfit, crossed the broad sea-channel to Kaol, a small village and fortress near the mouth of the Kingani river. Here, after a delay of eight or ten days, the expedition was roughly organized. It consisted of Sayd bin Salim, an officer appointed by the Sultan, who accompanied the travellers very much against his will, and partly consoled himself by taking a wife and four slaves with him ; Bombay and Mabruki, negroes from India ; two Portuguese half-caste servants from Goa ; thirteen Baloch soldiers, commanded by a Jemadàr, furnished by the Sultan ; eight interpreters, guides and " war-men," under an African freeman, named Kidogo ; five donkey-men, thirty-six porters, and a few supernumeraries, making a total of 88 persons.

After a great variety of minor worries, every one of which symbolized a greater trouble to come, all the heterogeneous elements of the party were collected and arranged in a temporary order ; and the travellers finally set their faces towards the unknown interior, on the 28th June. Only a year had elapsed since Livingstone reached the Indian Ocean, after his journey across Southern Africa ; and this was the beginning of a new series of discoveries, only less wonderful than his own.

CHAPTER III.

THE eastern coast of Africa is very low, and lined
with innumerable bays, reefs and lagoons.   The
flat soil of sand and crumbled rock is overgrown
with a dense bed of plants, the result of tropical
suns and abundant rains.   All the creeks and coves
are bordered with forests of mangrove trees ; when
the tide is out, the conical base of branching roots
supporting each tree, rises naked from the ooze,
often covered, at the water-line, with clusters of oys-
ters.   Where the coast rises a little higher above
the ocean level, it is a mass of verdure.   Clusters of
bald old trees, bent by the trade-winds, indicate
the position of native settlements, which, generally
hidden from sight, crowd along the coast like the
suburbs of a populous city.   Four or five miles inland there is an earlier sea margin, where the land
rises a little, making that blue line on the horizon
which is visible from Zanzibar.   The territory of
the native tribes commences here, only the narrow
coast-line being subject to the Arab sultan.
    After all the difficulty of getting his caravan in
motion, Burton only made a march of an hour and

a half to the frontier-village of Bimani, the first
day.   Here he was obliged to halt again, and attempt to reorganize his men.   "In Asia," he says,
" *two* departures usually suffice ; in Africa there
must be three—the little start, the great start, and
the start of the leaders.   Some clamored for tobacco—I gave up my cavendish ; others for guitar-
strings—they were silenced with beads ; and all,
born   donkey-drivers,   complained   loudly   of   the
hardship and indignity of having to load and lead
an ass."   The guide, after receiving twenty dollars,
refused to accompany the expedition, and even the
Baloch soldiers—a name given to the mixed breed
along the coast—began to speak insultingly of the
two European travellers.   In fact, during the subsequent progress of the exploration, there was not
one person attached to the party who did not, at
some time or other, attempt to desert.

The departure from Bimani was effected on the
1st of July, with some trouble ; it was like driving
a herd of wild cattle.   At length, by ejecting skulk-
ers from their huts, by dint of promises and threats,
of gentleness and violence, occasionally backed by
an application of the whip—all these methods employed for nine hours without intermission—the
sluggish and straggling body was set in motion.
After a march of only two miles, they reached a
village where provisions and muddy water were
plentiful, and where, consequently, the caravans are
accustomed to halt, have the weapons polished, and
prepare for encounters with the Wazaramo, as the
native tribes are called.   Here, however, Burton ob-

tained the services of Muinyi Wazírá, the nephew
of the chief, as guide and interpreter.

The next morning they made the final start, getting under way at dawn. "On the wayside appeared for the first time the *Khambi*, or substantial kraals, which give evidence of unsafe travelling
and the unwillingness of caravans to bivouac in the
villages. In this region they assumed the form of
round huts, and long sheds or booths of straw or
grass, supported by a framework of rough sticks
firmly planted in the ground and lashed together
with bark strips. The whole was surrounded with
a deep circle of thorns, which—the entrance or entrances being carefully closed at nightfall, not to
reopen until dawn—formed a complete defence
against bare feet and naked legs."

At the village of Nzasa, the first belonging to the
independent tribes, Burton was met by three p'ha-
zi, or head men of the place.

They came to ascertain whether he was bound
on peaceful errand, or—as the number of the guns
suggested—he was marching to revenge the murder of his "brother," (M. Maizan.) Assured of his
unwarlike intentions, they told him that he must
halt on the morrow and send forward a message
to the next chief. As this plan invariably loses
three days—the first being a *dies non*, the second being expended in dispensing information to all the
lieges squatting in solemn conclave, while on the third
the real message is privily whispered into the
chieftain's ear—Burton replied through Said that
he could not be bound by their rules, but was ready

to pay for their infraction. The proposition was accepted, the head men received a handsome present, and one of them agreed to accompany the party through the territory belonging to the tribe.

The advantage of this arrangement was made evident the very next day. At a village further on, they found the natives drawn up in line across the road, and prepared to dispute their passage. The Baloch were greatly alarmed, but the new guide and interpreter, Muinyi Waziri, with the head man, soon persuaded the natives to fall back and let the caravan pass. In the evening the latter reached a district called Kiranga-Ranga, which was considered dangerous. Before camping, tho Baloch soldiers and a temporary guard sent from the coast, began to quarrel, and thirteen men, led by a *jemadar*, (subaltern officer,) declared their intention of returning immediately. Burton summoned them before him, and wrote in their presence a letter to the Consul, describing their conduct ; thereupon they instantly changed their mind, and decided to remain. The difficulty, however, obliged the caravan to remain a day longer at the place. The weather already began to be unfavorable ; rains set in, and the exhalations from the dense vegetation of this low region invariably produce fevers.

A march of two days further brought the expedition to a place called Muhogive, one of the most dreaded in the whole Uzaramo country. Being thinly inhabited, on account of its malarious climate, it abounds in wild animals. "The guides," says

Burton, " speak of lions, and the cry of the fisi or cynhyena was frequently heard at night, threatening destruction to the asses. The fisi, the wuraba of the Somal, and the wilde honde of the Cape, is the wolf of Africa, common throughout the country, where it acts as scavenger. Though a large and powerful variety, it seldom assaults man, except when sleeping, and then it snatches a mouthful from the face, causing a ghastlier disfigurement even than the scalping of the bear. Three asses belonging to the expedition were destroyed by this beast. In all cases they were attacked by night with a loud wrangling shriek, and the piece of flesh was raggedly torn from the hind quarter. After affording a live rump-steak, they could not be driven like Bruce's far-famed bullock."

Struggling on through the low, unhealthy district, greatly delayed by the difficulty of procuring provisions, they reached, on the 8th of July, what the Arabs call the " Valley of Death and the home of Hunger "—the broad plain traversed by the Kingani River. Here the water was everywhere bad, and a mortal smell of decay was emitted by the dark, wet soil. Speke was already so affected with fever that he was unable to walk. The next day the road was again barred by a band of fifty natives, posted across it ; but they were dispersed by a present, as on the former occasion.

At a place called Tunda, it almost seemed as if the expedition would fail. Burton says : " After a night passed amid the rank vegetation, and within the malarious influence of the river, I arose weak and depressed, with aching head, burning eyes, and throbbing extremities. The new life, the alternations of damp heat and wet cold, the useless fatigue of walking, the sorry labor of waiting and reloading the asses, the exposure to sun and dew, and last, but not least, of morbific influences, the wear and tear of mind at the prospect of imminent failure, all were beginning to tell heavily upon me. My companion had shaken off his preliminary symptoms, but Said bin Salim, attacked during the rainy gusty night by a severe mkunguru or seasoning-fever, begged hard for a halt at Tunda—only for a day— only for half a day—only for an hour. Even this was refused. I feared that Tunda might prove fatal to us."

They fortunately passed the village where M. Maizan was murdered without encountering any difficulty. The next day's march brought them to a camping-place near a small hill, on the banks of the river, beyond which commenced a new region, called K'hutu, which is no longer considered dangerous by the caravans. Although the distance from the coast, by the road, was only 118 miles, the expedition had consumed 18 days in the journey, and was already greatly reduced by sickness and anxiety. Here the route left the main valley of the Kingani River, and followed a southern branch, the Mageta. A range of mountains, called the Duthumi, the summits of which had an altitude of between three and four thousand feet, now appeared in the northwest.

"Resuming our march on the 15th July, we entered the ' Doab,' (tract between two rivers) on the western bank of the Mgeta, where a thick and tangled jungle, with luxuriant and putrescent vegetation, is backed by low, grassy grounds, frequently inundated. Presently, however, the dense thicket opened out into a fine park country, peculiarly rich in game, where the calabash and the giant trees of the sea-board gave way to mimosas, gums, and stunted thorns. Large gnus, whom the porters regard with a wholesome awe, declaring that they are capable of charging a caravan, pranced about, pawing the ground, and shaking their formidable manes ; hartebeest and other antelopes clustered together on the plain, or travelled in herds to slake their thirst at the river. The homely cry of the partridge resounded from the brake, and the guinea-fowls looked like large blue-bells upon the trees. Small land-crabs took refuge in the pits and holes, which made the path a cause of frequent accidents ; while ants of various kinds, crossing the road in close columns, attacked man and beast ferociously, causing the caravan to break into a halting, trotting hobble, ludicrous to behold."

At Kiruru, the first village in this region, they were obliged to wait two days ; then the march was continued through a deep jungle, full of nearly impassable marshes. The fever which had already seized upon the travellers was so much increased by this travel that they were detained a whole week at Duthumi, near the foot of the mountains. Burton was in a semi-delirious state, and Speke had symptoms of sun-stroke. Both were so weak that, while they were scarcely able to walk, they could not bear the fatigue of riding upon asses. Burton's account shows that the African ass must be even more stubborn and intractable than his brethren in other parts of the world. " We had Zanzibar riding-asses, but the delicate animals soon chafed and presently died ; we were then reduced to the koroma or half-reclaimed beast of Wanyamwezi. The laden asses gave us even more trouble. The slaves would not attend to the girthing and the balancing of parcels—the great secret of donkey-loading—consequently the burdens were thrown at every mud or broken ground : the unwilling Baloch only grumbled, sat down and stared, leaving their jemadars with Said bin Salim and ourselves to re-load. My companion and I brought up the rear by alternate days, and sometimes we did not arrive before the afternoon at the camping-ground.

At Duthumi Burton prepared his first report to the Royal Geographical Society, and sent it to the coast with the temporary guard, which it was not considered necessary to retain. Although the goods and supplies with which the caravan started had been much reduced,—the stock for three months having been expended in as many weeks,—there was some consolation in knowing that both the most un-healthy and the most dangerous part of the route was now behind them. Luckily the travellers were provided with hammocks slung to poles, in which, carried by the native porters, they set forward again on the 24th of July. After two days more, through jungles where the earth constantly emitted a fetid odor, like that of decaying animal-matter, they reached the chief caravan station of Zungomero, at the foot of the first ranges of mountains.

This is the great centre of traffic for the eastern region. It lies upon the main route to the interior, communicating also with Quiloa on the coast, and during the caravan season, several thousand men pass through it every week. Burton found several companies encamped there, with their piles of ivory and crowds of porters. The place is on a plain of immensely fertile black soil, nearly enclosed by mountains. The air is very close and damp, soon corroding metal and reducing paper to a pulp : a prolonged halt always causes much sickness in a caravan. Moreover, provisions are not abundant, and proportionately dear. Burton's plan, therefore, was to move on as soon as possible ; but he was first obliged to procure additional porters, and he was daily expecting the arrival of the additional stock of goods, which were to have been forwarded from Bagamoya.

Here, reviewing his route, he gives the following account of the geography and population of what he calls the maritime region of Eastern Africa : "The first, or maritime region, extends from the shores of the Indian Ocean in E. long. 39° to the mountain chain forming the land of Usagara in E. long. 37° 28' ; its breadth is therefore 92 geographical miles, measured in rectilinear distance, and its mean length, bounded by the waters of the Kingani and the Rufiji Rivers, may be assumed at 110. The average rise is under four feet per mile. It is divided into two basins; that of the Kingani easterly, and westward that of the Mgeta stream, with its many tributaries; the former, which is the principal, is called the land of Uzaramo; the latter, which is of the second order, contains the province of K'hutu, by the Arabs pronounced Kutu, and Uziraha, a minor district. The natives of the country divide it into the three lowlands of Tunda, Dut'humi, and Zungomero.

"The present road runs, with few and unimportant deviations, along the whole length of the fluviatile valleys of the Kingani and the Mgeta. Native caravans, if lightly laden, generally accomplish the march in a fortnight, one halt included. On both sides of this line, whose greatest height above the sea-level was found to be 330 feet, rises the rolling ground, which is the general character of the country. Its undulations present no eminences worthy of notice; near the sea they are short and steep, farther inland they roll in longer waves, and everywhere they are covered with abundant and luxuriant vegetation, the result of decomposition upon the richest soil. In parts there is an appearance of park land; bushless and scattered forests, with grass rising almost to the lower branches of the smaller thorns; here and there clumps and patches of impassable shrubbery cluster round knots and knolls of majestic and thickly-foliaged trees. The narrow foot-paths connecting the villages often plunge into dark and dense tunnels, formed by overarching branch and bough, which delay the file of laden porters; the mud lingering long after a fall of rain in these low grounds fills them with a chilly, clammy atmosphere. Merchants traverse such spots with trembling : in these, the proper places for ambuscade, a few determined men easily plunder a caravan by opposing it in front, or by an attack in rear.

" The climate is hot and oppressive, and the daily sea-breeze, which extends to the head of the Mgeta valley, is lost in the lower levels. About Zungomero rain is constant, except for a single fortnight in the month of January ; it seems to the stranger as if the crops must infallibly decay, but they do not. At most times the sun, even at its greatest northern declination, shines through a veil of mist with a sickly blaze and a blistering heat, and the overcharge of electricity is evidenced by frequent and violent thunderstorms. In the western parts cold and cutting breezes descend from the rugged crags of Dut'humi.

" The negroids of this region are able-bodied men, tall and straight, compared with the coast-clans, but they are inferior in development to most of the inner tribes. The complexion, as usual, varies greatly. The chiefs are often coal-black, and but few are of light color. This arises from the country being a slave-importer rather than exporter ; and here, as among the Arabs, black skins are greatly preferred. The Mzaramo never circumcises, except when becoming a Moslem convert ; nor does this tribe generally tattoo, though some adorn the face with three long cicatrized cuts, like Mashali of Mecca, extending down each cheek from the ear-

lobes to the corners of the mouth. Their distinctive
mark is the peculiarity of dressing their hair. The
thick wool is plastered over with a cap-like coating
of ochreish and micaceous clay, brought from the
hills, and mixed to the consistency of honey with
the oil of the sesamum or the castor-bean. The
pomatum, before drying, is pulled out with the
fingers, to the ends of many little twists, which circle the head horizontally, and the mass is separated
into a single or a double line of knobs, the upper
being above and the lower below the ears.

"The habitations of the Wazaramo, who inhabit the region nearer the sea, are far superior in
shape and size to those of K'hutu, and, indeed, to
any on this side of Unyamwezi. Their buildings
generally resemble the humbler sort of English
cow-house, or an Anglo-Indian bungalow. In
poorer houses the outer walls are of holcus canes,
rudely puddled; the better description are built of
long and broad sheets of bark, propped against
strong uprights inside, and bound horizontally by
split bamboos, tied outside with fibrous cord. The
heavy pent-shaped roof, often provided with a double thatch of grass and reeds, projects eaves, which
are high enough to admit a man without stooping;
these are supported by a long cross-bar resting
on perpendiculars, tree-trunks, barked and smoothed,
forked above, and firmly planted in the ground.
Along the outer marginal length of this veranda
lies a border of large logs polished by long sit-
tings. The interior is dark and windowless, and

party-walls of stiff grass-cane divide it into several compartments.

"The Wazaramo are an ill-conditioned, noisy,
boisterous, violent and impracticable race. A few
years ago they were the principal obstacle to Arab
and other travellers entering into East Africa.
But the seizure of Kaole and other settlements by
the late Sultan Sayyid of Zanzibar has now given
strangers a footing in the land. After tasting the
sweets of gain, they have somewhat relented; but
quarrels between them and the caravans are still
frequent. The p'házi, or chief of the district, demands a certain amount of cloth for free passage
from all merchants on their way to the interior;
from those returning he takes cattle, jembe, or iron
hoes, shokah or hatchets, in fact, whatever he can
obtain. If not contented, his clansmen lie in ambush and discharge a few poisoned arrows at the
trespassers: they never have attempted, like the
Wagogo, to annihilate a caravan; in fact, the loss
of one of their number causes a general panic."

Two singular customs prevail among these tribes.
The first is that of adopted *brotherhood*, which has
some resemblance to a former custom in Scotland,
and one which is still found in some parts of India. It seems to spring from a natural social passion in the human race, as a partial remedy for the
feuds and discords of savage life. "In fact," says
Burton, "it is a contrivance for choosing relations
instead of allowing Nature to force them upon
man, and the flimsiness of the tie between brothers
born in polygamy has doubtless tended to perpet-

uate it. The ceremony, which is confined to adults of the male sex, is differently performed in the different tribes. Among the Wazaramo, the Wazegura, and the Wasagara, the two 'brothers' sit on a hide face to face, with the legs outstretched to the front and overlapping one another ; their bows and arrows are placed across their thighs ; while a third person, waving a sword over their heads, vociferates curses against any one that may 'break the brotherhood.' A sheep is then slaughtered, and its flesh, or more often its heart, is brought roasted to the pair, who, having made with a dagger incisions in each other's breasts close to the pit of the stomach, eat a piece of meat smeared with the blood. Among the Wanyamwezi and the Wajiji the cut is made below the left ribs or above the knee. Each man receives in a leaf his brother's blood, which, mixed with oil or butter, he rubs into his own wound. An exchange of small presents generally concludes the rite. It is a strong tie, as all men believe that death or slavery would follow its infraction. The Arabs, to whom the tasting of blood is unlawful, usually perform it by proxy. The slave 'fundi,' or fattori, of the caravans, become brothers, even with the Washenzi, whenever they expect an opportunity of utilizing the relationship.

"The second custom is more peculiar. The East African dares not appropriate an article found upon the road, especially if he suspect that it belongs to a fellow-tribeman. He believes that a 'kigámbo,' an unexpected calamity, slavery or

death, would follow the breach of this custom. At
Zungomero, a watch, belonging to the expedition,
was picked up by the country people in the jungle, and was punctually returned, well wrapped
round with grass and leaves. But subsequent experience makes the traveller regret that the superstition is not of a somewhat more catholic and
comprehensive character."

CHAPTER IV.

THE expedition halted two weeks at Zungomero, to await the arrival of supplies from the coast, and to obtain twenty-two porters who had been promised for the journey across the mountain ranges. It was the height of the rainy season, and the place was a hot-bed of pestilence. The travellers were lodged in a native hut, the roof of which was like a sieve, and the floor was a sheet of mud. This halt was demoralizing to the native guards and porters, and there was a repetition of the difficulties which had accompanied the first start of the caravan.

When the necessary natives had at last been collected and organized, the party numbered 132 individuals. On the 7th of August they left Zungomero and set out for the first ascent of the Usagara Mountains, now only distant a journey of five hours. Burton and Speke were so reduced by miasmatic fever that they could scarce sit upon the riding-asses, and their hearing, even, was much impaired. Crossing the M'geta River, they worked their way through the dense vegetation of the plain, and in three hours reached the commencement of a dry, open region. Here the slaves and porters had already housed themselves for the night, but they were dislodged and made to advance. In the afternoon the caravan ascended the first slant of the mountains, rising three or four hundred feet, and reached a station called Mzizi Mdogo, or "the little tamarind," to distinguish it from "the great tamarind," which lies further in the mountains. There was no vestige of building upon the spot; no sight nor sound of man; the blood-feud and the slave-trade had made desert of the land. They found, however, a hut erected by a former caravan, and encamped upon the spot.

Two of the laden asses had gone astray during the day, and when they were recovered, the salt and sugar had melted away, from their baths in the river; soap, cigars, and other articles were reduced to a paste, tea and gunpowder were spoiled, and even vegetables in water-tight cans became musty. On the other hand, there was much to console them in their troubles: "There was a wondrous change of climate at Mzizi Mdogo; strength and health returned as if by magic; even the Goanese shook off the obstinate bilious remittents of Zungomero. Truly delicious was the escape from the nebulous skies, the fog-driving gusts, the pelting rain, the clammy mists veiling a gross growth of fetor, the damp raw cold, rising as it were from the earth, and the alternations of fiery and oppressive heat; in fact, from the cruel climate of the river-valley, to the pure sweet mountain-air, alternately soft and

balmy, cool and reviving, and to the aspect of clear
blue skies, which lent their tints to highland ridges
well wooded with various greens.   Dull mangrove,
dismal jungle, and monotonous grass, were supplanted by tall solitary trees, among which the
lofty tamarind rose conspicuously graceful, and a
card-table-like swamp, cut by a net-work of streams,
nullahs, and stagnant pools, gave way to dry healthy
slopes, with short steep pitches and gently shelving
hills.   The beams of the large sun of the equator—
and nowhere have I seen the rulers of night and
day so large—danced gayly upon blocks and pebbles
of red, yellow, and dazzling snowy quartz, and the
bright sea-breeze waved the summits of trees, from
which depended graceful llianas, and wood-apples
large as melons, while creepers, like vine tendrils,
rising from large bulbs of brown-gray wood, clung
closely to their stalwart trunks.   Monkeys played at
hide-and-seek, chattering behind the bolls, as the
iguana, with its painted scale-armor, issued forth
to bask upon the sunny bank; white-breasted
ravens cawed when disturbed from their perching-
places; doves cooed on the well-clothed boughs,
and hawks soared high in the transparent sky.   The
field-cricket chirped like the Italian cigala in the
shady bush, and everywhere, from air, from earth,
from the hill slopes above, and from the marshes
below, the hum, the buzz, and the loud continuous
voice of insect life, through the length of the day
spoke out its natural joy.   Our gipsy encampment
lay

" By shallow rivers,' to whose falls
Melodious birds sing madrigals."

" By night, the soothing murmurs of the stream at the hill's base rose mingled with the faint rustling of the breeze, which, at times broken by the scream of the night-heron, the bellow of the bull-frog in his swampy home, the cynhyena's whimper, and the fox's whining bark, sounded through the silence most musical, most melancholy. Instead of the cold night rain, and the soughing of the blast, the view disclosed a peaceful scene, the moonbeams lying like sheets of snow upon the ruddy highlands, and the stars hanging like lamps of gold from the dome of infinite blue. I never wearied with contemplating the scene, for, contrasting with the splendors around me, still stretched in sight the Slough of Despond, unhappy Zungomero, lead-colored above, mud-colored below, wind-swept, fog-veiled, and deluged by clouds that dared not approach these delectable mountains."

After halting a day at this spot they pushed on over a succession of short, steep hills, dotted with clumps of tamarinds, aloes and thorny bushes. Along the path lay the skeletons, and even recent corpses, of porters who had perished of fatigue or starvation. A caravan which had lost fifty of its number from small-pox passed them, communicating the infection to a few of Burton's party, who halted at the lonely huts or tents set apart for those affected with the disease, and were never heard of afterwards.

Two more days were occupied in passing the first range of hills and the broken country beyond. The journey was very toilsome, on account of the frequent necessity of unloading the asses in order to cross the ravines and dry river-beds. The little beehive villages of the natives were visible all around, peeping out from the forests on the hillsides, but the country immediately bordering the road was deserted. For this reason it was almost impossible to procure provisions.

On the 12th of August they crossed a second range, the summit of which was 2,235 feet above the level of the sea. Rations had been issued to the natives for three days, but, with their usual improvidence, they had consumed everything as soon as possible, and were still a long day's journey distant from a place called Muhama, where the first supplies could be obtained. But, after a toilsome march which lasted the whole day, the native leader, Kidogo, led the caravan astray, and they were compelled to return some distance and camp at a little village called Zonhwe, where, by sending men out into the country in all directions, a partial supply of provisions was finally procured. This was the turning-point of the difficulties of the expedition. The Baloch guard revolted, making additional claims for their services, which Burton refused. Then they went off in a body, declaring they would return to Zanzibar. The natives promised to be faithful, although they also—as Burton afterwards discovered—had made up their minds to desert. Burton and Speke, however, had determined, in case of necessity, to bury their baggage, and push forward alone, accompanied only by the porters from Unyamwezi, the Land of the Moon. They therefore refused to submit to the new exactions which were attempted; the Baloch and their officers left the camp, and the remainder of the party, after a detention of three days at Zonhwe, started for the mountains.

About noon the next day the deserters suddenly made their appearance, submissive and penitent. They were now compelled to resume their services on the former terms, and Burton's independence on this occasion prevented a repetition of the same troubles. Muhama was reached the same evening, and after a halt there of three days to lay in a good stock of provisions, the expedition set out to cross a wide deserted tract of land which intervened between the place and the next range of mountains. For three days they travelled through an undulating region, sometimes interrupted by deep and difficult gullies, or the low, malarious beds of streams; sometimes a beautiful open park, where herds of zebras and antelopes grazed under the trees, and then a jungle of decaying reeds and exasperating thorns. At a place called Mbumi, they found a village which had been plundered and ruined only ten days before, apparently by some Arab slave-hunter.

On the 24th of August they reached the valley of the Mukondokwa River, a northern affluent of the Kingani. "The path was slippery with mud, and man and beast were rendered wild by the cruel stings of a small red ant and a huge black pismire. The former cross the road in dense masses, like the close columns of an army. They are large-headed, showing probably that they are the defenders of the republic, and that they perform the duties of soldiers in their excursions. Though they cannot spring, they show great quickness in fastening themselves to the foot or ankle as it brushes over them. The pismire, known to the people as the 'chungufundo,' is a horse-ant, about an inch in length, whose bull-dog-like head and powerful mandibles enable it to destroy rats and mice, lizards and snakes. It loves damp places upon the banks of rivers and stagnant waters; it burrows but never raises hills, and it appears scattered for miles over the paths. Like the other species, it knows neither fear nor sense of fatigue; it rushes to annihilation without hesitating, and it cannot be expelled from a hut except by fire or boiling water. Its bite, which is the preamble to its meal, burns like a pinch with a red-hot needle; and when it sets to work, twisting itself round and 'accroupi' in its eagerness for food, it may be pulled in two without relaxing its hold. The favorite food of this pismire is the termite : its mortal enemy is a large ginger-colored ant, called from its painful wound 'maji m'oto,' or 'hot-water.' In this foul jungle our men also suffered severely from the tzetze. This fly, the torment of Cape travellers, was limited, by Dr. Livingstone, to the regions south of the Zambezi River. A specimen brought home by me and submitted to Mr. Adam White, of the British Museum, was pro-

nounced by him to be a true *Glossina morsitans,* and
Mr. Petherick has fixed its limits about eight degrees
north of the equator."

They forded the river and camped in the low, damp
valley. The next morning, crippled by the night-
cold that rose from the water, and then wet through
by the chilly dew which dripped from the tall
jungle-grass, they traversed some fields of newly-
reaped grain and tobacco, and heard the frightened owners calling to each other from the neighboring hills. The path led up the valley of the
Mukondokwa, traversing broad marshes, and occasionally passing over the shoulders of stony hills.
The country was almost entirely depopulated, and
the parties sent out in search of provisions found
the people drawn up in battle array, to repel them.
The asses diminished in number, succumbing to
the hardships of the journey, and the natives suffered very much from the raw wind and chilly cold,
the result not of low temperature, but of humidity
and rapid evaporation.

Finally, on the 29th of August, the caravan
reached Rumuma, a favorite resting-place for
traders, on account of the comparative abundance
of its supplies. They halted there two days to
rest and feed the starving porters, and to repair
the sacks, pack-saddles and other articles. Here,
for the first time, the country people came in crowds
from the hills, bringing fowls, hauling along small,
but beautifully-formed goats, lank sheep and fine
bullocks, and carrying on their heads baskets full
of beans and ground-nuts. The climate of the

place is distinguished by its extremes. At night the thermometer, under the influence of dew and wind, sank to 48°, a killing temperature in those latitudes for half-naked and houseless men; while during the day the mercury ranged between 80° and 90°, with a fiery sun and strong south winds.

The natives of the region are described by Burton as " short, black, beardless men. They wear their hair combed off the forehead, and twisted into a fringe of little pig-tails, which extend to the nape of the neck. Few boast of cloth, the general body contenting themselves with a goatskin flap somewhat like a cobbler's apron tied over one shoulder, as we sling a game-bag. Their ornaments are zinc and brass ear-rings in rolls, which distend the ear-lobe, bangles, or armlets of similar metal, and iron chains with oblong links as anklets. Their arms are bows and arrows, assegais with long lanceated heads, and bull-hide shields three feet long by one broad, painted black and red in perpendicular stripes. I was visited by their Sultan Njasa, a small grizzled old man, with eyes reddened by liquor, a wide mouth, a very thin beard, a sooty skin, and long straggling hair, ' *à la malcontent.*' He was attired in an antiquated barsati, or blue and red Indian cotton, tucked in at the waist, with another thrown over his shoulders, and his neck was decked with many strings of beads. He insisted upon making 'sare' or brotherhood with Said bin Salim, who, being forbidden by his law to taste blood, made the unconscientious Muinyi Wazira his proxy."

On the 2nd of September the travellers reached another halting-place, near a spring of brackish water. The road lay through a plain which separates the second range from the Rubeho, or third and highest range of the mountains. The medium elevation of this plain is about 2,500 feet, which raises it above the fever-level; the dew diminishes, the fierce extremes of temperature disappear, and rain seldom falls heavily. Water, however, is scarce, and the caravans adopt the habit of starting at midday, and marching during the hours of greatest heat, in order to shorten the next morning's march to a watering-place. After camping one night in the thorny jungle, and hastening onward all the next day, the caravan rested in the valley of Iuenge, at the very foot of the Rubeho, or " Windy " Mountains.

In this basin, under the heights, the temperatures of day and night were again extreme, but the neighboring people brought in abundant supplies, including milk, butter, and honey. The next morning a caravan of 400 porters from the interior arrived, on their way to the sea, and Burton was enabled to procure some fresh supplies from the Arab merchants, together with asses and a few native porters. The merchants, moreover, kindly waited a few days to superintend Burton's preparations for crossing the Rubeho range; they gave useful hints for keeping the caravan together at places famous for desertion, and gave much valuable information in regard to travel in the interior. Burton took advantage of their departure to Zanzibar, to propose that the

four most intractable members of his Baloch guard
should be sent back with them, but the latter, with
many protestations of fidelity, refused to make use
of the opportunity.   Dispatches for the Royal Geographical Society were also prepared at this place,
and nothing remained but to make a new start and
overcome the final barrier between the dangerous
coast region and the unknown Land of the Moon.

" The great labor still remained.   Trembling with
ague, with swimming heads, ears deafened by weakness, and limbs that would hardly support us, we
contemplated with a dogged despair the apparently
perpendicular path that ignored a zigzag, and the
ladders of root and boulder, hemmed in with tangled vegetation, up which we and our starving,
drooping asses were about to toil.   On the 10th of
September we hardened our hearts, and began to
breast the Pass Terrible.   My companion was so
weak that he required the aid of two or three supporters; I, much less unnerved, managed with one.
After rounding in two places wall-like sheets of rock
—at their bases green grass and fresh water were
standing close to camp, and yet no one had driven
the donkeys to feed—and crossing a bushy jungly
step, we faced a long steep of loose white soil and
rolling stones, up which we could see the Wanyamwezi porters swarming, more like baboons scaling a
precipice than human beings, and the asses falling
after every few yards.   As we moved slowly and
painfully forward, compelled to lie down by cough,
thirst, and fatigue, the 'sayhah' or war-cry rang
loud from hill to hill, and Indian files of archers and

spearmen streamed like lines of black ants in all
directions down the paths. The predatory Wahumba, awaiting the caravan's departure, had seized the
opportunity of driving the cattle and plundering the
villages of Inenge. Two passing parties of men,
armed to the teeth, gave us this information; whereupon the negro 'Jelai' proposed, fear-maddened, a
sauve qui peut—leaving to their fate his employers,
who, bearing the mark of Abel in this land of Cain,
were ever held to be the head and front of all
offence. Khudabakhsh, the brave of braves, being
attacked by a slight fever, lay down, declaring himself unable to proceed, moaned like a bereaved
mother, and cried for drink like a sick girl. The
rest of the Baloch, headed by the jemadar, were in
the rear; they levelled their matchlocks at one of
the armed parties as it approached them, and, but
for the interference of Kidogo, blood would have
been shed.

" By resting after every few yards, and by cling-
ing to our supporters, we reached, after about six
hours, the summit of the Pass Terrible, and there
we sat down among the aromatic flowers and bright
shrubs—the gift of mountain dews—to recover
strength and breath. My companion could hardly
return an answer; he had advanced mechanically
and almost in a state of coma. The view from the
summit appeared eminently suggestive, perhaps un-
usually so, because disclosing a retrospect of severe
hardships, now past and gone. Below the foreground of giant fractures, huge rocks, and detached
boulders, emerging from a shaggy growth of moun-

tain vegetation, with forest glens and hanging woods, black with shade gathering in the steeper folds, appeared, distant yet near, the tawny basin of Inenge, dotted with large square villages, streaked with lines of tender green, that denoted the water-courses, mottled by the shadows of flying clouds, and patched with black where the grass had been freshly fired. A glowing sun gilded the canopy of dense smoke which curtained the nearer plain, and in the background the hazy atmosphere painted with its azure the broken wall of hill which we had traversed on the previous day.

"Somewhat revived by the *tramontana* which rolled like an ice-brook down the Pass, we advanced over an easy step of rolling ground, decked with cactus and the flat-topped mimosa, with green grass and bright shrubs, to a small and dirty camp, in a hollow flanked by heights, upon which several settlements appeared. At this place, called the 'Great Rubeho,' in distinction from its western neighbor, I was compelled to halt." Speke had become delirious from fever, but fortunately recovered sufficiently to push on the next day. An ascent almost as difficult as the first pass led to the dividing-ridge of the mountains, 5,700 feet above the sea.

On this ridge there was a small village of thievish natives. The caravan was delayed there a whole day, at great inconvenience, since all the water had to be carried from the ravines below. Burton's men had furious quarrels with other parties, on account of the danger of infection from small-pox, and it was with great difficulty that any of the natives could be persuaded to carry Speke in a hammock slung to a pole.

" On the 14th of September," Burton continues, " our tempers being sensibly cooled by the weather, we left the hill-top and broke ground upon the counter-slope or landward descent of the Usagara Mountains. Following a narrow footpath that wound along the hill-flanks, on red earth growing thick clumps of cactus and feathery mimosa, after forty-five minutes' march we found a kraal in a swampy green gap, bisected by a sluggish rivulet that irrigated scanty fields of grain, gourds, and watermelons, the property of distant villagers. For the first time since many days I had strength enough to muster the porters and to inspect their loads. The outfit, which was expected to last a year, had been half exhausted in three months. I summoned Said bin Salim, and passed on to him my anxiety. Like a veritable Arab, he declared, without the least emotion, that we had enough to reach Unyanyembe, where we certainly should be joined by the escort of twenty-two porters. ' But how do you know that ?' I inquired. ' Allah is all-knowing,' replied Said ; ' but the caravan *will* come.' Such fatalism is infectious. I ceased to think upon the subject.

" On the 15th, after sending forward the luggage, and waiting as agreed upon for the return of the porters to carry my companion, I set out about noon, through hot sunshine tempered by the cool hill-breeze. Emerging from the grassy hollow, the path skirted a well-wooded hill and traversed a small savanna, overgrown with stunted straw and hedged in by a bushy forest. At this point massive trees, here single, there in holts and clumps, foliaged more gloomily than church-yard yews, and studded with delicate pink flowers, rose from the tawny sun-burned expanse around, and defended from the fiery glare braky rings of emerald shrubbery, sharply defined as if by the forester's hand. The savanna extended to the edge of a step, which, falling deep and steep, suddenly disclosed to view, below and far beyond the shaggy ribs and the dark ravines and folds of the foreground, the plateau of Ugogo and its eastern desert. The spectacle was truly impressive. The vault above seemed 'an ample æther,' raised by its exceeding transparency higher than it is wont to be. Up to the curved rim of the western horizon, lay, burnished by the rays of a burning sun, plains rippled like a yellow sea by the wavy reek of the dancing air, broken toward the north by a few detached cones rising island-like from the surface, and zebra'd with long black lines, where bush and scrub and strip of thorn jungle, supplanted upon the water-courses, trending in mazy net-work southward to the Rwaha River, the scorched grass and withered cane-stubbles, which seemed to be the staple growth of the land. There was nothing of effeminate or luxuriant beauty, nothing of the flush and fullness characterizing tropical nature, in this first aspect of Ugogo. It appeared, what it is, stern and wild—the rough nurse of rugged men—and perhaps the anticipation of dangers and difficulties ever present to the minds of those preparing to endure the waywardness of its children, contributed not a little to the fascination of the scene."

There was another forced halt of a day on the western declivity of the mountains ; then, resuming the march, the path fell into a deep glen, down which the caravan wandered until night, finally encamping among the rocks. A march of fours hours more, on the 18th, brought them to the plains of Ugogo, the point beyond which the Arab merchants of Zanzibar had predicted they would be unable to penetrate. Here the tent was pitched under a group of mimosas, and all members of the party prepared for a brief rest, new supplies, new disputes and difficulties.

From Burton's account of this second or mountain region, and the tribes who inhabit it, we take the following particulars : " The second or mountain region extends from the western frontier of K'hutu, at the head of the alluvial valley, in E. long. 37° 28', to the province of Ugogi, the eastern portion of the flat tableland of Ugogo, in E. long. 36° 14'. Its diagonal breadth is 85 geographical and rectilinear miles ; the native caravans, if lightly laden, generally traverse it in three weeks, including three or four halts. Its length cannot be estimated. According to the guides, Usagara is a prolongation of the mountains of Nguru, or Ngu, extending southward, with a gap forming the fluviatile valley of the Rwaha or Rufiji River : thus the feature would correspond with the Eastern Ghauts of the Indian Peninsula. The Usagara chain is of the first order in East Africa ; it is indeed the only important elevation in a direct line from the coast to Western Unyamwezi ; it would hold, however, but a low grade in the general system of the earth's mountains. The highest point above sea-level, was 5,700 feet ; there are, however, peaks which may rise to 6,000 and even to 7,000 feet, thus rivalling the inhabited portion of the Neilgherries, in southern India.

"From the mingling of lively colors, Usagara is delightful to the eye, after the monotonous tracts of verdure which pall upon the sight at Zanzibar and in the river valleys. The subsoil, displayed in the deeper cuts and ravines, is either of granite, greenstone, schiste, or a coarse incipient sandstone, brown or green, and outcropping from the ground with strata steeply tilted up. In the higher elevations the soil varies in depth from a few inches to thirty feet ; it is often streaked with long layers of pebbles, apparently water-rolled.

"The plains, basins, and steps, or facets of table-land found at every elevation, are fertilized by a stripe-work of streams, runnels, and burns, which, anastomosing in a single channel, flow off into the main drain of the country. Cultivation is found in patches isolated by thick belts of thorny jungle, and the villages are few and rarely visited. As usual in hilly countries, they are built upon high ridges and the slopes of cones, for rapid drainage after rain, a purer air and fewer mosquitoes, and, perhaps, protection from kidnappers. The country people bring down their supplies of grain and pulse for caravans. There is some delay and difficulty on the first day of arrival at a station, and provisions for a party exceeding a hundred men are not to be depended upon after the third or fourth marketing, when the people have exhausted their stores. Fearing the thievish disposition of the Wasagara, who will attempt even to snatch away a cloth from a sleeping man, travellers rarely lodge near their settlements. Kraals of thorn, capacious circles inclosing straw boothies, are found at every march, and, when burned or destroyed by accident, they are rebuilt before the bivouac. The roads, as usual in East Africa, are tracks trodden down by caravans and cattle, and the water-course is ever the favorite pass. Many of the ascents and descents are so proclivitous that donkeys must be relieved of their loads ; and in fording the sluggish streams, where no grass forms a causeway over the soft, viscid mire, the animals sink almost to the knees. The steepest paths are those in the upper regions ; in the lower, though the inclines are often severe, they are generally longer, and consequently easier. At the foot of each hill there is either a mud or a water-course dividing it from its neighbor. These obstacles greatly reduce the direct distance of the day's march.

" The clans now tenanting these East African ghauts are the Wasagara—with their chief sub-tribe the Wakwivi—and the Wahehe ; the latter a small body inhabiting the southwestern corner, and extending into the plains below.

" The limits of Wasagara have already been laid down by the names of the plundering tribes that surround them. These mountaineers, though a noisy and riotous race, are not overblessed with courage : they will lurk in the jungle with bows and arrows to surprise a stray porter ; but they seem ever to be awaiting an attack—the best receipt for inviting it. In the higher slopes they are fine, tall, and sturdy men ; in the lowlands they appear as degraded as the Wak'hutu. They are a more bearded race than any other upon this line of East Africa, and, probably from extensive intercourse with the Wamrima, most of them understand the language of the coast. The women are remarkable for a splendid development of limb, while the bosom is lax and pendent.

"The Wasagara display great varieties of complexion, some being almost black, while the others are chocolate-colored. This difference cannot be accounted for by the mere effects of climate—level and temperature. Some shave the head ; others wear the Arab's shushah, a kind of skull-cap growth, extending more or less from the poll. Among them is seen, for the first time on this line, the classical coiffure of ancient Egypt. The hair, allowed to attain its fullest length, is twisted into a multitude of the thinnest ringlets, each composed of two thin lengths wound together ; the wiry stiffness of the curls keeps them distinct and in position. Behind, a curtain of pigtails hangs down to the nape ; in front the hair is either combed off the forehead, or it is brought over the brow and trimmed short. No head-dress has a wilder nor a more characteristically African appearance than this, especially when, smeared with a pomatum of micaceous ochre, and decorated with beads, brass balls, and similar ornaments, it waves and rattles with every motion of the head. Young men and warriors adorn their locks with the feathers of vultures, ostriches, and a variety of bright-plumed jays, and some tribes twist each ringlet with a string of reddish fibre. It is seldom combed out, the operation requiring for a head of thick hair the hard work of a whole day."

CHAPTER V.

BURTON halted three days at the camp called Ugogi, to recruit the party and to lay in rations for four long desert marches. Apparently there was an abundance of provisions, but the people at first declined to part with their grain and cattle, even at exorbitant prices. The travellers received a visit from Sultan Makande, a Ugogo chief, settled at the place, who came, as he said, to offer his services. But he walked like an idiot; he begged for every article that met his eye; and he tried to persuade Burton to follow the longest of the three roads leading onward to Unyamwezi, evidently since he hoped to share some additional plunder with the many chiefs living on that road.

Ugogo is the half-way district between the coast and Unyanyembe (the central province of the Land of the Moon), and it is usually reached in two months by the caravans travelling inland. The people are a mongrel race, mixed of the tribes of the mountains and the interior table-land. The plains are rich in grain and the hills in cattle, when not

THE ENCAMPMENT IN UGOGO.

plundered by the neighboring tribes. The inhabitants offer for sale milk and honey, eggs and *ghee*, or clarified butter, but in such a condition that the articles are hardly fit for use. There is a good supply of game : guinea fowls are in abundance, and elephants and giraffes are frequent in the plains.

The place is about 2,760 feet above the sea-level, and the climate, after the raw cold of the mountain-range, is agreeable from its elastic air and dry, healthy warmth. The nights are fresh and without dew, and the rays of a tropical sun are tempered by the winds which sweep down from the mountains, as regularly as the monsoons of the coast. Burton and Speke both began to improve in health, and the partridges and guinea-fowls which the latter furnished for their table, were a welcome change from their lean fare of the previous months. The Baloch guards, the native servants and porters, began to throw off the effects of the pleurisies and other complaints which they attributed to hardship and exposure on the mountain-tops.

"Immediately before our departure," says Burton, "when almost in despair at the rapid failure of our carriage—the asses were now reduced to nine—I fortunately secured, for the sum of four cloths per man, the services of fifteen Wanyamwezi porters. In all a score, they had left at Ugogi their employer, in consequence of a quarrel concerning *the* sex. They dreaded forcible seizure and sale if found without protection travelling homeward through Ugogo ; and thus they willingly agreed to carry our goods as far as their own country, Unyanyembe. Truly is travelling like campaigning—a pennyweight of luck is better than a talent of all the talents! And if marriages, as our fathers used to say, are made in the heavens, the next-door manufactory must be devoted to the fabrication of African explorations. Notwithstanding, however, the large increase of conveyance, every man appeared on the next march more heavily laden than before; they carried grain for six days, and water for one night.

" We left Ugogi on the 22d September, at three P. M., instead of at noon. As all the caravan hurried recklessly forward, I brought up the rear, accompanied by Said bin Salim, the jemadar, and several of the sons of Ramji, who insisted upon driving the asses for greater speed at a long trot, which, after lasting a hundred yards, led to an inevitable fall of the load. Before emerging from Ugogi, the road wound over a grassy country, thickly speckled with calabashes. Square dwellings appeared on both sides, and there was no want of flocks and herds. As the villages and fields were left behind, the land became a dense, thorny jungle, based upon a sandy red soil. The horizon was bounded upon both sides by gradually thinning lines of lumpy, outlying hill, the spurs of the Rubeho Range, that extended, like a scorpion's claws, westward; and the plain, gently falling in the same direction, was broken only by a single hill-shoulder and by some dwarf descents. As we advanced through the shades—a heavy cloud-bank had shut out the crescent moon—our difficulties increased ; thorns and spiky twigs threatened the eyes : the rough and rugged road led to many a stumble, and the frequent whine of the cynhyena made the asses wild with fear. About 8 P. M., directed by loud shouts and flaring fires, we reached a kraal, a patch of yellow grass, offering clear room in the thorny thicket. That night was the perfection of a bivouac, cool from the vicinity of the hills, genial from their shelter, and sweet as forest air in these regions ever is.

"On the next day we resumed our labor betimes; for a dreary and thirsty stage lay before us. Toiling through the sunshine of the hot waste I could not but remark the strange painting of the land around. At a distance the plain was bright yellow with stubble, and brown-black with patches of leafless wintry jungle based upon a brick-dust soil. A closer approach disclosed colors more vivid and distinct. Over the ruddy plain lay scattered untidy heaps of grey granite boulders, surrounded and capped by tufts of bleached white grass. The copse showed all manner of strange hues, calabashes purpled and burnished by sun and rain, thorns of a greenish coppery bronze, dead trees with trunks of ghastly white, and gums of an unnatural sky-blue, the effect of the yellow outer pellicle being peeled off by the burning rays, while almost all were reddened up to a man's height, by the double galleries, ascending and descending, of the white ants."

In the afternoon they climbed a steep, stony range of hills, and after a few hours' travel reached a western slope, descending to the great, rolling ta-ble-land of Central Africa. The caravan encamped at night in the wilderness, having still a long day's march to a small pond called the Ziwa, the first place where a good supply of water could be found. The next morning Burton learned that he had sus-tained an apparently irreparable loss. A part of the caravan had been attacked by a swarm of wild bees, and a porter who had been engaged at Menge took the opportunity of deserting. He carried a portmanteau, containing the Nautical Almanac, the surveying books, and most of the paper, pens and ink. The caravan was delayed several hours, a search was made at the place where the man must have deserted, but without result. Much saddened by the disaster, Burton pushed on until sunset, and encamped on the dry plain, within a few miles of the pond of Ziwa.

Before settling for the night, Kidogo, the native leader and guide, stood up, and to loud cries of "Maneno! maneno!"—words! words! equivalent to the parliamentary hear! hear!—delivered him-self of the following speech :

"Listen, O ye whites! and ye children of Sayyi-di Majidi! and ye sons of Ramji! hearken to my words, O ye offspring of the night! The journey entereth Ugogo—Ugogo (the orator threw out his arm westward.) Beware, and again beware (he made violent gesticulations.) You don't know the Wagogo, they are ——s and ——s! (he stamped.) Speak not to those Washenzi pagans ; enter not into their houses (he pointed grimly to the ground.)

Have no dealings with them, show no cloth, wire, nor beads (speaking with increasing excitement.) Eat not with them, drink not with them, and make not love to their women (here the speech became a scream.) Kirangozi of the Wanyamwezi, restrain your sons ! Suffer them not to stray into the villages, to buy salt out of camp, to rob provisions, to debauch with beer, or to sit by the wells !" And thus, for nearly half an hour, now violently, then composedly, he poured forth the words of wisdom, till the hubbub and chatter of voices which at first had been silenced by surprise, brought his eloquence to an end.

" We left the jungle-kraal early on the 26th September, and, after hurrying through thick bush, we debouched upon an open stubbly plain, with herds of gracefully-bounding antelopes and giraffes, who stood for a moment with long outstretched necks to gaze, and presently broke away at a rapid, striding camel's trot, their heads shaking as if they would jerk off, their limbs loose, and their joints apparently dislocated. About 9 P.M. we sighted the much-talked-of Ziwa. The Arabs, fond of ' showing a green garden,' had described to me at Inenge a piece of water fit to float a man-of-war. I was not therefore surprised to find a shallow pool, which in India would barely merit the name of tank.

" The Ziwa, which lies 3,100 feet above the sea, occupies the lowest western level of Marenga Mk'háli, and is the deepest of the many inundated grounds lying to its north, northeast and northwest. The extent greatly varies : in September, 1857, it

was a slaty sheet of water, with granite projections
on one side, and about 300 yards in diameter; the
centre only could not be forded. The bottom and
the banks were of retentive clay; a clear ring,
whence the waters had subsided, margined the
pool and beyond it lay a thick thorny jungle. In
early December, 1858, nothing remained but a surface of dry, crumbling, and deeply-cracked mud,
and, according to travellers, it had long, in consequence of the scanty rains, been in that state. Caravans always encamp at the Ziwa when they find
water there. The country around is full of large
game, especially elephants, giraffes, and zebras.

"At the Ziwa the regular system of kuhonga, or
black-mail, so much dreaded by travellers, begins in
force. Up to this point all the chiefs are contented
with little presents; but in Ugogo tribute is taken
by force, if necessary. None can evade payment;
the porters, fearing lest the road be cut off to them
in future, would refuse to travel unless each chief is
satisfied; and when a quarrel arises they throw down
their packs and run away. Ugogo, since the closing
of the northern line through the Wahumba and the
Wamasai tribes, and the devastation of the southern
regions by the Warori, is the only open line, and the
sultans have presumed upon their power of stopping
the way. There is no regular tariff of taxes: the
sum is fixed by the traveller's dignity and outfit,
which, by means of his slaves, are as well known to
every sultan as to himself. Properly speaking, the
exaction should be confined to the up-caravans;
from those returning, a head or two of cattle, a few

hoes, or some similar trifle, are considered ample. Such, however, was not the experience of the expedition. When first travelling through the country the ' Wazungu ' (white men) were sometimes mulcted to the extent of fifty cloths by a single chief, and the Arabs congratulated them upon having escaped so easily."

When the chief of the place had been propitiated by a present of cloth and beads, the country people made their appearance, bringing bullocks, sheep, goats, and poultry, watermelons and pumpkins, honey, buttermilk and curds, and an abundance of holcus and calabash flour. The latter is made from the hard, dry pulp surrounding the seeds in the ripe gourd : its taste is slightly acid, and it is considered very nourishing. On account of the supplies, the caravan halted four days, and there was the usual amount of quarrelling between the leaders of the various nationalities composing it. The detention, however, proved to be fortunate. On the last day, September 30th, a caravan headed by several Arab traders arrived from the coast, bringing not only later news from the world, but—a singular good fortune—the valuable portmanteau which had been lost.

Burton's caravan joined the latter for the journey to the Land of the Moon, making a total of 190 men, thus affording greater security to both. They had chosen the middle route through Ugogo, for the reason that it was the beaten path, and only infested by four chiefs to whom black-mail must be paid. " On the 1st of October, (1857,)" Burton continues,

" we left the Ziwa late in the morning, and after passing through the savannas and the brown jungles of the lower levels, where giraffe again appeared, the path crested a wave of ground and debouched upon the table-land of Ugogo. The aspect was peculiar and unprepossessing. Behind still towered in sight the delectable mountains of Usagara, mist-crowned and robed in the lightest azure, with streaks of a deep plum-color, fronting the hot low land of Marenga Mk'hali, whose tawny face was wrinkled with lines of dark jungle. On the north was a tabular range of rough and rugged hill, above which rose three distant cones pointed out as the haunts of the robber Wahumba : at its base was a deep depression, a tract of brown brush patched with yellow grass, inhabited only by the elephant, and broken by small outlying hillocks. Southward, scattered eminences of tree-crowned rock rose a few yards from the plain which extended to the front, a clearing of deep red or white soil, decayed vegetation based upon rocky or sandy ground, here and there thinly veiled with brown brush and golden stubbles : its length, about four miles, was studded with square villages, and with the stately but grotesque calabash. This giant is to the vegetable what the elephant is to the animal world : the Persians call it the " practice-work of nature "—its disproportionate conical bole rests upon huge legs exposed to view by the washing away of the soil.

" From the day of our entering to that of our leaving the country, every settlement turned out its swarm of gazers, men and women, boys and girls,

some of whom would follow us for miles with explosions of Hi!—i!—i! screams of laughter and
cries of excitement, at a long high trot—most un-
graceful of motion !—and with a scantiness of toilette which displayed truly unseemly spectacles.
The matrons, especially the aged matrons, and the
old men were ever the most pertinacious and in-
trusive, the most surly and quarrelsome. Vainly
the escort attempted to arrest the course of this
moving multitude of semi-nude barbarity. I afterward learned that the two half-caste Arabs who
had passed us at Muhama, had, while preceding us,
spread through Ugogo malevolent reports concerning the Wazungu (white men.) They had one eye
each and four arms ; they were full of 'knowledge,' which in these lands means magic ; they
caused rain to fall in advance and left droughts in
their rear ; they cooked watermelons and threw
away the seeds, thereby generating small-pox ; they
heated and hardened milk, thus breeding a murrain
among cattle ; and their wire, cloth, and beads
caused a variety of misfortunes ; they were kings
of the sea, and therefore white-skinned and straight-
haired—a standing mystery to these curly-pated
people—as are all men who live in salt water ; and
next year they would return and seize the country.
Suspicion of our intentions touching 'territorial
aggrandizement' was a fixed idea : everywhere the
value attached by barbarians to their homes is in
inverse ration to the real worth of the article.
Hence mountaineers are proverbially patriotic.
Thus the lean Bedouins of Arabia and the lank

Somal, though they own that they are starving, never sight a stranger without suspecting that he is spying out the wealth of the land. 'What will happen to us?' asked the Wagogo; 'we never yet saw this manner of man!'' But the tribe cannot now forfeit intercourse with the coast: they annoyed us to the utmost, they made the use of their wells a daily source of trouble, they charged us double prices, and when they brought us provisions for sale, they insisted upon receiving the price of even the rejected articles; yet they did not proceed to open outrage.'

At a station called Kilfukuru they were detained a day, and at the next, Kanyenye, four days, to settle the amount of black-mail with the chiefs. Magomba, the chief of the latter district, was one of the most powerful and dreaded in the Land of Ugogo, and was not satisfied until he had received, from first to last, presents of the value of fifty dollars. Burton's account of his meeting with this rapacious "head man" will serve as a specimen of an experience which was renewed, every few days, during his progress through the country. "I received, when encamped at the Ziwa," he says, "a polite message declaring his desire to see white men; but—' the favor of the wind produces dust'—I was obliged to acknowledge the compliment with two cottons. On arrival at his head-quarters I was waited upon by an oily cabinet of viziers and elders, who would not depart without their 'respects'—four cottons. The next demand was made by his favorite wife, a peculiarly hideous old princess, with more wrinkles than hairs, with no hair black and no tooth white, and attended by ladies in waiting as unprepossessing as herself : she was not to be dismissed without a fee of six cottons. At last, accompanied by a mob of courtiers, who crowded in like an African House of Commons, appeared in person the magnifico. He was the only sultan that ever entered my tent in Ugogo—pride and a propensity for strong drink prevented other visits. He was much too great a man to call upon the Arab merchants, but in our case curiosity had mastered state considerations. Magomba was a black and wrinkled elder, drivelling and decrepit, with a half-bald head, from whose back and sides depended a few straggling corkscrews of iron grey ; he wore a coat of castor-oil and a loin-cloth, which grease and use had changed from blue to black. A few bead strings decorated his neck, large flexible anklets of brass wire adorned his legs, solid brass rings, single and in coils, which had distended his ear-lobes almost to splitting, were tied by a string over his cranium, and his horny soles were defended by single-soled sandals, old, dirty, and tattered. He chewed his quid and he expectorated without mercy ; he asked many a silly question, yet he had ever an eye to the main chance."

On the 8th of October, during the delay at Kanyenye, a caravan bound for the coast arrived from the interior, and Burton was enabled to. send dispatches home. On the 10th he set forward again, over a plain covered with thorny jungles which were very difficult to pass. Two days of such marching brought the caravan to the territory of the next chief, where there was another forced halt of five days, partly to arrange the inevitable black-mail, and partly to lay in provisions for four days through a desert region. Every such halt was accompanied with quarrels and attempts at desertion, many of which Burton describes in detail, until, from their continual repetition, they finally become as wearisome to the reader as they must have been to the explorer.

Leaving the pestilent jungle, where they had been encamped, they journeyed onward in the heat, stung by the *tsetse* fly, and annoyed with swarms of wild bees and gadflies. On one occasion an army of large poisonous ants drove them out of the tent, until they were banished by the use of boiling water. The nights were cold and raw, and almost every morning they found that some valuable article had been rendered useless by the termites. During the first night, fifteen porters who had been hired at Ugogi deserted, Burton's riding-ass was torn by a hyena, and his fever returned. The next day he was obliged to walk over the burning soil, through a wild country where the frankincense was used for fuel, lying down every half hour to rest; but late in the evening he reached the district of Mdaburu, the westernmost part of the Land of Ugogo, where another halt of two days was prescribed. Here there was less difficulty in settling with the resident chief. The risk of being attacked seemed to diminish, in proportion as the caravan penetrated further into the interior.

A wide desert tract called Mgunda Mk'hali—
"the Fiery Field"—separates Ugogo from Unyamwezi, the Land of the Moon. It is traversed
by three roads, of which Burton chose the central
one. Eight marches are required to cross it, only
the first three of which, however, are especially fatiguing, although caravans are threatened with
drouth and the death of cattle during the whole
journey. The natives, for their own safety, adopted
a better organization on entering this region.

"From east to west," says Burton, "the diagonal breadth of the Fiery Field is 140 miles. The
general aspect is a dull uniform bush, emerald-col-
ored during the rains, and in the heats a network
of dry and broom-like twigs. Except upon the
banks of nullahs—'rivers' that are not rivers—the
trees, as in Ugogo, wanting nutriment, never afford
timber, and even the calabash appears stunted. The
trackless waste of scrub, called the 'bush' in Southern Africa, is found in places alternating with thin
gum-forest; the change may be accounted for by
the different depths of water below the level of the
ground. It is a hardy vegetation of mimosas and
gums mixed with evergreen succulent plants, cacta-
ceæ, aloes, and euphorbias; the grass, sometimes
tufty, at other times equally spread, is hard and
stiff; when green it feeds cattle, and when dry it is
burned in places by passing caravans to promote
the growth of another crop.

"On the 20th October we began the transit of
the 'Fiery Field,' whose long broad line of brown
ungle, painted blue by the intervening air, had, for

two days previous, formed our western horizon.
The waste here appeared in its most horrid phase.
The narrow goat-path serpentined in and out of a
growth of poisonous thorny jungle, with thin, hard
grass-straw, growing on a glaring white and rolling
ground; the view was limited by bush and brake,
as in the alluvial valleys of the maritime region,
and in weary sameness the spectacle surpassed
everything that we had endured in Marenga Mk'-
hali. We halted through the heat of the day at
some water-pits in a broken course; and resuming
our tedious march early in the afternoon, we arrived
about sunset at the bed of a shallow nullah, where
the pure element was found in sand-holes about five
feet deep."

On the 22d of October they reached Jiwe la
Mkoa, the half-way station in the desert. A few
villages, inhabited by emigrants of mongrel tribes,
were passed on the way, but no incident occurred
beyond the usual fatigues of such a journey. Jiwe
Mkoa, or the Round Rock, is a dome-shaped hill
of grey syenite, two miles in length and about 300
feet high. Here a little water is obtained from pits,
and there is a small village, which does not furnish
any supplies to caravans.

After six days more of slow and toilsome progress, the caravan exchanged the dry, thorny plains
for a region of jungle, tall grass and scattered forests, with indications of abundance of water. At
the first appearance of cultivation the natives halted, in order to form in orderly style, and present a
more dignified character. " Then," says Burton,

" ensued a clearing, studded with large stockaded villages, peering over tall hedges of dark-green milk-bush, fields of maize and millet, manioc, gourds, and watermelons, and showing numerous flocks and herds, clustering around the shallow pits. The people swarmed from their abodes, young and old hustling one another for a better stare ; the man forsook his loom and the girl her hoe, and for the remainder of the march we were escorted by a tail of screaming boys and shouting adults ; the males almost nude, the women bare to the waist and clothed only· knee-deep in kilts, accompanied us, puffing pipes the while, with wallets of withered or flabby flesh flapping the air, striking their hoes with stones, crying ' Beads ! beads !' and ejaculating their wonder in strident explosions of ' Hi ! hi !—Hui ! ih !' and ' Ha !—a !—a !' It was a spectacle to make an anchorite of a man—it was at once ludicrous and disgusting.

"At length the kirangozi (leader) fluttered his red flag in the wind, and the drums, horns, and larynxes of his followers began the fearful uproar which introduces a caravan to the admiring ' natives.' Leading the way, our guide, much to my surprise—I knew not then that such was the immemorial custom of Unyamwezi—entered uninvited and sans ceremony the nearest large village ; the long string of porters flocked in with bag and baggage, and we followed their example. The guests at once dispersed themselves through the several courts and compounds into which the interior hollow was divided, and lodged themselves with as much regard for self and disregard for their grumbling hosts as possible. We were placed under a wall-less roof, bounded on one side by the bars of the village palisade, and the mob of starers that relieved one another from morning till night made me feel like the denizen of a menagerie."

This was at last Unyamwezi, the Land of the Moon, and Burton and Speke were the first Europeans who ever visited it. Before accompanying them to new adventures, we will give the most interesting particulars of Burton's account of the geography and ethnology of Ugogo.

"The third division of the country visited is a flat table-land extending from the Ugogi valley, at the western base of the Wasagara Mountains, in E. longitude 36° 14', to Tura, the eastern district of Unyamwezi, in E. longitude 33° 57'; occupying a diagonal breadth of 155 geographical rectilinear miles. The length from north to south is not so easily estimated. The average of the heights observed is 3,650 feet, with a gradual rise westward to Jiwe la Mkoa, which attains an altitude of 4,200 feet (?).

"This third region, situated to leeward of a range whose height compels the southeast trades to part with their load of vapors, and distant from the succession of inland seas which, stationed near the centre of the African continent, act as reservoirs to restore the balance of humidity, is an arid, sterile land, a counterpart in many places of the Kalahari and the Karroo, or South African desert-plains. The general aspect is a glaring yellow flat, darkened by long growths of acrid, saline, and succulent plants, thorny bush, and stunted trees, and the coloring is monotonous in the extreme. It is sprinkled with isolated dwarf cones, bristling with rocks and boulders, from whose interstices springs a thin forest of gums, thorns, and mimosas.

" The climate of Ugogo is markedly arid. During the transit of the expedition in September and October, the best water-colors faded and hardened in their pans ; India-rubber, especially the prepared article in squares, became viscid, like half-dried bird-lime ; ' Macintosh ' was sticking-plaster, and the best vulcanized elastic bands tore like brown paper. During almost the whole year a violent east wind sweeps from the mountains. There are great changes in the temperature, while the weather apparently remains the same, and alternate currents of hot and cold air were observed.

" Arab and other travellers unaccustomed to the country at first suffer from the climate, which must not, however, be condemned. They complain of the tourbillons, the swarms of flies, and the violent changes from burning heat to piercing cold, which is always experienced in that region when the thermeter sinks below 60°–55° F. Their thin tents, pitched under a ragged calabash, cannot mitigate the ardor of an unclouded sun ; the salt-bitter water, whose nitrous and saline deposits sometimes tarnish a silver ring like the fumes of sulphur, affects their health ; while the appetite, stimulated by a purer atmosphere and the coolness of the night air, is kept within due bounds only by deficiency in the means of satisfying it. Those who have seen Africa farther west are profuse in their praises of the climate on their return-march from the interior.

" The superiority of climate, and probably the absence of that luxuriant vegetation which distinguishes the eastern region, have proved favorable to the physical development of the races living in and about Ugogo. The Wagogo, and their northern neighbors the Wahumba, are at once distinguishable from the wretched population of the alluvial valleys, and of the mountains of Usagara ; though living in lower altitudes, they are a fairer race—and therefore show better blood—than the Wanyamwezi. These two tribes, whose distinctness is established by difference of dialect, will be described in order.

" The Wagogo display the variety of complexion usually seen among slave-purchasing races : many of them are fair as Abyssinians ; some are black as negroes. In the eastern and northern settlements they are a fine, stout, and light-complexioned race. Their main peculiarity is the smallness of the cranium compared with the broad circumference of the face at and below the zygomata : seen from behind, the appearance is that of a small half bowl fitted upon one of considerably larger bias ; and this, with the widely-extended ears, gives a remarkable expression to the face. Nowhere in eastern Africa is the lobe so distended. Pieces of cane an inch or two in length, and nearly double the girth of a man's finger, are so disposed that they appear like handles to the owner's head. The distinctive mark of the tribe is the absence of the two lower incisors ; but they are more generally recognized by the unnatural enlargement of their ears. In Eastern·Africa the ' aures perforatæ ' are the signs not of slavery, but of freedom.   There is no regular tattoo, though some of the women have two parallel lines running from below the bosom down the abdomen, and the men often extract only a single lower incisor.   The hair is sometimes shaved clean, at others grown in mop-shape ; more generally it is dressed in a mass of tresses, as among the Egyptians, and the skin, as well as the large bunch of corkscrews, freely stained with ochre and micaceous earths.

" The strength of the Wagogo lies in their comparative numbers. As the people seldom travel to the coast, their scattered villages are full of fighting men.   Moreover, uchawi or black magic here numbers few believers, consequently those drones of the social hive, the waganga, or medicine-men, are not numerous.   The Wagogo seldom sell their children and relations, yet there is no order against the practice.   They barter for slaves their salt and ivory, the principal produce of the country.

" The Wagogo are celebrated as thieves -who will, like the Wahehe, rob even during the day. They are importunate beggars, who specify their long list of wants without stint or shame : their principal demand is tobacco, which does not grow in the land ; and they resemble the Somal, who never sight a stranger without stretching out the hand for ' bori.'   The men are idle and debauched, spending their days in unbroken crapulence and drunkenness, while the girls and women hoe the fields, and the boys tend the flocks and herds. They mix honey with their pombe, or beer, and each man provides entertainment for his neighbors in turn. After midday it would be difficult throughout the country to find a chief without the thick voice, fiery eyes, and moidered manners, which prove that he is either drinking or drunk.

"The Wahumba are a fair and comely race, with the appearance of mountaineers, long-legged and lightly made. They have repeatedly ravaged the lands of Usagara and Ugogo; in the latter country, near Usek'he, there are several settlements of this people, who have exchanged the hide-tent for the hut, and the skin for the cotton cloth. They stain their garments with ochrish earth, and their women are distinguished by wearing kitindi of full and half size above and below the elbows. The ear-lobes are pierced and distended by both sexes, as among the Wagogo. In their own land they are purely pastoral; they grow no grain, despise vegetable food, and subsist entirely upon meat or milk according to the season. Their habitations are hemispheres of boughs lashed together and roofed with a cow's hide; it is the primitive dwelling-place, and the legs of the occupant protrude beyond the shelter. Their arms, which are ever hung up close at hand, are broad-headed spears of soft iron, long 'sine,' or double-edged daggers, with ribbed wooden handles fastened to the blade by a strip of cow's tail shrunk on, and 'rungu,' or wooden knob-kerries, with double bulges that weight the weapon as it whirls through the air. They ignore and apparently despise the bow and arrows, but in battle they carry the pavoise, or large hide-shield, affected by the Kafirs of the Cape. The Arabs, when in force, do not fear their attacks.

[NOTE.—Burton, in describing the different regions of Central Africa and their inhabitants, always makes use of the prefixes peculiar to the native languages. *U* signifies the country, *Wa* the tribe occupying it, *Ki* the language, and *M* an individual of the tribe. Thus, *Ugogo,* the first region west of the mountains; *Wagogo,* the general designation of the inhabitants; *Kigogo,* their language, and *M'gogo,* a single individual.]

CHAPTER VI.

AFTER the gloomy jungles and interminable thornforests of the " Fiery Field," the fair open country, bounded on either hand by low, rolling hills, with a succession of villages and fields of sesame, maize, millet, watermelons and pumpkins, seemed like a veritable Paradise to the weary caravan. No halt was made at Tura, however ; supplies were certain each day, and the travellers pushed on to reach Unyanyembe, the central district of the Land of the Moon, where the Arab merchants have built a small town, called Kazeh, as an entrepot for their trade with all the interior regions.

At the end of the third day's march from Tura, they were overtaken by a flying caravan, belonging to an Arab who had left the coast nearly three months after their departure. He warned them against returning beyond Kazeh, on account of the great dangers of the journey. At a village called Rubuga, the chief gave Burton a splendid fat bullock, and the native porters so gorged themselves that they were hardly able to march. Advancing slowly through a fertile and populous country, on the 6th of November, they entered a dreaded forest, beyond which lay Unyanyembe. One of the neighboring chiefs, a sort of African Rob Roy, was in the habit of waylaying caravans in this forest, and almost every Arab merchant had been plundered. Burton therefore started at 1 A.M., but in spite of every precaution against surprise, one of the porters was robbed of a leathern portmanteau, containing clothes, books, notes of travel and botanical collections.

Finally the wilderness of granite hills, gum trees, and mimosas was left behind, and the caravan encamped on the banks of a stream, in a pleasant and well-cultivated country. The next day,—the 7th of November, 1857, the 134th day from the date of leaving the coast, they approached Kazeh, the one important town of Unyamwezi. Burton's account of his arrival, and his reception by the Arab merchants, is both interesting and refreshing after his long catalogue of quarrels and suspicions :

"About 8 A.M. we halted for stragglers at a little village, and when the line of porters, becoming compact, began to wriggle, snake-like, its long length over the plain, with floating flags, booming horns, muskets ringing like saluting-mortars, and an uproar of voice which nearly drowned the other noises, we made a truly splendid and majestic first appearance. The road was lined with people who attempted to vie with us in volume and variety of sound : all had donned their best attire, and with such luxury my eyes had been long unfamiliar. Advancing, I saw several Arabs standing by the way-

side; they gave the Moslem salutation, and cour-
teously accompanied me for some distance. Among
them were the principal merchants.

"I had directed Said bin Salim to march the
caravan to the tembe kindly placed at my disposal
by the Arabs met at Inenge. The caravan-leader
and the porters, however, led us on by mistake to
the house of "Musa Mzuri "—handsome Moses—an
Indian merchant settled at Unyanyembe, for whom
I bore an introductory letter, graciously given by
H. H. the Sayyid Majid of Zanzibar. As Musa
was then absent on a trading journey to Karagwah,
his agent, Snay bin Amir, came forward to perform
his guest-rites, and led me to the vacant house.

After allowing me, as is the custom, a day to rest
and to dismiss the porters, who at once separated
to their homes, all the Arab merchants, then about
a dozen, made the first ceremonious call, and to
them was officially submitted the circular addressed
by the Prince of Zanzibar to his subjects resident
in the African interior. Contrary to the predictions
of others, nothing could be more encouraging than
the reception experienced from the Omani Arabs;
striking, indeed, was the contrast between the open-
handed hospitality and the hearty good-will of this
truly noble race, and the niggardness of the savage
and selfish African—it was heart of flesh after
heart of stone. A goat and a load of the fine white
rice grown in the country were the normal prelude
to a visit and to offers of service which proved
something more than a mere *vox et præterea nihil.*
Whatever I alluded to, onions, plantains, limes, ve-

getables, tamarind-cakes, coffee from Karagwah, and similar articles, only to be found among the Arabs, were sent at once, and the very name of payment would have been an insult. Snay bin Amir, determined to surpass all others in generosity, sent two goats to us and two bullocks to the Baloch and the sons of Ramji : sixteen years before, he had begun life a confectioner at Muscat, and now he had risen to be one of the wealthiest ivory and slave dealers in Eastern Africa.

" Unyanyembe, the central and principal province of Unyamwezi, is, like Zungomero in Khutu, the great bandari or meeting-place of merchants, and the point of departure for caravans which thence radiate into the interior of Central Intertropical Africa. Here the Arab merchant from Zanzibar meets his compatriot returning from the Tanganyika Lake and from Uruwwa. Northward well-travelled lines diverge to the Nyanza Lake, and the powerful kingdoms of Karagwah, Uganda, and Unyoro ; from the south Urori and Ubena, Usanga and Usenga, send their ivory and slaves ; and from the southwest the Rukwa Water, K'hokoro, Ufipa, and Marungu must barter their valuables for cottons, wires, and beads.

" Unyanyembe, which rises about 3,480 feet above sea-level, and lies 356 miles in rectilinear distance from the eastern coast of Africa, resembles in its physical features the lands about Tura. The plain or basin of Ihárá, or Kwihárá, a word synonymous with the ' bondei ' or lowland of the coast, is bounded on the north and south by low, rolling hills, which converge toward the west, where, with the characteristically irregular lay of primitive formations, they are crossed almost at right angles by the Mfuto chain. The position has been imprudently chosen by the Arabs; the land suffers from alternate drought and floods, which render the climate markedly malarious. The soil is aluminous in the low levels—a fertile plain of brown earth, with a subsoil of sand and sandstone, from eight to twelve feet below the surface; the water is often impregnated with iron, and the higher grounds are uninhabited tracts covered with bulky granite boulders, bushy trees, and thorny shrubs.

"It is difficult to average the present number of Arab merchants at Unyanyembe, who, like the British in India, visit but do not colonize; they rarely, however, exceed twenty-five in number; and during the travelling season, or when a campaign is necessary, they are sometimes reduced to three or four; they are too strong to yield without fighting, and are not strong enough to fight with success. Whenever the people have mustered courage to try a fall with the strangers, they have been encouraged to try again. Hitherto the merchants have been on friendly terms with Fundikira, the chief. Their position, however, though partly held by force of prestige, is precarious.

"The Arabs live comfortably, and even splendidly, at Unyanyembe. The houses, though single-storied, are large, substantial, and capable of defence. Their gardens are extensive and well planted; they receive regular supplies of merchandise, comforts,

and luxuries from the coast; they are surrounded
by troops of concubines and slaves, whom they
train to divers crafts and callings; rich men have
riding-asses from Zanzibar, and even the poorest
keep flocks and herds. At Unyanyembe, as at
Msene, and sometimes at Ujiji, there are itinerant
fundi, or slave artisans — blacksmiths, tinkers,
masons, carpenters, tailors, potters, and rope-
makers—who come up from the coast with Arab
caravans. These men demand exorbitant wages.

"One drawback to the Arab's happiness is the
failure of his constitution; a man who escapes illness for two successive months boasts of the immu-
nity; and, as in Egypt, no one enjoys robust health.
The older residents have learned to moderate their
appetites. They eat but twice a day—after sunrise, and at noon. The midday meal concluded,
they confine themselves to chewing tobacco or the
dried coffee of Karagwah. They avoid strong
meats, especially beef and game, which are considered heating and bilious, remaining satisfied with
light dishes, omelets and pillaus, harísah, firni, and
curded milk; and the less they eat the more likely
they are to escape fever.

"From Unyanyembe, twenty marches, which are
seldom accomplished under twenty-five days, conduct the traveller to Ujiji, upon the Tanganyika. Of
these the fifth station is Msene, the great bandari of
Western Unyamwezi. It is usually reached in
eight days; and the twelfth is the Malagarazi River,
the western limit of the fourth region.

"Throughout Eastern Africa made roads, the first

test of progress in a people, are unknown. The most frequented routes are foot-tracks, like goat-walks, one to two spans broad, trodden down during the travelling season by man and beast, and during the rains the path, in African parlance, ' dies,' that is to say, it is overgrown with vegetation. In open and desert places four or five lines often run parallel for short distances. In jungly countries they are mere tunnels in thorns and under branchy trees, which fatigue the porter by catching his load. Where fields and villages abound, they are closed with rough hedges, horizontal tree-trunks, and even rude stockades, to prevent trespassing and pilferage." These difficulties, added to the short marches of the caravan-porters, render it almost impossible for an exploring party to advance at a more rapid rate than six geographical miles per day.

Burton was detained at Kazeh from the 8th of November to the 14th of December, and the delay was one long trial of patience. It is customary for caravans proceeding towards Ujiji, on the Tanganyika Lake, to make a halt of six weeks or two months, for rest, reorganization, and the enjoyment of a more civilized society. Burton was anxious, on account of the approaching rainy season, to push onward as rapidly as possible, but all circumstances combined to prevent him. On the morning after his arrival at Kazeh, the native porters, hired at the coast, all left for their homes; the guide took a leave of absence for fifteen days; and the Baloch guards, with the remaining servants, persisted in declaring Unyanyembe, and not the Lake, to be the limit of the expedition. Kazeh, in fact, proved to be a second point of departure, only less difficult than the original start, because the travellers had gained much experience in the meantime. The greatest trouble was occasioned by Said bin Salim, the officer furnished by the Sultan of Zanzibar ; and without the hearty and unremitting assistance of the Arab merchant, Snay bin Amir, the expedition might have been prevented from advancing beyond Kazeh.

The rainy season commenced in November, but, although it is considered healthy in those interior régions, Burton was so prostrated by malarious fever that he felt more dead than alive. He was attacked by partial paralysis of the limbs, the effects of which he felt for more than a month afterwards. After reaching Yombo, two short marches west of Kazeh, the prospect of going onward gradually improved. Twenty porters were hired, five of whom immediately deserted, and eleven of the Baloch guards joined the party. Three more short marches brought Burton to a village called Irora, where, on the 22nd of December, he was joined to Speke, who had remained behind to receive some scanty supplies which had arrived from the coast, and who had also engaged an additional number of porters. The latter, contrary to the usual habits of the class, were clamorous to proceed to the district of Msene without delay.

In three days more Burton, who had been carried in a hammock slung upon poles, regained strength enough to ride upon an ass. The day's stages were very short ; the country through which he passed was moderately populated and supplied the most necessary food. On the 30th of December he reached the country of Msene, which is the chief trading-place of Western Unyamwezi. It is governed by a ruler who calls himself Sultan Masanza, and who is not hostile to strangers. "This chief," says Burton, "has considerable power, and the heads of many criminals elevated upon poles in front of his several villages show that he rules with a firm hand. He is never approached by a subject without the clapping of hands and the kneeling which, in these lands, are the honors paid to royalty. He was a large-limbed, gaunt, and sinewy old man, dressed in a dirty subai or Arab check over a coating of rancid butter, with a broad brass disk, neatly arabesqued, round his neck, with a multitude of little pig-tails where his head was not bald, and with some thirty sambo or flexible wire rings deforming, as if by elephantiasis, his ankles. Like the generality of sultans, he despises beads as an article of decoration, preferring coils of brass or copper. He called several times at the house occupied by the expedition, and on more than one occasion brought with him a bevy of wives whose deportment was, I regret to say, rather *naive* than decorous.

"There was 'cold comfort' at Msene, where I was delayed twelve days. The clay-roof of the tembe was weed-grown like a deserted grave, and in the foul central court-yard only dirty puddles set in black mud met the eye. The weather was what only they can realize who are familiar with a rainy monsoon. The temptations of the town rendered it almost impossible to keep a servant or a slave within doors ; the sons of Ramji vigorously engaged themselves in trading, and Muinyi Wazira in a debauch, which ended in his dismissal."

The delay at least enabled Burton to celebrate New Year's day, 1858, with a roast of beef, and a pudding in which there was neither flour nor plums. When he started again, on the 10th of January, the usual experience with runaway guides, refractory porters, and quarrels between the leaders of the various portions of the party, was repeated. Three whole days elapsed, during which they made short marches to the westward, before the natives were tolerably organized and reduced to obedience. The country was generally open and rolling, with here and there a forest, a tract of thorny jungle, or a marsh. The native villages were simply circles of low huts, shaped like bee-hives, and surrounded with thickets of euphorbia. Burton's fever returned, with another partial paralysis, which prevented him from walking ; so there was another detention until hammock-bearers could be procured. The native leaders, believing him to be at the point of death, became both careless and insolent, so that it was the 21st of January before they reached the village of Usagozi, a little more than one third of the distance from Kazeh to the Tanganyika Lake.

Here they were detained four days by an inflammation of Speke's eyes, which temporarily clouded his sight. Finally, after crossing a fertile and populous region, where, nevertheless, it was difficult to procure provisions, on the 31st of January they saw before them the broad plain of the Malagarazi River. This stream, which rises among mountains far to the northward, and winds through yet unexplored regions of Central Africa, empties into the Tanganyike Lake on its eastern side. It is not navigable, but so rapid and broken in its current, and so infested with crocodiles, that the natives rarely attempt to ford it.

At Ugaga, where the travellers struck the river (which is there about 50 yards wide), the chief who owned the ferry subjected them to fresh exactions. The boats were miserable canoes of bark, five to seven feet in length, and could only support the weight of two persons. Nevertheless, after a great deal of time and trouble, the whole caravan was safely transported to the northern bank, and there was now no serious physical obstacle thenceforward to the lake.

Although the nominal western frontier of the Land of the Moon had been crossed a few days before, Burton considers the Malagazi River the boundary of the fourth region which he traversed. The name of Unyamwezi, which it retains, was first mentioned by the Portuguese navigators, nearly three centuries ago, and there can be little doubt that the " Mountains of the Moon " of Ptolemy referred to the range which bounds this central table-land on the east and the highest peaks of which are Kilimandjaro and Kenia. Burton's account of the geography of the region, and the tribes which inhabit it, must now be given, before we follow him on his toilsome but successful march to Lake Tanganyika.

The fourth division is a hilly table-land, extending from the western skirts of the desert Mgunda Mk'hali, in E. long. 33° 57′, to the eastern banks of the Malagarazi River, in E. long. 31° 10′; it thus stretches diagonally over 155 rectilinear geographical miles. Bounded on the north by Usui and the Nyanza Lake, to the southeastward by Ugala, southward by Ukimbu, and southwestward by Uwende, it has a depth of from twenty-five to thirty marches. Native caravans, if lightly laden, can accomplish it in twenty-five days, including four halts. The maximum altitude observed was 4,050 feet, the minimum 2,850. This region contains the two great divisions of Unyamwezi and Uvinza.

"There is the evidence of barbarous tradition for a belief in the existence of Unyamwezi as a great empire united under a single despot. The elders declare that their patriarchal ancestor became after death the first tree, and afforded shade to his children and descendants. According to the Arabs, the people still perform pilgrimage to a holy tree, and believe that the penalty of sacrilege in cutting off a twig would be visited by sudden and mysterious death. All agree in relating that during the olden time Unyamwezi was united under a single sovereign, whose tribe was the Wakalaganza, still inhabiting the western district, Usagozi. According to the people, whose greatest chronical measure is a *masika*, or rainy season, in the days of the grandfathers of their grandfathers the last of the Wanyamwezi emperors died. His children and nobles divided and dismembered his dominions, further partitions ensued, and finally the old empire fell into the hands of a rabble of petty chiefs. Their wild computation would point to an epoch of 150 years ago —a date by no means improbable.

"These glimmerings of light thrown by African tradition illustrate the accounts given by the early Portuguese concerning the extent and the civilization of the Unyamwezi empire. Moreover, African travellers in the seventeenth century concur in asserting that, between 250 and 300 years ago, there was an outpouring of the barbarians from the heart of Æthiopia and from the shores of the Central Lake toward the eastern and southern coasts of the peninsula, a general waving and wandering of tribes, which caused great ethnological and geographical confusion, public demoralization, dismemberment of races, and change, confusion, and corruption of tongues.

"The general character of Unyamwezi is rolling ground, intersected with low conical and tabular hills, whose lines ramify in all directions. No mountain is found in the country. The superjacent stratum is clay, overlying the sandstone based upon various granites, which in some places crop out, picturesquely disposed in blocks and boulders, and huge domes and lumpy masses; iron-stone is met with at a depth varying from five to twelve feet, and at Kazeh, the Arab settlement in Unyanyembe, bits of coarse ore were found by digging not more than four feet in a chance spot.

During the rains a coat of many-tinted greens conceals the soil; in the dry season the land is grey, lighted up by golden stubbles, and dotted with wind-distorted trees, shallow swamps of emerald grass, and wide sheets of dark mud. Dwarfed stumps and charred 'black-jacks' deform the fields, which are sometimes ditched or hedged in, while a thin forest of parachute-shaped thorns diversifies the waves of rolling land and earth-hills spotted with sun-burnt stone. The reclaimed tracts and clearings are divided from one another by strips of primeval jungle varying from two to twelve miles in length. As in most parts of Eastern Africa, the country is dotted with 'fairy mounts'—dwarf mounds, the ancient sites of trees now crumbled to dust, and the débris of insect architecture; they appear to be rich ground, as they are always diligently cultivated. The yield of the soil, according to the Arabs, averages sixty-fold, even in unfavorable seasons.

"The Land of the Moon, which is the garden of Central Inter-tropical Africa, presents an aspect of peaceful rural beauty which soothes the eye like a medicine after the red glare of barren Ugogo, and the dark monotonous verdure of the western provinces. The inhabitants are comparatively numerous in the villages, which rise at short intervals above their impervious walls of the lustrous green milk-bush, with its coral-shaped arms, variegating the well-hoed plains; while in the pasture-lands frequent herds of many-colored cattle, plump, round-barrelled, and high-humped, like the Indian breeds,

and mingled flocks of goats and sheep dispersed
over the landscape, suggest ideas of barbarous comfort and plenty. There are few scenes more soft
and soothing than a view of Unyamwezi in the
balmy evenings of spring. As the large yellow sun
nears the horizon, a deep stillness falls upon earth :
even the zephyr seems to lose the power of rustling the lightest leaf. The milky haze of midday
disappears from the firmament, the flush of departing day mantles the distant features of scenery
with a lovely rose-tint, and the twilight is an orange
glow that burns like distant horizontal fires, passing upward through an imperceptibly graduated
scale of colors—saffron, yellow, tender green, and
the lightest azure—into the dark blue of the infinite space above. The charm of the hour seems
to affect even the unimaginative Africans, as they
sit in the central spaces of their villages, or, stretched
under the forest-trees, gaze upon the glories
around.

   " The rainy monsoon is here ushered in, accompanied, and terminated by storms of thunder and
lightning, and occasional hail-falls. The blinding
flashes of white, yellow, or rose color play over the
firmament uninterruptedly for hours, during which
no darkness is visible. In the lighter storms thirty
and thirty-five flashes may be counted in a minute :
so vivid is the glare that it discloses the finest
shades of color, and appears followed by a thick
and palpable gloom, such as would hang before a
blind man's eyes, while a deafening roar, simultaneously following the flash, seems to travel, as it

were, to and fro overhead. Several claps sometimes sound almost at the same moment, and as if coming from different directions. The same storm will, after the most violent of its discharges, pass over, and be immediately followed by a second, showing the superabundance of electricity in the atmosphere.

" Travellers from Unyamwezi homeward returned often represent that country to be the healthiest in Eastern and Central Africa : they quote, as a proof, the keenness of their appetites, and the quantity of food which they consume. The older residents, however, modify their opinions : they declare that digestion does not wait upon appetite ; and that, as in Egypt, Mazanderan, Malabar, and other hot-damp countries, no man long retains rude health. The sequelæ of their maladies are always severe ; few care to use remedies, deeming them inefficacious against morbific influences to them unknown ; convalescence is protracted, painful, and uncertain, and at length they are compelled to lead the lives of confirmed invalids. The gifts of the climate, lassitude and indolence, according to them, predispose to corpulence ; and the regular warmth induces baldness, and thins the beard, thus assimilating strangers in body as in mind to the aborigines. They are unanimous in quoting a curious effect of climate, which they attribute to a corruption of the ' humors and juices of the body.' Men who, after a lengthened sojourn in these regions, return to Oman, throw away the surplus provisions brought from the African coast, burn their clothes and bedding, and for the first two or three months eschew society ; a peculiar effluvium rendering them, it is said, offensive to the finer olfactories of their compatriots.

"The races requiring notice in this region are two, the Wakimbu and the Wanyamwezi.

"The Wakimbu, who are immigrants into Unyamwezi, claim a noble origin, and derive themselves from the broad lands running south of Unyanyembe as far westward as K'hokoro. About twenty masika, wet monsoons, or years ago, according to themselves, they left Nguru, Usanga, and Usenga, in consequence of the repeated attacks of the Warori, and migrated to Kipiri, the district lying south of Tura ; they have now extended into Mgunda Mk'hali and Unyanyembe, where they hold the land by permission of the Wanyamwezi. In these regions there are few obstacles to immigrants. They visit the sultan, make a small present, obtain permission to settle, and name the village after their own chief ; but the original proprietors still maintain their rights to the soil. The Wakimbu build firmly-stockaded villages, tend cattle, and cultivate sorghum and maize, millet and pulse, cucumbers and watermelons. Apparently they are poor, being generally clad in skins. They barter slaves and ivory in small quantities to the merchants, and some travel to the coast. They are considered treacherous by their neighbors, and Mapokera, the Sultan of Tura, is, according to the Arabs, prone to commit ' *avanies*.' They are known by a number of small lines formed by raising the skin with a needle, and opening it by points laterally between the hair of the temples and the eyebrows. In appearance they are dark and uncomely; their arms are bows and arrows, spears, and knives stuck in the leathern waistbelt; some wear necklaces of curiously-plaited straw, others a strip of white cowskin bound around the brow—a truly savage and African decoration. Their language differs from Kinyamwezi.

" The Wanyamwezi tribe, the proprietors of the soil, is the typical race in this portion of Central Africa: its comparative industry and commercial activity have secured to it a superiority over the other kindred races.

" The aspect of the Wanyamwezi is alone sufficient to disprove the existence of very elevated lands in this part of the African interior. They are usually of a dark sepia-brown, rarely colored like diluted Indian ink, as are the Wahiao and slave races to the south, with negroid features markedly less Semitic than the people of the eastern coast. The effluvium from their skins, especially after exercise or excitement, marks their connection with the negro. The hair curls crisply, but it grows to the length of four or five inches before it splits; it is usually twisted into many little ringlets or hanks; it hangs down like a fringe to the neck, and is combed off the forehead after the manner of the ancient Egyptians and the modern Hottentots.

" There are but few ceremonies among the Wanyamwezi. A woman about to become a mother retires from the hut to the jungle, and after a few hours returns with a child wrapped in goat-skin upon her back, and probably carrying a load of firewood on her head. The medical treatment of the Arabs with salt and various astringents for forty days is here unknown. Twins are not common as among the Kafir race, and one of the two is invariably put to death; the universal custom among these tribes is for the mother to wrap a gourd or calabash in skins, to place it to sleep with, and to feed it like, the survivor. If the wife die without issue, the widower claims from her parents the sum paid to them upon marriage; if she leave a child, the property is preserved for it. When the father can afford it, a birth is celebrated by copious libations of pombe. Children are suckled till the end of the second year. Their only education is in the use of the bow and arrow; after the fourth summer the boy begins to learn archery with diminutive weapons, which are gradually increased in strength. Names are given without ceremony, and, as in the countries to the eastward, many of the heathens have been called after their Arab visitors. Circumcision is not practiced by this people. The children in Unyamwezi generally are the property not of the uncle but of the father, who can sell or slay them without blame; in Usukuma or the northern lands, however, succession and inheritance are claimed by the nephews or sisters' sons. The Wanyamwezi have adopted the curious practice of leaving property to their illegitimate children by slave-girls or concubines, to the exclusion of their issue by wives; they justify it by the fact of the former requiring their assistance more than the latter, who have friends and relatives to aid them. As soon as the boy can walk he tends the flocks ; after the age of ten he drives the cattle to pasture, and, considering himself independent of his father, he plants a to-bacco-plot and aspires to build a hut for himself. There is not a boy ' which can not earn his own meat.'

" Another peculiarity of the Wanyamwezi is the position of the wahárá or unmarried girls. Until puberty they live in the father's house ; after that period the spinsters of the village, who usually number from seven to a dozen, assemble together and build for themselves at a distance from their homes a hut where they can receive their friends without parental interference. There is but one limit to community in single life ; if the mhárá or ' maiden ' be likely to become a mother, her ' young man' must marry her under pain of mulct ; and if she die in childbirth, her father demands from her lover a large fine for having taken away his daughter's life. Marriage takes place when the youth can afford to pay the price for a wife ; it varies, according to circumstances, from one to ten cows.

" The habitations of the Eastern Wanyamwezi are the *tembe,* which in the west give way to the circular African hut ; among the poorer sub-tribes the dwelling is a mere stack of straw. The best tembe have large projecting eaves supported by uprights : cleanliness, however, can never be expected in them. Having no limestone, the people ornament the inner and outer walls with long lines of ovals formed by pressure of the finger-tips, after dipping them in ashes and water for whitewash, and into red clay or black mud for variety of color. With this primitive material they sometimes attempt rude imitations of nature—human beings and serpents. In some parts the cross appears, but the people apparently ignore it as a symbol. Rude carving is also attempted upon the massive posts at the entrances of villages, but the figures, though to appearance idolatrous, are never worshipped.

" The characteristic of the Mnyamwezi village is the *iwánzá* "—a convenience resulting probably from the instinct of the sexes, who prefer not to mingle, and for the greater freedom of life and manners. Of these buildings there are two in every settlement, generally built at opposite sides, fronting the normal mrimba-tree, which sheds its filmy shade over the public court-yard. That of the women being a species of harem, was not visited ; as travellers and strangers are always admitted into the male iwánzá, it is more readily described. This public house is a large hut, somewhat more substantial than those adjoining, often smeared with smooth clay, and decorated here and there with broad columns of the ovals before described, and the prints of palms dipped in ashes and placed flat like the hands in ancient Egyptian buildings. The roof is generally a flying thatch raised a foot above the walls—an excellent plan for ventilation in these regions. Outside, the iwánzá is defended against, the incursions of cattle by roughly-barked trunks of trees resting upon stout uprights : in this space men sit, converse, and smoke. The two doorways are protected by rude charms suspended from the lintel, hares' tails, zebras' manes, goats' horns, and other articles.

" The Wanyamwezi have won for themselves a reputation by their commercial industry. Encouraged by the merchants, they are the only professional porters of East Africa ; and even among them the Waklaganza, Wasumbwa, and Wasukuma are the only tribes who regularly visit the coast in this capacity. They are now no longer 'honest and civil to strangers '—semi-civilization has hitherto tended to degradation. They seem to have learned but little by their intercourse with the Arabs. Commerce with them is still in its infancy. They have no idea of credit, although in Karagwah and the northern kingdoms payment may be delayed for a period of two years. They cannot, like some of their neighbors, bargain : a man names the article which he requires, and if it be not forthcoming he will take no other."

CHAPTER VII.

BURTON—DISCOVERY AND EXPLORATION OF THE TANGANYIKA LAKE.

AFTER crossing the Malagarazi River, the journey lay through a howling wilderness, once populous and fertile, but now laid waste by hostile tribes. Snay bin Amir, the friendly Arab merchant at Kazeh, had warned Burton that it would be the most difficult part of the route. The expedition made a short march, the first day, and then, on the 5th of February, set out, over the marshy lowlands on the northern bank of the river and the bordering hills, which were difficult on account of the steep ascents and descents. The soil was marvellously fertile, and the same endless luxuriance of vegetation clothed the heights as the valleys.

For two or three days they pushed onward through this region, sometimes drenched with showers of rain, and exposed to accident from the asses falling in the deep and slippery ravines. Then they reached the Rusugi River, a northern affluent of the Malagarazi, about 100 yards wide, very swift and breast-deep. The porters plunged boldly into the stream, for their numbers protected them from the crocodiles, while the two travellers were transported across on the shoulders of men. When they reached the camping-place, it appeared that one of the Goanese servants, with six porters, and some of the supplies of baggage, were missing. The native guides, however, insisted on advancing, and it was a week before the lost men rejoined the caravan, on the banks of the lake.

On the 9th of February they descended from the ridge beyond the Rusugi River, and traversed a deep swamp of black mud, dotted in the more elevated parts with old salt-pans and pits, where broken pottery and blackened lumps of clay still showed traces of human labor. Then followed deep and rocky ravines, with luxuriant vegetation above and rivulets at the bottom, all very difficult to cross. The porters, who were in a place of famine, insisted on pushing on to the utmost of their strength; but after a march of six hours they were persuaded to halt on a rocky hill, with water near at hand. The guide succeeded in procuring a kaffer ox from a neighboring valley, in the evening, which was a welcome addition to the nearly-exhausted supplies.

The next day there was a similar experience of travel, but it led them to the Ruguvu River, which was crossed with some difficulty, all the goods being thoroughly soaked in the water. Here, however, Burton procured some ears of corns from a native caravan. Then, " a desert march, similar to the stage last travelled, led us to the Unguwwe River a shallow, muddy stream, girt in, as usual, by dense vegetation; and we found a fine large kraal on its left bank. After a cold and rainy night we resumed our march by fording the Unguwwe. Then came the weary toil of fighting through tiger and spear grass, with reeds, rushes, a variety of ferns before unseen, and other lush and lusty growths, clothing a succession of rolling hills, monotonous swellings, where the descent was ever a reflection of the ascent. The paths were broken, slippery, and pitted with deep holes; along their sides, where the ground lay exposed to view, a conglomerate of ferruginous red clay—suggesting a resemblance to the superficies of Londa, as described by Dr. Livingstone—took the place of the granites and sandstones of the eastern countries, and the sinking of the land toward the lake became palpable."

The next day they found grapes and plantains growing wild: scattered fields and plantations gave token of habitation, although no villages were visible. The country was still rough and difficult to traverse, but cliffs and mountains rose in the far distance, like beacons announcing the existence of a vast lake at their feet. Finally, on the 13th of February, after entering an open, grassy plain, thinly sprinkled with trees, Burton saw one of the native guides run forward and change the direction of the caravan. He rode on to ascertain the meaning of this manœuvre, and presently reached a steep and stony hill, in climbing which Speke's riding-ass fell and died. When they gained the summit, the other animals, utterly exhausted, refused to proceed. Burton turned to his servant, Bombay, and asked:

" What is that streak of light which lies below ?"
" I am of the opinion," said Bombay, " that that is
the water." Burton gazed in dismay; the remains of
his temporary blindness, the intervening veil of
trees, and a broad ray of sunshine illuminating but
one reach of the lake, seemed to have greatly diminished its extent. Somewhat prematurely he began
to lament that he had risked life and lost health for
so poor a prize : it was all Arab exaggeration, and
his first thought was to return immediately and endeavor to reach the Nyanza, or Northern Lake.

But, after advancing a few yards further, the
whole scene suddenly burst upon his view, filling
him with admiration, wonder and delight. " Nothing,
in sooth," he says, " could be more picturesque
than this first view of the Tanganyika Lake, as it
lay in the lap of the mountains, basking in the gorgeous tropical sunshine. Below and beyond a
short foreground of rugged and precipitous hill-
fold, down which the footpath zigzags painfully,
a narrow strip of emerald green, never sere and
marvellously fertile, shelves toward a ribbon of
glistening yellow sand, here bordered by sedgy
rushes, there cleanly and clearly cut by the breaking wavelets. Farther in front stretch the waters,
an expanse of the lightest and softest blue, in
breadth varying from thirty to thirty-five miles, and
sprinkled by the crisp east wind with tiny crescents
of snowy foam. The background in front is a
high and broken wall of steel-colored mountain,
here flecked and capped with pearly mist, there
standing sharply pencilled against the azure air ; its

yawning chasms, marked by a deeper plum-color, fall toward dwarf hills of mound-like proportions, which apparently dip their feet in the wave. To the south, and opposite the long low point behind which the Malagarazi River discharges the red loam suspended in its violent stream, lie the bluff head-lands and capes of Uguhha, and, as the eye dilates, it falls upon a cluster of outlying islets speckling a sea-horizon. Villages, cultivated lands, the fre-quent canoes of the fishermen on the waters, and on a nearer approach the murmurs of the waves breaking upon the shore, give a something of va-riety, of movement, of life to the landscape, which, like all the fairest prospects in these regions, wants but a little of the neatness and finish of art— mosques and kiosks, palaces and villas, gardens and orchards—contrasting with the profuse lavishness and magnificence of nature, and diversifying the unbroken *coup d'œil* of excessive vegetation, to rival, if not to excel, the most admired scenery of the classic regions, the riant shores of this vast crevasse appeared doubly beautiful to me after the silent and spectral mangrove-creeks on the East African sea-board, and the melancholy, monotonous expe-rience of desert and jungle scenery, tawny rock and sun-parched plain or rank herbage and flats of black mire. Truly it was a revel for soul and sight."

That evening they reached a village on the shore, called Ukaranga, somewhat to the south-ward of Ujiji, their destination, having been led astray by the native guide. Burton, however, lost

no time in procuring a boat for the remainder of
the journey, and set off next morning over the
quiet, beautiful water, enjoying the views of the distant purple mountains which enclose it. He was
greatly disappointed in finding no signs of an important commercial mart, on approaching Ujiji.
Only a few log canoes, and some groups of curious
fishermen, denoted the landing-place, and the ghaut
or quay of disembarkation was the sand of the
shore.

" Around the ghaut a few scattered huts, in the
humblest bee-hive shape, represented the port-town.
Advancing some hundred yards through a din of
shouts and screams, tom-toms, and trumpets, which
defies description, and mobbed by a swarm of black
beings, whose eyes seemed about to start from their
heads with surprise, I passed a relic of Arab civilization, the ' bazaar.' It is a plot of higher ground,
cleared of grass, and flanked by a crooked tree ; there
between 10 A.M and 3 P.M.—weather permitting—
a mass of standing and squatting negroes buy and
sell, barter and exchange, offer and chaffer with a
hubbub heard for miles, and there a spear or dag-
ger-thrust brings on, by no means unfrequently, a
skirmishing faction-fight. The articles exposed for
sale are sometimes goats, sheep, and poultry, generally fish, vegetables, and a few fruits, plantains, and
melons ; palm-wine is a staple commodity, and occasionally an ivory or a slave is hawked about ;
those industriously disposed employ themselves during the intervals of bargaining in spinning a coarse
yarn with the rudest spindle, or in picking the cot-

ton, which is placed in little baskets on the ground.
I was led to a ruinous tembe, built by an Arab
merchant, Hamid bin Salim, who had allowed it to
be tenanted by ticks and slaves. Situated, however, half a mile from, and backed by, the little village of Kawele, whose mushroom-huts barely pro-
truded their summits above the dense vegetation,
and placed at a similar distance from the water in
front, it had the double advantage of proximity to
provisions, and of a view which at first was highly
enjoyable. The Tanganyika is ever seen to advantage from its shores; upon its surface the sight
wearies with the unvarying tintage—all shining
greens and hazy blues—while continuous parallels
of lofty hills, like the sides of a huge trough, close
the prospect and suggest the idea of confinement.

" At Ujiji terminates, after twelve stages, which
native caravans generally finish in a fortnight, all
halts included, the transit of the fifth region. The
traveller has now accomplished a total number of
85 long, or 100 short stages, which, with necessary
rests, but excluding detentions and long halts, oc-
cupy 150 days. The direct longitudinal distance
from the coast is 540 geographical miles, which the
sinuosities of the road prolong to 955, or in round
numbers 950 statute miles. The number of days
expended by the expedition in actual marching was
100, of hours 420, which gives a rate of 2.27 miles
per hour. The total time was seven and a half
months, from the 27th of June, 1857, to the 18th of
February, 1858; thus the number of the halts ex-
ceeded by one third the number of the marches. In

practice Arab caravans seldom arrive at the Tanganyika, for reasons before alluded to, under a total period of six months. Those lightly laden may make Unyamyembe in between two and a half and three months, and from Unyanyembe to Ujiji in twenty-five stages, which would reduce their journey to four months.

" Ujiji—also called Manyofo, which appears, however, peculiar to a certain sultanat or district—is the name of a province, not, as has been represented, of a single town. It was first visited by the Arabs about 1840, ten years after they had penetrated to Unyamwezi; they found it conveniently situated as a mart upon the Tanganyika Lake, and a central point where their depots might be established, and whence their factors and slaves could navigate the waters and collect slaves and ivory from the tribes upon its banks.

" Abundant humidity and a fertile soil, evidenced by the large forest-trees and the profusion of ferns, render Ujiji the most productive province in this section of Africa : vegetables, which must elsewhere be cultivated, here seem to flourish almost spontaneously. Rice of excellent quality was formerly raised by the Arabs upon the shores of the Tanganyika; it grew luxuriantly, attaining, it is said, the height of eight or nine feet. The inhabitants, however, preferring sorghum, and wearied out by the depredations of the monkey, the elephant, and the hippopotamus, have allowed the more civilized cereal to degenerate.

" The bazaar at Ujiji is well supplied. Fresh

fish of various kinds is always procurable, except during the violence of the rains : the people, however, invariably cut it up and clean it out before bringing it to market. Good honey abounds after the wet monsoon. By the favor of the chief, milk and butter may be purchased every day. Long-tailed sheep and well-bred goats, poultry and eggs— the two latter are never eaten by the people—are brought in from the adjoining countries : the Arabs breed a few Manilla ducks, and the people rear, but will not sell, pigeons.

"The Wajiji are a burly race of barbarians, far stronger than the tribes hitherto traversed, with dark skins, plain features, and straight, sturdy limbs : they are larger and heavier men than the Wanyamwezi, and the type, as it approaches Central Africa, becomes rather negro than negroid. Their feet and hands are large and flat, their voices are harsh and strident, and their looks as well as their manners are independent even to insolence. The women, who are held in high repute, resemble, and often excel, their masters in rudeness and violence ; they think little in their cups of entering a stranger's hut, and of snatching up and carrying away an article which excites their admiration. Many of both sexes, and all ages, are disfigured by the small-pox —the Arabs have vainly taught them inoculation— and there are few who are not afflicted by boils and various eruptions.

"The lakists are an almost amphibious race, excellent divers, strong swimmers and fishermen, and vigorous ichthyophagists all. At times, when excited by the morning coolness and by the prospect of a good haul, they indulge in a manner of merriment which resembles the gambols of sportive water-fowls : standing upright and balancing themselves in their hollow logs, which appear but little larger than themselves, they strike the water furiously with their paddles, skimming over the surface, dashing to and fro, splashing one another, urging forward, backing, and wheeling their craft, now capsizing, then regaining their position with wonderful dexterity. They make coarse hooks, and have many varieties of nets and creels. Conspicuous on the waters and in the villages is the dewa, or ' otter ' of Oman, a triangle of stout reeds, which shows the position of the net. A stronger kind, and used for the larger ground-fish, is a cage of open basket-work, provided like the former with a bait and two entrances. The fish once entangled cannot escape, and a log of wood used as a trimmer, attached to a float-rope of rushy plants, directs the fisherman.

" The Wajiji are considered by the Arabs to be the most troublesome race in these black regions. They are taught by the example of their chiefs to be rude, insolent, and extortionate ; they demand beads even for pointing out the road ; they will deride and imitate a stranger's speech and manner before his face ; they can do nothing without a long preliminary of the fiercest scolding ; they are as ready with a blow as with a word ; and they may often be seen playing at ' rough and tumble,' fighting, pushing, and tearing hair, in their boats. A Mjiji uses his dagger or his spear upon a guest with little hesitation ; he thinks twice, however, before drawing blood, if it will cause a feud. Their roughness of manner is dashed with a curious ceremoniousness. When the sultan appears among his people, he stands in a circle and claps his hands, to which all respond in the same way. Women courtesy to one another, bending the right knee almost to the ground. When two men meet, they clasp each other's arms with both hands, rubbing them up and down, and ejaculating for some minutes, ' Nama sanga ? nama sanga ?—art thou well ?' They then pass the hands down to the forearm, exclaiming, ' Wáhke ? wáhke ?—how art thou ?' and finally they clap palms at each other, a token of respect which appears common to these tribes of Central Africa. The children have all the frowning and unprepossessing look of their parents ; they reject little civilities, and seem to spend life in disputes, biting and clawing like wild-cats. There appears to be little family affection in this undemonstrative race.

"My first care after settling in Hamid's tembe, was to purify the floor by pastilles of asafœtida and fumigations of gunpowder ; my second was to prepare the roof for the rainy season. Improvement, however, progressed slowly ; the ' children ' of Said bin Salim were too lazy to work ; and the Wanyamwezi porters, having expended their hire in slaves, and fearing loss by delay, took the earliest opportunity of deserting. By the aid of a Msawahili artisan, I provided a pair of cartels, with substitutes for chairs and tables. Benches of clay were built round the rooms, but they proved useless, being found regularly every morning occupied in force by a swarming, struggling colony of the largest white ants. The roof, long overgrown with tall grass, was fortified with an extra coat of mud : it never ceased, however, leaking like a colander ; presently the floor was covered with deep puddles, then masses of earth dropped from the sopped copings and sides of the solid walls, and, at last, during the violent showers, half the building fell in. The consequence of the extreme humidity was, that every book which had English paste in it was rendered useless by decay ; writing was rendered illegible by stains and black mildew ; moreover, during my absence while exploring the lake, Said bin Salim having neglected to keep a fire, as was ordered, constantly burning in the house, a large botanical collection was irretrievably lost.

" At first the cold damp climate of the Lake Regions did not agree with us ; perhaps, too, the fish diet was over-rich and fat, and the abundance of vegetables led to little excesses. All energy seemed to have abandoned us. I lay for a fortnight upon the earth, too blind to read or write except with long intervals, too weak to ride, and too ill to converse. My companion who, when arriving at the Tanganyika Lake was almost as ' groggy ' upon his legs as I was, suffered from a painful ophthalmia, and from a curious distortion of face, which made him chew sideways, like a ruminant. Valentine was nearly blind ; and he also had a wry mouth, by no means the properest for the process of mastication. Gaetano, who arrived at Ujiji on the 17th of February, was half starved, and his anxiety to make up for lost time brought on a severe attack of fever. The Baloch complained of influenzas and catarrhs : too lazy to build huts after occupying Kannena's 'Traveller's Bungalow' for the usual week, they had been turned out in favor of fresh visitors, and their tempers were as sore as their lungs and throats.''

Burton's preparations for exploring the lake were greatly hindered by the suspicion and rapacity of the chief, Kannena, who levies a duty upon all trade, and could not understand the motive of the traveller in refusing to purchase ivory and slaves. The latter endeavored to make up by presents for the chief's possible loss, but he admits that his policy was a mistake, and that he ought to have feigned some commercial character. Since it seemed almost impossible to procure a large boat for navigating the lake, at Ujiji, Burton dispatched Speke on the 2nd of March in a large canoe across the water, to hire a sailing boat which was reported to be owned by an Arab merchant on the other side.

Speke returned on the 29th, having reached the opposite shore at the island of Kivira, about 70 miles south of Ujiji. But he did not succeed in obtaining the boat : all his supplies were ruined by the rains, and he was, physically, in a melancholy plight. By this time, however, Burton was very anxious to examine the northern end of the lake, where, he was assured by the natives, there was a

large river flowing out of it to the north. This, he
naturally supposed, could only be one of the affluents
—if not the main stream—of the Nile. By making
renewed presents to the chief, and paying an exorbitant hire, he finally obtained two large canoes and
fifty-five oarsmen. Preparations were hastened, on
account of the approaching departure of an armed
Arab caravan to the northern end of the lake, and
on the 9th of April everything was in readiness.

" Early on the next morning," he writes, " we embarked on board the canoes : the crews had been
collected, paid, and rationed ; but as long as they
were near home it was impossible to keep them
together. Each man thinking solely of his own
affairs, and disdaining the slightest regard for the
wishes, the comfort, or the advantage of his employers, they objected systematically to every article
which I had embarked. Kannena had filled the
canoes with his and his people's salt, consequently
he would not carry even a cartel. Various points
settled, we hove anchor, or rather hauled up the
block of granite doing anchoral duty, and, with the
usual hubbub and strife, the orders which every
man gives, and the advice which no man takes, we
paddled in half an hour to a shingly and grassy
creek defended by a sand-pit and backed by a few
tall massive trees. Opposite, and but a few yards
distant, rose the desert islet of Bangwe, a quoin-
shaped mass of sandstone and red earth, bluff to
the north, and gradually shelving toward the water
at the other extremity : the prolific moisture above
and around had covered its upper ledge with a

coat of rich thick vegetation.   Landward the country rises above the creek, and upon its earth-waves, which cultivation shares with wild growth, appear a few scattered hamlets."

For the first three days they had calm weather, except at night, and slowly coasted along the eastern shore, to a village called Nyasanga.   "This is the place," says Burton, "for a few words concerning boating and voyaging upon the Tanganyika Lake.   The Wajiji, and indeed all these races, never work silently or regularly.   The paddling is accompanied by a long, monotonous melancholy howl, answered by the yells and shouts of the chorus, and broken occasionally by a shrill scream of delight from the boys which seems violently to excite the adults.   The bray and clang of the horns, shaums, and tom-toms, blown and banged incessantly by one or more men in the bow of each canoe, made worse by brazen-lunged imitations of these instruments in the squeaking trebles of the younger paddlers, lasts throughout the livelong day, except when terror induces a general silence.

These 'Wáná Máji'—sons of water—work in 'spirts,' applying lustily to the task till the perspiration pours down their sooty persons.   Despite my remonstrances, they insisted upon splashing the water in shovelfuls over the canoe.   They make terribly long faces, however, they tremble like dogs in a storm of sleet, and they are ready to whimper when compelled by sickness or accident to sit with me under the endless cold wave-bath in the hold. After a few minutes of exertion, fatigued and worn,

they stop to quarrel, or they progress languidly till recruited for another effort. When two boats are together they race continually till a bump—the signal for a general grin—and the difficulty of using the entangled paddles afford an excuse for a little loitering, and for the loud chatter and violent abuse without which apparently this people cannot hold converse. At times they halt to eat, drink, and smoke : the bhang-pipe is produced after every hour, and the paddles are taken in while they indulge in the usual screaming convulsive whooping-cough. They halt for their own purposes but not for ours ; all powers of persuasion fail when they are requested to put into a likely place for collecting shells or stones. For some superstitious reason they allow no questions to be asked, they will not dip a pot for water into the lake, fearing to be followed and perhaps boarded by crocodiles, which are hated and dreaded by these black navigators, much as is the shark by our seamen, and for the same cause not a scrap of food must be thrown overboard—even the offal must be cast into the hold. " Whittling " is here a mortal sin : to chip or break off the smallest bit of even a condemned old tub drawn up on the beach causes a serious disturbance. By the advice of a kind and amiable friend, I had supplied myself with the desiderata for sounding and ascertaining the bottom of the lake : the crew would have seen me under water rather than halt for a moment when it did not suit their purpose. The wild men lose half an hour, when time is most precious, to secure a dead fish as it floats past the canoe entangled in its net.   They never pass a village without a dispute ; some wishing to land, others objecting because some wish it. The captain, who occupies some comfortable place in the bow, stern, or waist, has little authority ; and if the canoe be allowed to touch the shore, its men will spring out, without an idea of consulting aught beyond their own inclinations.   Arrived at the halting-place they pour on shore ; some proceed to gather firewood, others go in search of rations, and others raise the boothies."

On the 15th of April they reached a village called Wafanya, the southernmost settlement in a new region, called Urundi.   The inhabitants were noisy and troublesome, but not hostile, and provisions were abundant.   Beyond this point, however, the people are reported to be robbers, and the trading-boats therefore cross the lake, which is much narrower to the northward.   The transit is divided into two stages by an island called Ubwari, which is eighteen miles from the eastern and seven from the western shore.   This is the only island near the centre of the Tanganyika Lake—a long, narrow ridge of rock, from twenty to twenty-five miles in length.   It is covered with the most luxuriant vegetation, and there are signs of cultivation upon its slopes ; but the boatmen only touch at one or two points at the northern extremity, believing that cannibals inhabit the main portion.

After a rest of two days at Wafanya, the expedition prepared to cross the lake, but was again delayed by an altercation among the natives and the threatening appearance of the sky. Finally, on the 19th, the men rowed westward towards Ubwari, "which appeared a long strip of green directly opposite Urundi, and distant from eighteen to twenty miles. A little wind caused a heavy chopping swell; we were wet to the skin, and as noon drew nigh, the sun shone stingingly, reflected by a mirrory sea. At 10 A.M. the party drew in their paddles and halted to eat and smoke. About two P.M. the wind and waves again arose—once more we were drenched, and the frail craft was constantly baled out to prevent water-logging. A long row of nine hours placed the canoes at a roadstead, with the usual narrow line of yellow sand, on the western coast of Ubwari Island. The men landed to dry themselves, and to cook some putrid fish which they had caught as it floated past the canoe, with the reed triangle that buoyed up the net. It was 'strong meat' to us, but to them its staleness was as the 'taste in his butter' to the Londoner, the pleasing toughness of the old cock to the Arab, and the savory 'fumet' of the aged he-goat to the Baloch. After a short halt we moved a little northward to Mzimu, a strip of low land dividing the waters from their background of grassy rise, through which a swampy line winds from the hills above. Here we found canoes drawn up, and the islanders flocked from their hamlets to change their ivory and slaves, goats and provisions, for salt and beads, wire and cloth. The Wabwari are a peculiar, and by no means a comely race. The men are habited in the usual mbugu, tigered with black stripes, and tailed like leopard-skins : a wisp of fine grass acts as fillet, and their waists, wrists, and ankles, their knob-sticks, spears, and daggers, are bound with ratan-bark, instead of the usual wire."

They halted another day on the opposite side of the island, and then made for a point on the western shore of the lake, which appeared to be 15 miles distant. The village of Murivumba was reached after a row of nine hours, but the native boatmen refused to stop there, asserting that the people were cannibals. The party encamped on the sand at a safe distance, and the next day the boatmen paddled northward for ten hours along the shore, the increasing nearness of the mountains in the east showing that they were approaching the head of the lake. Still another long day of paddling against a head-wind, another night on the sand, and a row of three hours and a half, on the 26th of April, landed them at the little roadstead, where the trade of the Uvira country is carried on,—the point generally reached by Arab merchants from the coast.

" Great rejoicings ushered in the end of our outward bound voyage. Crowds gathered on the shore to gaze at the new merchants arriving at Uvira, with the usual concert, vocal and instrumental, screams, shouts, and songs, shaums, horns, and tom-toms. The captains of the two canoes performed with the most solemn gravity a bear-like dance upon the mat-covered benches which form the " quarter-decks," extending their arms, pirouetting upon both heels, and springing up and squatting down till their hams touched the mats. The crews, with a general grin which showed all their ivories, rattled their paddles against the sides of their canoes in token of greeting, a custom derived probably from the ceremonious address of the lakists, which is performed by rapping their elbows against their ribs.

" We had now reached the " ne plus ultra," the northermost station to which merchants have as yet been admitted. The people are generally on bad terms with the Wavira, and in these black regions a traveller coming direct from an enemy's territory is always suspected of hostile intentions—no trifling bar to progress. Opposite us still rose, in a high broken line, the mountains of inhospitable Urundi, apparently prolonged beyond the northern extremity of the waters. The head, which was not visible from the plain, is said to turn north-northwestward, and to terminate after a voyage of two days, which some informants, however, reduce to six hours. The breadth of the Tanganyika is here between seven and eight miles. On the 28th of April all my hopes —which, however, I had hoped against hope—were rudely dashed to the ground. I received a visit from the three stalwart sons of the Sultan Maruta : they were the noblest type of negroid seen near the lake, with symmetrical heads, regular features, and pleasing countenances ; their well-made limbs and athletic frames of a shiny jet black, were displayed to advantage by their loose aprons of red and dark-striped bark-cloth, slung, like game-bags, over their shoulders, and were set off by opal-colored eye-balls, teeth like pearls, and a profusion of broad, massive rings of snowy ivory round their arms, and conical ornaments like dwarf marling-spikes of hippopotamus-tooth suspended from their necks. The subject of the mysterious river issuing from the lake was at once brought forward. They all declared that they had visited it, they offered to forward me, but they unanimously asserted, and every man in the host of bystanders confirmed their words, that 'Rusizi' *enters into*, and does not *flow out of* the Tanganyika. I felt sick at heart. I had not, it is true, undertaken to explore the Coy Fountains by this route ; but the combined assertions of the cogging shaykh and the false Msawahili had startled me from the proprieties of reason, and—this was the result.

"Uvira is much frequented on account of its cheapness ; it is the great northern depot for slaves, ivory, grain, bark cloth, and iron-ware, and, in the season, hardly a day elapses without canoes coming in for merchandise or provisions. The imports are the kitindi, salt, beads, tobacco, and cotton cloth. Rice does not grow there, holcus and maize are sold at one to two fundo of common beads per masuta or small load—perhaps sixteen pounds—and one khete is sufficient during the months of plenty to purchase five pounds of manioc, or two and even three fowls. Plantains of the large and coarse variety are common and cheap, and one cloth is given for two goodly earthen pots full of palm-oil."

Burton spent nine days at Uvira, vainly endeavoring to reach the northern extremity of the lake, which according to some accounts was distant two days' journey, and according to others, only six hours. The native boatmen could be neither bribed nor bullied into accompanying him, and two Arab agents at the place equally refused. The people of Urundi, on the opposite shore, are dreaded by those of Uvira, and there appeared to be no regular trade opened with the northern regions. Moreover, Burton was suffering from an ulceration of the tongue, which made speaking very painful, and the tongue, in those parts, is the traveller's chief offensive and defensive weapon. It is a characteristic of African travel that the explorer may be stopped on the very threshold of success, by a single remaining stage, as effectively as if all the waves of the Atlantic or the sands of Arabia lay between.

There were signs of gales brewing in the north, and on the forenoon of the 6th of May, they set out on the return voyage. The boats touched at the same points on the western shore, and crossed the western arm of the lake to the island of Ubwari, with no other trouble than that arising from occasional rough weather. Near their former camping-place on the island the crews procured a large supply of palm-oil from the natives. On the 10th, the sky was gloomy, the air oppressive, and all things foreboded a violent storm ; the travellers wished to wait a day longer at the island, but the natives were so anxious to reach home that they insisted on crossing the lake.

" We left Mzimu at sunset," says Burton, " and for two hours coasted along the shore. It was one of those portentous evenings of the tropics—a calm before a tempest—unnaturally quiet; we struck out, however, boldly toward the eastern shore of the Tanganyika, and the western mountains rapidly lessened on the view. Before, however, we reached the mid-channel, a cold gust—in these regions the invariable presage of a storm—swept through the deepening shades cast by the heavy rolling clouds, and the vivid nimble lightning flashed, at first by intervals, then incessantly, with a ghastly and blinding glow, illuminating the ' vast of night,' and followed by a palpable obscure and a pithy darkness, that weighed upon the sight. As terrible was its accompaniment of rushing, reverberating thunder, now a loud roar, peal upon peal, like the booming of heavy batteries, then breaking into a sudden crash, which was presently followed by a rattling discharge like the sharp pattering of musketry. The bundles of spears planted upright amidships, like paratonnerres, seemed to invite the electric fluid into the canoes. The waves began to rise, the rain descended, at first in warning drops, then in torrents, and had the wind steadily arisen, the cockle-shell craft never could have lived through the short, chopping sea which characterizes the Tanganyika in heavy weather. The crew, though blinded by the showers and frightened by the occasional gusts, held their own gallantly enough; at times, however, the moaning cry, " Oh, my wife !" showed what was going on within. Bombay, a noted Voltairian in fine weather, spent the length of that wild night in reminiscences of prayer. I sheltered myself from the storm under my best friend, the Mackintosh, and thought of the far-famed couplet of Hafiz— with its mystic meaning I will not trouble the reader :

" This collied night, these horrid waves, these gusts that sweep
    the whirling deep !
What reck they of our evil plight, who on the shore securely
    sleep ?"

Fortunately the rain beat down wind and sea, otherwise nothing short of a miracle could have preserved us for a dry death."

On the morning of the 10th they reached Wafan-ya, where the welcome rest after the storm, was broken by a violent altercation among the natives. During the confusion, one of the Goanese servants fired a pistol into the crowd, shooting one of the Ujiji boatmen through the body. Burton considered himself lucky in paying a fine of cloth and beads, of the value of forty-eight dollars. It was fortunate for him that the man was a slave ; had it been a free native, the trouble, expense, and possible danger, would have been far greater. Three days afterwards the boats returned triumphantly to Ujiji, welcomed by all the people of the place, men, women and children, who rushed into the water to greet their relatives or friends among the crews.

" We had expended upwards of a month," Burton writes, from the 10th of April to the 13th of May, 1858, in this voyage of 15 days outward bound, nine at Uvira, and nine in returning. The boating was rather a severe trial. We had no means of resting the back ; the holds of the canoes, besides being knee - deep in water, were disgracefully crowded : they had been appropriated to us and our four servants by Kannena, but by degrees he introduced, in addition to the sticks, spears, broken vases, pots, and gourds, a goat, two or three small boys, one or two sick sailors, the little slave-girl and the large sheep. The canoes were top-heavy with the number of their crew, and the shipping of many seas spoiled our tents, and, besides, wetted our salt and soddened our grain and flour ; the gunpowder was damaged, and the guns were honey-combed with rust. Besides the splashing of the paddles and the dashing of waves, heavy showers fell almost every day and night, and the intervals were bursts of burning sunshine.

" The discomfort of the halt was not less than that of the boat. At first we pitched tents near the villages, in tall fetid grass, upon ground never level, where stones were the succedanea for tent-pegs stolen for fuel, and where we slept literally upon mire. The temperature inside was ever in extremes, now a raw rainy cold, then a steam-bath that damped us like an April shower. The villagers, especially in the remoter districts, were even more troublesome, noisy, and inquisitive than the Wagogo. A ' notable passion of wonder ' appeared in them. We felt like baited bears : we were mobbed in a moment, and scrutinized from every point of view by them ; the inquisitive wretches stood on tiptoe, they squatted on their hams, they bent sideways, they thrust forth their necks like hissing geese to vary the prospect. Their eyes, ' glaring lightning-like out of their heads,' as old Homer hath it, seemed to devour us ; in the ecstasy of curiosity they shifted from one muzungu to his ' brother,' till, like the well-known ass between the two bundles of hay, they could not enjoy either. They were pertinacious as flies ; to drive them away was only to invite a return, while—worst grief of all—the women were plain, and their grotesque salutations resembled the ' encounter of two dog-apes.' "

In spite of all these privations, the health of the explorers was much improved by the voyage. Speke was still hard of hearing, but he had fully recovered his sight, and Burton's paralysis had almost left him. The rainy season broke up, the day after their return to Ujiji, and the climate became dry, bracing and agreeable. Everything was favorable, except the almost exhausted state of their supplies. They could neither make preparations for the exploration of the southern portion of the lake, nor for the return to Kazeh, before the arrival of fresh goods from the latter place. Suddenly, on the 22nd of May, a discharge of muskets announced the arrival of a caravan, and the hut was presently surrounded with boxes and bales, slaves and porters. Most welcome of all, the travellers received letters and papers from Zanzibar and England, their first mail in eleven months. Among other packages, there was a " Low Church " tract, sent by the American Consul at Zanzibar !

" This was an unexpected good fortune, happening at a crisis when it was really wanted. My joy was somewhat damped by inspecting the packs of the fifteen porters. Twelve were laden with ammunition which was not wanted, and with munitions *de bouche*, which were : nearly half the bottles of curry-powder, spices, and cognac were broken, tea coffee, and sugar had been squeezed out of their tin canisters, and much of the rice and coffee had disappeared. The three remaining loads were one of American domestics—sixty shukkahs—and the rest contained fifteen coral bracelets and white beads. All were the refuse of their kind : the good Hindoos at Zanzibar had seized this opportunity to dispose of their flimsy, damaged, and unsalable articles. This outfit was sufficient to carry us comfortably to Unyanyembe. I saw, however, with regret, that it was wholly inadequate for the purpose of exploring the two southern thirds of the Tanganyika Lake, much less for returning to Zanzibar, via the Nyassa or Maravi Lake, and Kilwa, as I had once dreamed."

Burton thus sums up his observations of the size and character of the lake : " The Tanganyika occupies the centre of the length of the African continent, which extends from 32° N. to 33° S. latitude, and it lies on the western extremity of the eastern third of the breadth. Its general direction is parallel to the inner African line of volcanic action drawn from Gondar southward through the regions about Kilima-ngáo (Kilimanjáro) to Mount Njesa, the eastern wall of the Nyassa Lake. The general formation suggests, as in the case of the Dead Sea, the idea of a volcano of depression—not, like the

Nyanza or Ukerewe, a vast reservoir formed by the drainage of mountains. Judging from the eye, the walls of this basin rise in an almost continuous curtain, rarely waving and infracted, to 2,000 or 3,000 feet above the water-level. The lower slopes are well wooded : upon the higher summits large trees are said not to grow ; the deficiency of soil, and the prevalence of high, fierce winds would account for the phenomena. The lay is almost due north and south, and the form a long oval, widening in the central portions and contracting systematically at both extremities. The length of the bed was thus calculated : From Ujiji (in S. lat. 4° 55') to Uvira (in S. lat. 3° 25'), where the narrowing of the breadth evidences approach to the northern head, was found by exploration a direct distance of 1° 30'=90 miles, which, allowing for the interval between Uvira and the River Rusizi, that forms the northernmost limit, may be increased to 100 rectilinear geographical miles. According to the Arab voyagers, who have frequently rounded the Lake Ujiji in eight stages from the northern and twelve from the southern end of the lake, the extent from Ujiji to the Marungu River, therefore, is roughly computed at 150 miles. The total of length, from Uvira, in S. lat. 3° 25', to Marungu, in S. lat. 7° 20·, would then be somewhat less than 250 rectilinear geographical miles. About Ujiji the water appears to vary in breadth from 30 to 35 miles, but the serpentine form of the banks, with a succession of serrations and indentations of salient and re-entering angles—some jutting far and irregularly into the

bed—render the estimate of average difficult.   The
Arabs agree in correctly stating, that opposite Ujiji
the shortest breadth of the lake is about equal to
the channel which divides Zanzibar from the main
land, or between 23 and 24 miles.   At Uvira the
breadth narrows to eight miles.   Assuming, therefore, the total length at 250, and the mean breadth
at 20 geographical miles, the circumference of the
Tanganyika would represent, in round numbers, a
total of 550 miles ; the superficial area, which
seems to vary little, covers about 5,000 square miles ;
and the drainage from the beginning of the great
Central African depression in Unyamwezi, in E.
long. 33° 58′, numbers from the eastward about 240
miles.

"By B. P. thermometer the altitude of the Tanganyika is 1,850 feet above the sea-level, and about
2,000 feet below the adjacent plateau of Unyamwezi
and the Nyanza, or northern lake.

"A careful investigation and comparison of statements leads to the belief that the Tanganyika receives and absorbs the whole river-system—the net-
work of streams, nullahs, and torrents—of that portion of the Central African depression whose water-
shed converges toward the great reservoir.   Geographers will doubt that such a mass, situated at so
considerable an altitude, can maintain its level without an effluent.   Moreover, the freshness of the
water would, under normal circumstances, argue the
escape of saline matter washed down by the in-
fluents from the area of drainage.   But may not
the Tanganyika, situated, like the Dead Sea, as the

reservoir for supplying with humidity the winds which have parted with their moisture in the barren and arid regions of the south, maintain its general level by the exact balance of supply and evaporation? And may not the saline particles deposited in its waters be wanting in some constituent which renders them evident to the taste?"

This statement of Burton is entirely corroborated by more recent discoveries. The Victoria Nyanza, according to Speke, is 3,308 feet above the sea, and the Albert Nyanza, discovered by Baker, 2,720 feet. It is therefore impossible that the Tanganyika discharges into the latter lake, or, in fact, northward. Although the great lake Nyassa, explored by Livingstone, has an altitude of only 1,300 feet above the sea, yet its northern end is enclosed by an unbroken sweep of high mountains, beyond which, according to all native accounts, there are dry table-lands. The probability of a connection between the Tanganyika and the Kasai River, or some other affluent of the Congo, or Zaire, is almost too slight to be entertained : the lake is undoubtedly the centre of a Central Africa basin belonging to itself.

CHAPTER VIII.

BURTON.——RETURN TO KAZEH——DISCOVERY OF THE VICTORIA NYANZA.

IMMEDIATELY after the arrival of the caravan, Burton made preparations for quitting Ujiji. During the three months and a half which had elapsed since his first view of the lake, every one of the attendants hired at the coast—the Baloch guards, guides and servants—had been investing in slaves, and they united in turning the departure into a sort of flight, fearing lest their human merchandise should seize the opportunity to run off with itself. On the 26th of May the travellers saw the Tanganyika Lake at sunrise, for the last time. Masses of brown clouds, luminously fringed with purple, covered the eastern sky, and behind them the sun shot out his rays like the spokes of a huge aërial wheel, pouring a broad flood of gold over the light blue water. The consciousness of having succeeded in the main object of the journey balanced their regret at being obliged to leave something undone, and they turned eastward with light hearts.

An Arab merchant, Said bin Majid, joined them

with his caravan for the return to Kazeh. Button's own party, however, had hurried onward with such nervous haste, leaving part of the stores behind, that he did not overtake and succeed in organizing them for two days, during which time many things were lost. Said bin Majid insisted, also, on hurrying past the appointed stations, and by his neglect to lay in the necessary supplies was detained afterwards. The caravans took a more northerly route, in order to avoid the deeper portions of the affluents of the Malagarazi River, but the country, though less broken, was very similar in character to what they had already seen. After a few violent thunder-storms, the land rapidly dried up, and as they approached the river, conflagrations became frequent. A sheet of flame, beginning with the size of a spark, would overspread the hill-side, advancing on the wings of the wind with the roaring rushing sound of many hosts where the grass lay thick; shooting huge forky tongues high into the dark air where the great trees were caught; smouldering and darkening as it struck a line of rocks, then blazing and soaring again until, topping the brow of a hill, the sheet became a thin line of fire and gradually vanished from the view.

Resuming their march along the cold and foggy valley of the Malagarazi, they reached the old and dreaded ferry-place on the river, on the 4th of June. The stream was much broader and deeper than before, which gave the fierce native chief an opportunity of making greater exactions. The crossing occupied seven hours; but when it was finished the caravans were at ease, for no further obstacle now intervened between them and Kazeh.

"An eventless march of twelve days led from the Malagarazi Ferry to Unyanyembe. Avoiding the *détour* to Msene we followed this time the more direct southern route. I had expected again to find the treacle-like surface over which we had before crept, and perhaps even in a worse state; but the inundations compelled the porters to skirt the little hills bounding the swamps. Provisions—rice, holcus, and panicum, manioc, cucumbers, and sweet potatoes, pulse, ground-nuts, and tobacco—became plentiful as we progressed; the arrow-root and the bhang-plant flourished wild, and plantains and palmyras were scattered over the land. On the 8th of June, emerging from inhospitable Uvinza into neutral ground, we were pronounced to be out of danger, and on the next day, when in the meridian of the Usagozi, we were admitted for the first time to the comfort of a village. Three days afterward we separated from Said bin Majid. Having a valuable store of tusks, he had but half loaded his porters; he also half fed them: the consequence was that they marched like madmen, and ours followed like a flock of sheep. He would not incur the danger and expense of visiting a settlement, and he pitched in the bush, where provisions were the least obtainable. When I told him that we must part company, he deprecated the measure with his stock statement, viz., that at the distance of an hour's march there was a fine safe village full of provisions and well fitted for a halt.

" On the 17th of June, the caravan, after sundry difficulties caused by desertion, passed on to Irora, the village of Salim bin Salih, who this time received us hospitably enough. Thence we first sighted the blue hills of Unyanyembe, our destination. The next day saw us at Yombo, where, by good accident, we met a batch of seven clothbales and one box *en route* to Ujiji, under charge of our old enemy Salim, bin Sayf of Dut'humi. We also received the second packet of letters which reached us that year : as usual, they were full of evil news. Almost every one had lost some relation or friend near and dear to him : even Said bin Salim's hearth had been spoiled of its chief attraction, an only son, who, born it was supposed in consequence of my ' barakat ' (propitious influence,) had been named Abdullah.

" After a day's halt to collect porters at Yombo, we marched from it on the 20th of June, and passing the scene of our former miseries, the village under the lumpy hill, ' Zimbili,' we re-entered Kazeh. There I was warmly welcomed by the hospitable Snay bin Amir, who, after seating us to coffee, as is the custom, for a few minutes in his barzah or ante-room, led us to the old abode, which had been carefully repaired, swept, and plastered. There a large metal tray, bending under succulent dishes of rice and curried fowl, giblets and manioc boiled in the cream of the ground-nut, and sugared omelets flavored with ghee and onion shreds, presented peculiar attractions to half-starved travellers.

"Our return from Ujiji to Unyanyembe was thus accomplished in twenty-two stations, which, halts included, occupied a total of twenty-six days, from the 26th of May to the 20th of June, 1858, and the distance along the road may be computed at 265 statute miles."

Immediately after arriving, everybody was attacked with fevers or disorders of the liver. These, however, soon yielded to the medicines and stimulants received from the coast. Several Arab merchants were preparing to start eastward, in order to reach Zanzibar in time for the Indian trading-season, and Burton might have returned with them. But several reasons induced him to remain for a while at Kazeh. He had not given up the hope of being able to make the journey from that place to Quiloa (Kilwa); he desired to collect from the Arab merchants and native guides all procurable information of the interesting countries lying to the north and south of the line he had traversed. "During my first halt at Kazeh," he says, "the merchants had related to me their discovery of a large bahr—a sea or lake—lying fifteen or sixteen marches to the north; and from their descriptions and bearings, my companion had laid down the water in a hand-map forwarded to the Royal Geographical Society. All agreed in claiming for it superiority of size over the Tanganyika Lake. I saw at once that the existence of this hitherto unknown basin would explain many discrepancies promulgated by speculative geographers, more especially the notable and deceptive differences of distances, caused by the confusion of the two waters. My companion, who had recovered strength from the repose and the comparative comfort of our headquarters, appeared a fit person to be detached upon this duty; moreover, his presence at Kazeh was by no means desirable."

The usual difficulties accompanied the performance of this undertaking. The officers and guides brought from the coast endeavored to avoid the necessity of accompanying Speke; the native porters were engaged only to desert again; and even the old and faithful servant, Bombay, knowing that his services could not be-dispensed with, exacted a new present of cloth. By dint of much patience and severe exertion all these difficulties were finally overcome, and on the 10th of July Speke left Kazeh, at the head of a small party. During his absence Burton applied himself industriously to the collection of information, and the accounts he gives of the kingdoms of Usui, Karagwe, and Uganda, lying to the northward, have since been verified in all essential particulars by Speke's second journey. It is therefore unnecessary to quote them here.

After having exhausted the knowledge of the chief men of Kazeh, Burton devoted his time to the preparations for the return journey. The tattered tents were repaired, the rude, simple furniture of travel put in order, new garments made, hammocks, bags, and pack-saddles overhauled, and such supplies procured betimes, as might be difficult to obtain on the eve of departure. "On the 14th of

July," he writes, " the last Arab caravan of the season left Unyanyembe, under the command of Sayf bin Said el Wardi. As he obligingly offered to convey letters and any small articles which I wished to precede me, and knowing that under his charge effects were far safer than with our own people, I forwarded the useless and damaged surveying instruments, certain manuscripts, and various inclosures of maps, field and sketch-books, together with reports to the Royal Geographical Society.

" This excitement over I began to weary of Kazeh. Snay bin Amir and most of the Arabs had set out on an expedition. . My Goanese servant, who connected my aspect with hard labor, avoided it like a pestilence. Already I was preparing to organize a little expedition to K'hokoro and the southern provinces, when unexpectedly—in these lands a few cries and gun-shots are the only credible precursors of a caravan—on the morning of the 25th of August reappeared my companion.

" At length my companion had been successful, his ' flying trip ' had led him to the northern water, and he had found its dimensions surpassing our most sanguine expectations. We had scarcely, however, breakfasted, before he announced to me the startling fact that he had discovered the sources of the White Nile. It was an inspiration perhaps : the moment he sighted the Nyanza, he felt at once no doubt but that the ' lake at his feet gave birth to that interesting river which has been the subject of so much speculation and the object of so many explorers.' "

Speke, considering that the distance he had to traverse was nearly as great as from Kazeh to Lake Tanganyika, had made a remarkably successful trip. The usual impediments of African travel, troubles with porters, guides, and native chiefs, were diminished in his case by the comparative smallness of his party, the greater necessity of their keeping together, and the lighter equipment and supplies. For several days he traversed the fertile and populous uplands of northern Unyamwezi, and then entered a region called Usukuma, more thinly peopled, and with great tracts of thorny jungle and open, grassy plains. Beyond this was the small district of Uquimba, where he found workers in iron, and learned that the great lake was near at hand. On the 30th of July, 1858, he stood upon its shores. At first a bay, filled with small islands, the waters grew in breadth as he advanced, until, from the summit of a cape 250 feet in height, he saw a broad sea-horizon to the north. The exaggerated statements of the natives, however, led him to assign for it a much greater length from north to south, than proved to be the case, on his second journey.

Burton, whose notices of Speke in his narrative are always in singularly bad taste, and often unjustly disparaging, gives, on the whole, an impartial account of the great lake, the discovery of which—not by himself—seems to have seriously annoyed him. "This fresh-water sea," he says, "is known throughout the African tribes as Nyanza, and the similarity of the sound to 'Nyassa,' the indigenous name of the little Maravi or Kilwa

Lake, may have caused in part the wild confusion in which speculative geographers have involved the lake regions of Central Africa.   The Arabs, after their fashion of deriving comprehensive names from local and minor features, call it Ukerewe, in the Kisukuma dialect meaning the 'place of ke-rewe' (kelewe,) an islet. As has been mentioned, they sometimes attempt to join by a river, a creek, or some other theoretical creation, the Nyanza with the Tanganyika, the altitude of the former being 3,750 feet above sea-level, or 1,900 above the latter, and the mountain regions which divide the two having been frequently travelled over by Arab and African caravans.   The Nyanza, as regards name, position, and even existence, has hitherto been unknown to European geographers ; but, as will presently appear, descriptions of this sea by native travellers have been unconsciously transferred by our writers to the Tanganyika of Ujiji, and even to the Nyassa of Kilwa.

"The Nyanza is an elevated basin or reservoir, the recipient of the surplus monsoon-rain which falls in the extensive regions of the Wamasai and their kinsmen to the east, the Karagwah line of the Lunar Mountains to the west, and to the south Usukuma or Northern Unyamwezi.   Extending to the equator in the central length of the African peninsula, and elevated above the limits of the depression in the heart of the continent, it appears to be a gap in the irregular chain which, running from Usumbara and Kilimangao to Karagwah, represents the formation anciently termed the Mountains of the Moon. The physical features, as far as they were observed, suggest this view. The shores are low and flat, dotted here and there with little hills; the smaller islands also are hill-tops, and any part of the country immediately on the south would, if inundated to the same extent, present a similar aspect. The lake lies open and elevated, rather like the drainage and the temporary deposit of extensive floods than a volcanic creation like the Tanganyika, a long, narrow, mountain-girt basin. The waters are said to be deep, and the extent of the inundation about the southern creek proves that they receive during the season an important accession. The color was observed to be clear and blue, especially from afar in the early morning; after 9 A.M., when the prevalent southeast wind arose, the surface appeared greyish, or of a dull milky white, probably the effect of atmospheric reflection. The tint, however, does not, according to travellers, ever become red or green like the waters of the Nile. But the produce of the lake resembles that of the river in its purity; the people living on the shores prefer it, unlike that of the Tanganyika, to the highest and the clearest springs; all visitors agree in commending its lightness and sweetness, and declare that the taste is rather of river or of rain-water than resembling the soft slimy produce of stagnant muddy bottoms, or the rough, harsh flavor of melted ice and snow.

"At Kazeh, sorely to my disappointment, it was finally settled, in a full conclave of Arabs, that we must return to the coast by the tedious path with

which we were already painfully familiar.   At Ujiji
the state of our finances had been the sole,
though the sufficient ˋobstacle to our traversing
Africa from east to west ; we might—had we possessed the means—by navigating the Tanganyika
southward, have debouched, after a journey of
three months, at Kilwa.   The same cause prevented us from visiting the northern kingdoms of
Karagwah and Uganda ; to effect this exploration,
however, we should have required not only funds
but time.   The rains there setting in about September render travelling impossible ; our two years'
leave of absence was drawing to a close, and even
had we commanded a sufficient outfit, we were not
disposed to risk the consequences of taking an extra twelve months.   No course, therefore, remained
but to regain the coast.   We did not however,
give up hopes of making our return useful to geography, by tracing the course of the Rwaha or Ru-
fijí River, and of visiting the coast between the
Usagara Mountains and Kilwa, an unknown line
not likely to attract future travellers."

CHAPTER IX.

BURTON.—THE RETURN TO THE COAST.

AS early as the 6th of September, the officer Said bin Salim, impatient to commence the homeward march, began forming a camp outside of Kazeh. But day after day passed by, and, although the stragglers from the original party began to collect, there was the usual delay in finding porters. Finally, on the 25th of the month, it was reported that the caravan was ready, and the two travellers sent their baggage to the camp. Burton, finding it almost impossible to procure hammock-bearers for a long journey, adopted the expedient of taking them from one district to another. The only objection to this plan was its great expense, three cloths being demanded by each porter for thirty miles, equivalent to eighteen dollars for the necessary six porters.

In addition to a good stock of beads and cloth, they had sixteen cows and calves, for milk and as presents for the native chiefs; but the cows all became dry in a few days, some of the calves soon died of fatigue, and whenever an animal lay down in the road it was immediately slaughtered by the porters, who then feasted upon the flesh.

"The 26th of September, 1858, saw us on foot betimes. The hospitable Snay bin Amir, freshly recovered from an influenza which had confined him for some days to his sleeping-mat, came personally to superintend our departure. As no porters had returned for property left behind, and as all the "cooking-pots" had preceded us on the yester, Snay supplied us with his own slaves, and provided us with an Arab breakfast, well cooked, and, as usual, neatly served on porcelain plates, with plaited and colored straw dish-covers, pointed like Chinese caps. Then, promising to spend the next day with me, he shook hands and followed me out of the compound."

This seemed like a departure, but it was not. After innumerable halts and delays, constantly being obliged to send back for articles left behind, it was the 4th of October before they reached the village of Hanga, only a long day's march from Kazeh. Here Speke was so overcome by the fever, that he became violently delirious, and was seized with a kind of convulsions, accompanied with terrible pains in the body. A messenger was sent back to Kazeh for medicine adapted to the case, but the attack gradually exhausted itself, and at the end of a week the sufferer was able to bear transportation in a hammock. In these troubles Burton received no aid from Said bin Salim, who had already forfeited his confidence, but the journey had developed good qualities in another of his attendants.

"Seedy Mubarak Bombay," he says,—" in the interior the name became Mamba (a crocodile) or Pombe (small beer)—had long before returned to his former attitude, that of a respectful and most ready servant. He had, it is true, sundry uncomfortable peculiarities. He had no memory : an article once taken by him was always thrown upon the ground and forgotten : in a single trip he broke my elephant-gun, killed my riding-ass and lost its bridle. Like the Eastern Africans generally, he lacked the principle of immediate action; if beckoned to for a gun in the field he would probably first delay to look round, then retire, and lastly advance. He had a curious inverted way of doing all that he did. The water-bottle was ever carried on the march either uncorked or inverted ; his waistcoat was generally wound round his neck, and it appeared fated not to be properly buttoned ; while he walked bareheaded in the sun, his fez adorned the tufty poll of some comrade ; and at the halt he toiled like a char-woman to raise our tents and to prepare them for habitation, while his slave, the large lazy Maktubu, a boy-giant from the mountains of Urundi, sat or dozed under the cool shade. Yet with all his faults and failures, Bombay, for his unwearied activity, and especially from his undeviating honesty—there was no man, save our " negro rectitude," in the whole camp who had not proved his claim to the title triliteral—was truly valuable."

The stages now appeared shorter, the sun cooler, the breeze warmer ; after fourteen months of excessive fevers, the party had become tolerably acclimated ; all were loud in praise, as they had formerly been violent in censure, of the air and water. Before entering the Fiery Field, the hire for carrying the hammocks became so exorbitant that Burton dismissed his bearers, mounted an ass, and once more took his place at the head of the caravan. Speke gradually recovered the same way. Leaving Hanga on the 13th of October, they consumed fifteen days in making the seven short marches to Tura, the Eastern village of Unyamwezi, on account of the native porters running to the right and left, to visit their homes. There were also constant rumors of robbers, and the members of the caravan always flew to arms at the slightest report of danger.

" At Eastern Tura," says Burton, " where we arrived on the 28th of October, a halt of six days was occasioned by the necessity of providing and preparing food, at that season scarce and dear, for the week's march through the Fiery Field. The caravan was then mustered, when its roll appeared as follows. We numbered in our own party two Europeans, two Goanese, Bombay with two slaves—the childman Nasibu, and the boy-giant Maktubu—the bull-headed Mabruki, Nasir, a half-caste Mazuri Arab, who had been sent with me by the Arabs of Kazeh to save his morals, and Taufiki, a Msawahili youth, who had taken service as gun-carrier to the coast : they formed a total of 10 souls. Said bin Salim was accompanied by 12—the charmers Halimah and Zawada, his five children, and a little gang of five fresh captures, male and female. The Baloch, 12

in number, had 15 slaves and 11 porters, composing
a total of 38.   The sons of Ramji, and the ass-
drivers under Kidogo their leader, were in all 24,
including their new acquisitions.   Finally, 68 Wanyamwezi porters, carrying the outfit and driving the
cattle, completed the party to 152 souls.

"On the 3rd of November the caravan, issuing
from Tura, plunged manfully into the Fiery Field,
and after seven marches in as many days, halted for
breath and forage at Jiwe la Mkoa, the Round
Stone.   A few rations having been procured in its
vicinity, we resumed our way on the 12th of November, and in two days exchanged, with a sensible
pleasure, the dull expanse of dry brown bush and
brushwood, dead thorn-trees, and dry nullahs, for
the fertile red plain of Mdaburu.   After that point
began the transit of Ugogo, where I had been taught
to expect accidents ; they resolved themselves, however, into nothing more than the disappearance of
cloth and beads in inordinate quantities.   We were
received by Magomba, the Sultan of Kanyenye,
with a charge of magic, for which, of course, it was
necessary to pay heavily.   The Wanyamwezi porters seemed even more timid on the down-journey
than on the up-march.   They slank about like curs,
and the fierce look of a Mgogo boy was enough to
strike a general terror.   Twanigana, when safe in
the mountains of Usagara, would frequently indulge
me in a dialogue like the following, and it may
serve as a specimen of the present state of conversation in East Africa :

" ' The state, Mdula ?' (*i. e.*, Abdullah, a word un-pronounceable to negroid organs.)

" ' The state is very ! (well) and thy state ?'

" ' The state is very ! (well) and the state of Spik-ka ?' (my companion).

" ' The state of Spikka is very ! (well).'

" ' We have escaped the Wagogo (resumes Twani-gana), white man, O !'

" ' We have escaped, O my brother !'

" ' The Wagogo are bad.'

" ' They are bad.'

" ' The Wagogo are very bad.'

" ' They are very bad.'

" ' The Wagogo are not good.'

" ' They are not good.'

" ' The Wagogo are not at all good.'

" ' They are not at all good.'

" ' I greatly feared the Wagogo, who kill the Wan-yamwezi.'

" ' Exactly so !'

" ' But now I don't fear them.   I call them ——s and ——s, and I would fight the whole tribe, white man, O !'

" ' Truly so, O my brother !'

"And thus for two mortal hours, till my ennui turned into marvel.

" This form of conversation, however, was sur-passed by the attempt of one of the Baloch guards, Gul Mohammed by name, to convert a native called *Muzungu Mbaya*, (' The Wicked White Man,') to the Moslem faith.   At the close of a day's march, if the former found the latter sitting alone, he invariably squatted down beside him, and opened the conversation with the remark :

" ' And thou, Muzungu Mbaya, thou also must die !'

" ' Ugh ! ugh !' replies the native, personally offended, ' don't speak in that way ! Thou must die too.'

" ' It is a sore thing to die,' resumes Gul Mohammed.

" ' Hoo ! hoo !' exclaims the other, ' it is bad, very bad, never to wear a nice cloth, no longer to dwell with one's wife and children, not to eat and drink, snuff, and smoke tobacco. Hoo ! hoo ! it is bad, very bad !'

" ' But we shall eat,' says the Moslem, ' the flesh of birds, mountains of meat, and delicate roasts, and drink sugared water, and whatever we hunger for.'

" The African's mind is disturbed by this tissue of contradictions. He considers birds somewhat low feeding, roasts he adores, he contrasts mountains of meat with his poor half pound in pot, he would sell himself for sugar ; but, on the other hand, he hears nothing of tobacco : still, he takes the trouble to ask : ' Where, O my brother ?'

" ' There !' exclaims Gul Mohammed, pointing to the skies.

" This is a stumbling-block to Muzungu Mbaya. The distance is great, and he can scarcely believe that his questioner has visited the firmament to see the provisions : he therefore ventures upon the

query : 'And hast thou been there, O my brother ? '

" ' I beg pardon of Allah !' ejaculates Gul Mohammed, half angry, half amused. ' What a pagan
this is ! No, my brother, I have not exactly been
there ; but my Allah told my apostle, who told his
descendant, who told my father and mother, who
told me, that when we die we shall go up to a
plantation, where——'

" ' Oof !' grunts Muzungu Mbaya, ' it is good of
you to tell us all this upumbafu (nonsense) which
your mother told you. So there are plantations
in the skies ?'

" ' Assuredly,' replies Gul Mohammed, who ex-
pounds at length the Moslem idea of paradise to
the African's running commentary of ' Nenda we !'
(be off !) ' Mama-e !' (O my mother !) and ' Tumba-
nina,' which may not be translated.

" Muzungu Mbaya, who for the last minute has
been immersed in thought, now suddenly raises
his head, and, with somewhat of a goguenard air,
inquires—

" ' Well, then, my brother, thou knowest all things !
answer me, is thy Mulungu black like myself, white
like this muzungu, or whity-brown as thou art ?'

" Gul Mohammed is fairly floored : he ejaculates
sundry la haul ! to collect his wits for the reply :

" ' Verily, the Mulungu hath no color.'

" ' To-o-oh ! Tuh !' exclaims the Muzungu, contorting his wrinkled countenance, and spitting with
disgust upon the ground. He was now justified in
believing that he had been made a laughing-stock.

The mountain of meat had, to a certain extent, won over his better judgment : the fair vision now fled, and left him to the hard realities of the half pound."

The transit through the Land of Ugogo occupied three weeks, from the 14th of November to the 5th of December. Immediately after reaching the old camping-ground at Ugogi, at the foot of the Rubeho Mountains, a caravan arrived from the coast, bringing fresh letters and papers. The porters, learning that there was a famine in the Rubeho country, unanimously declared that they would take the Kiringawana route, which lies about 43 miles south of the former, across the mountains ; and Burton was obliged to consent.

"The Kiringawana route," he says, "numbers nineteen short stages, which may be accomplished without hardship in twelve days, at the rate of about five hours per diem. Provisions are procurable in almost every part, except when the Warori are 'out ;' and water is plentiful, if not good. Travel is rendered pleasant by long stretches of forest land without bush or fetid grass. The principal annoyances are the thievish propensities of the natives and the extortionate demands of the chief. A minor plague is that of mosquitoes, that haunt the rushy banks of the hill rivulets, some of which are crossed nine or ten times in the same day ; moreover, the steep and slippery ascents and descents of black earth and mud. or rough blocks of stone, make the porters unwilling to work."

After a halt of only a day at Ugogi, they continued the journey. The first stages were over an undulating plateau, with settlements and cultivation in the hollows. Gradually the country became wilder, the hills more frequent and abrupt, and storms began to gather about the higher peaks. The march was made without any accident, or incident of importance, except the following, which is a lively description of many similar experiences :

" The morning of the 15th of December commenced with a truly African scene. The men were hungry and the air was chill. They prepared, however, to start quietly betimes. Suddenly a bit of rope was snatched, a sword flashed in the air, a bow-horn quivered with nocked arrow, and the whole caravan rushed frantically with a fearful row to arms. As no one dissuaded the party from 'fighting it out,' they apparently became friends, and took up their loads. My companion and I rode quietly forward : scarcely, however, had we emerged from the little basin which the camp had been placed, than a terrible hubbub of shouts and yells announced that the second act had commenced. After a few minutes, Said bin Salim came forward in trembling haste to announce that the jemadar had again struck a pagazi, who, running into the nullah, had thrown stones with force enough to injure his assailant, consequently that the Baloch had drawn their sabres and had commenced a general massacre of porters. Well understanding this misrepresentation, we advanced about a mile, and thence sent back two of the sons of Ramji to declare that we would not be delayed, and that if not at once followed, we would engage other porters at the nearest village. This brought on a denouement : presently the combatants appeared, the Baloch in a high state of grievance, the Africans declaring that they had not come to fight but to carry. I persuaded them both to defer settling the business till the evening, when both parties, well crammed with food, listened complacently to that gross personal abuse, which, in these lands, represents a reprimand.

" Resuming our journey, we crossed two high and steep hills, the latter of which suddenly disclosed to the eye the rich and fertile basin of Mororo."

This place, which is nearly half the distance from Ugogi to Zungomero, is the most considerable station on the road. They halted there a day to rest and recruit, and then pressed forward through the valleys of streams which flowed to the southward—apparently affluents of the Rufiji River, which empties into the sea near Quiloa—and across rocky hills, covered with thorns and cactus. On the 19th they crossed the Rufita Pass, finding it much less steep and difficult than the Rubeho, or Windy Pass, to the northward. In the valley beyond, the chief of the region received the travellers with courtesy, demanding the usual blackmail, but afterwards presenting them with a bullock.

On Christmas Day they crossed the Mabruki Pass, the last which intervened between them and the lower country east of the mountains. The first descent was by a sharp ridge, between wooded heights, commanding wide and beautiful views over a great extent of landscape; then followed a precipitous steep of red earth, torn by water-courses. The end of the day's journey saw the travellers over the range. The bullock which had been reserved for their Christmas dinner was lost on the way. "I had ordered," says Burton, "the purchase of half a dozen goats wherewith to cele-brate the day; the porters, however, were too lazy to collect them. My companion and I made good cheer upon a fat capon, which acted as roast-beef, and a mess of ground-nuts sweetened with sugar-cane, which did duty as plum-pudding. The con-trast of what was with what might be now, how-ever, suggested only pleasurable sensations; long odds were in favor of our seeing the Christmas day of 1859, compared with the chances of things at Msene on the Christmas-day of 1857.

"From Uziraha sixteen hours distributed into fourteen marches conducted us from Uziraha, at the foot of the Usagara Mountains, to Central Zungomero. The districts traversed were Eastern Mbwiga, Marundwe, and Kirengwe. The road again realizes the European idea of Africa in its most hideous and grotesque aspect. Animals are scarce amid the portentous growth of herbage, not a head of black cattle is seen, flocks and poultry are rare, and even the beasts of the field seem to flee the land. The people admitted us into their villages, whose wretched straw hovels, contrasting with the luxuriant jungle which hems them in, look like

birds'-nests torn from the trees : all the best settlements, however, were occupied by parties of tou-
ters. At the sight of our passing caravan the
goatherd hurried off his charge, the peasant prepared to rush into the grass, the women and children slunk and hid within the hut, and no one ever
left his home without a bow and a sheath of arrows, whose pitchy-colored bark-necks denoted a
fresh layer of poison.

"We entered Zungomero on the 29th of December, after sighting on the left the cone at
whose base rises the Maji ya W'heta, or Fontaine
qui bouille."

At Zungomero Burton made a final but equally
ineffectual attempt to take the route to Quiloa instead of Zanzibar. The principal result was the desertion, in a body, of the native porters. This
obliged the party to wait three weeks at Zungomero ; in the meantime messengers were despatched
to the coast. However, before any assistance arrived, a caravan from the interior made its appearance, and a fresh supply of porters was obtained
without difficulty.

"The 21st of January, 1859, enabled us to bid
adieu to Zungomero and merrily to take the footpath way. We made Konduchi on the 3rd of February, after twelve marches, which were accomplished in fifteen days. There was little of interest
or adventure in this return line, of which the nine
first stations had already been visited and described.
As the yegea mud, near Dut'humi, was throat-deep,
we crossed it lower down : it was still a weary

trudge of several miles through thick slabby mire, which admitted a man to his knees. In places, after toiling under a sickly sun, we crept under the tunnels of thick jungle-growth, veiling the Mgazi and other streams ; the dank and fetid cold caused a deadly sensation of faintness, which was only relieved by a glass of ether-sherbet, a pipe or two of the strongest tobacco, and half an hour's repose. By degrees it was found necessary to abandon the greater part of the remaining outfit and the luggage : the Wanyamwezi, as they neared their destination, became even less manageable than before, and the sons of Ramji now seemed to consider their toils at an end. On the 25th of January we forded the cold, strong, yellow stream of the Mgeta, whose sandy bed had engulfed my elephant-gun, and we entered with steady hearts the formerly-dreaded Uzaramo.

" On the 30th of January our natives of Zanzibar screamed with delight at the sight of the mango-tree, and pointed out to one another, as they appeared in succession, the old familiar fruits, jacks and pine-apples, limes and cocos. On the 2nd of February we greeted, with doffed caps and three times three and one more, as Britons will do on such occasions, the kindly smiling face of our father Neptune, as he lay basking in the sunbeams between earth and air. Finally the 3rd of February, 1859, saw us winding through the poles decorated with skulls —they now grin in the Royal College of Surgeons, London—a negro Temple-bar which pointed out the way into the little maritime village of Konduchi.

" Our entrance was attended with the usual ceremony, now familiar to the reader : the warmen
danced, shot, and shouted, a rabble of adults,
youths and boys crowded upon us, the fair sex lulli-
loo'd with vigor, and a general procession conducted
their strangers to the hut, swept cleaned, and gar-
nished for us by old Premji, the principal Banyan
of the head-quarter village, and there stared and
laughed till they could stare and laugh no more.

" On the 9th of February the battela and the
stores required for our trip arrived at Konduchi
from Zanzibar, and the next day saw us rolling
down the coast, with a fair fresh breeze toward
classic Kilwa, the Quiloa of De Gama, of Camoens,
and of the Portuguese annalists. I shall reserve an
account of this most memorable shore for a future
work, devoted especially to the sea-board of Zanzibar—coast and island : in the present tale of adventure the details of a *cabotage* would be out of place.
Suffice it to say that we lost nearly all our crew by
the cholera, which, after ravaging the eastern coast
of Arabia and Africa, and the islands of Zanzibar
and Pemba, had almost depopulated the southern
settlements on the main land. We were unable to
visit the course of the great Rufiji River, a counterpart of the Zambezi in the south, and a water-road
which appears destined to become the highway of
nations into Eastern equatorial Africa. No man
dared to take service on board the infected vessel ;
the Hindoo Banyans, who directed the copal trade
of the river regions, aroused against us the chiefs of
the interior ; moreover, the stream was in flood,

overflowing its banks, and its line appeared marked by heavy purple clouds, which discharged a deluge of rain. Convinced that the travelling season was finished, I turned the head of the battela northward, and on the 4th of March, 1859, after a succession of violent squalls and pertinacious calms, we landed once more upon the island of Zanzibar.

" On the 22nd of March, 1859, the clove-shrubs and the cocoa-trees of Zanzibar again faded from my eyes. After crossing and recrossing three times the tedious line, we found ourselves anchored, on the 16th of April, near the ill-omened black walls of the Aden crater.

" The crisis of my African sufferings had taken place during my voyage upon the Tanganyika Lake : the fever, however, still clung to me like the shirt of Nessus. Mr. Apothecary Frost, of Zanzibar, had advised a temporary return to Europe : Dr. Steinhaeuser, the civil surgeon, Aden, also recommended a lengthened period of rest. I bade adieu to the coal-hole of the East on the 28th of April, 1859, and in due time greeted with becoming heartiness the shores of my native land."

CHAPTER X.

CAPTAIN JOHN HANNING SPEKE, of the Indian Army, who was Burton's companion, was also his successor. The two men appear to have been of totally different temperament and character, and therefore it was impossible for them to agree upon the same system of dealing with the native tribes. This was evidently the main cause of their disagreement during the journey to Lake Tanganyika; but it was intensified by Burton's disparagement of the importance which Speke attached to his discovery of the Nyanza. The latter was sure that this lake was one of the feeders of the White Nile, and when he reached England in May, 1859, he immediately called upon Sir Roderick Murchison, President of the Royal Geographical Society, who accepted his views without hesitation.

A council of the Society was immediately convened for the purpose of considering Speke's plan of a new exploration. Some of the members thought it would be best to go up the Nile, which seemed to them the natural course to pursue, especially as the White Nile was said to have been navigated (although geographers had their doubts about the matter) by the expeditions sent up by Mohammed Ali, in 1841 and '42, to 3° 22′ N. To this Speke objected, as so many had since tried the same route, and always failed; but at the same time he proposed, if the Society would allow him £5,000, to return to Zanzibar at the end of the year, march back to Kazeh, and make a complete exploration of the Victoria Nyanza. Although he proposed to spend three years in the undertaking, examining the country and ascertaining its main geographical features, the Society considered the sum demanded much too large; whereupon Speke accepted the half, saying that whatever the expedition might cost, he would make up the rest from his own resources.

Speke's object in delaying the expedition for a year was that he might send on fifty men, with a load of beads and brass wire, under the charge of Arab ivory-traders, to the kingdom of Karagwe, and fifty more, in the same manner, to Kazeh; so that, leaving the coast at the best season (May to July), he would be able to push on expeditiously, and thus escape the great disadvantages of travelling with a large caravan, with the accompanying amount of desertion and theft. The project, which was a very good one, failed, because nine months elapsed before the grant of £2,500 was made, and the command of the expedition given to Speke. The Indian branch of the Government, however, supplied fifty carbines, with ammunition, all the surveying instruments, and several gold watches, as presents for the native chiefs. Captain Grant, also of the Indian army, and a personal friend of Speke, was, at the latter's request, detailed to accompany him.

At the same time, Mr. Petherick, an English ivory merchant, who had spent many years in the equatorial regions of Central Africa, offered to have boats ready to meet the expedition at Gondokoro, the highest trading-station on the White Nile, and to send a party of men into the unknown interior beyond that point to collect ivory, and assist the explorers in case of need—should the latter succeed in penetrating so far. Later events proved that Mr. Petherick made this agreement without any expectation that he would ever be required to fulfill it.

On the 27th of April, 1860, Speke and Grant left England in the steam-frigate *Forte,* and after a long voyage reached the Cape of Good Hope on the 4th of July. There the Governor, Sir George Grey, who took a warm interest in the expedition, induced the Cape Parliament to grant a sum of £300 for the purchase of baggage-mules, and detached ten volunteers from the Native Rifle Corps, to accompany the travellers. After touching at Delagoa Bay, Mozambique, and the island of Johanna, they reached Zanzibar on the 17th of August. Here the most welcome news was that the English Consul had thirteen days before dispatched fifty-six loads of cloth and beads to Kazeh.

Said Majid, the Sultan of Zanzibar, received the

travellers in a very friendly manner, and offered them all needful assistance. The success of the first expedition, Speke found, greatly facilitated the preparations for the second. " Said bin Salim," he says, " our late caravan captain, was appointed to that post again, as he wished to prove his character for honor and honesty; and it now transpired that he had been ordered not to go with me when I discovered the Victoria Nyanza. Bombay and his brother Mabruki were bound to me of old, and the first to greet me on my arrival here; while my old friends the Balochs begged me to take them again. The Hottentots, however, had usurped their place. I was afterward sorry for this, though, if I ever travel again, I shall trust to none but natives, as the climate of Africa is too trying to foreigners."

Col. Rigby, the English Consul, also allowed Speke to select from his boat's crew any men he could find who had served in men-of-war. " For this purpose," Speke continues, " my factotum, Bombay, prevailed on Baraka, Frij, and Rahan— all of them old sailors, who, like himself, knew Hindostanee—to go with me. With this nucleus to start with, I gave orders that they should look out for as many Wanguana (freed men—*i. e.*, men emancipated from slavery) as they could enlist, to carry loads, or do any other work required of them, and to follow me in Africa wherever I wished, until our arrival in Egypt, when I would send them back to Zanzibar. Each was to receive one year's pay in advance, and the remainder when their work was completed."

By the 21st of September everything was ready at Zanzibar, and Sheikh Said and the men, together with the Hottentots, mules and baggage, were sent across to Bagamoyo, on the mainland. Speke and Grant followed on the 25th, and found the caravan already in a tolerable state of organization. Several native merchants availed themselves of the opportunity, to make the same journey with greater security, and they were all anxious to set out without delay, as it was a time of year when famine might be expected in the interior. A very few days, therefore, sufficed for the remaining preparations, and on the 2nd of October the march began, but not with the doubt and uncertainty of the first start, four years before.

Speke gives the following description of his caravan, its habit of travel, and his own and Grant's duties on the way :

" Starting on a march with a large mixed caravan, consisting of one corporal and nine privates, Hottentots—one jemadar and 25 privates, Balochs —one Arab Cafila Bashi and 75 freed slaves—one kirangozi or leader, and 100 negro porters—12 mules untrained, three donkeys, and 22 goats— one could hardly expect to find everybody in his place at the proper time for breaking ground ; but, at the same time, it could hardly be expected that ten men, who had actually received their bounty-money, and had sworn fidelity, should give one the slip the very first day. Such, however, was the case. Ten out of the thirty-six given by the sultan ran away, because they feared that the white men, whom they believed to be cannibals, were only taking them into the interior to eat them ; and one pagazi, more honest than the freed men, deposited his pay upon the ground, and ran away too. Go we must, however, for one desertion is sure to lead to more : and go we did. Our procession was in this fashion : the kirangozi, with a load on his shoulder, led the way, flag in hand, followed by the pagazis carrying spears or bows and arrows in their hands, and bearing their share of the baggage in the shape either of bolster-shaped loads of cloth and beads covered with matting, each tied into the fork of a three-pronged stick, or else coils of brass or copper wire tied in even weights to each end of sticks which they laid on the shoulder ; then helter-skelter came the Wanguana, carrying carbines in their hands, and boxes, bundles, tents, cooking-pots—all the miscellaneous property on their heads ; next the Hottentots, dragging the refractory mules laden with ammunition-boxes, but very lightly, to save the animals for the future ; and, finally, Sheikh Said and the Baloch escort, while the goats, sick women and stragglers brought up the rear. From first to last, some of the sick Hottentots rode the hospital donkeys, allowing the negroes to tug their animals ; for the smallest ailment threw them broadcast on their backs.

" My first occupation was to map the country. This was done by timing the rate of march with a watch, taking compass-bearings along the road or on any conspicuous marks—as, for instance, hills off it

—and by noting the watershed—in short, all topographical objects. On arrival in camp every day
came the ascertaining, by boiling a thermometer, of
the altitude of the station above the sea-level; of
the latitude of the station by the meridian altitude
of a star taken with a sextant; and of the compass
variation by azimuth. Occasionally there was the
fixing of certain crucial stations, at intervals of sixty
miles or so, by lunar observations, or distances of
the moon either from the sun or from certain given
stars, for determining the longitude, by which the
original-timed course can be drawn out with certainty on the map by proportion. Should a date be
lost, you can always discover it by taking a lunar
distance and comparing it with the Nautical Almanac, by noting the time when a star passes the
meridian if your watch is right, or by observing the
phases of the moon, or her rising and setting, as
compared with the Nautical Almanac. The rest of
my work, besides sketching and keeping a diary,
which was the most troublesome of all, consisted in
making geological and zoological collections. With
Captain Grant rested the botanical collections and
thermometrical registers. He also boiled one of
the thermometers, kept the rain-gauge, and under-
took the photography; but after a time I sent the
instruments back, considering this work too severe
for the climate, and he tried instead sketching with
water-colors, the results of which form the chief
part of the illustrations in this book. The rest of
our day went in breakfasting after the march was

over—a pipe, to prepare us for rummaging the fields and villages to discover their contents for scientific purposes—dinner close to sunset, and tea and pipe before turning in at night."

CHAPTER XI.

DURING the first days of the march Speke experienced a repetition of Burton's troubles with the porters and native attendants. They stole his goats ; they demanded extra pay ; they refused to march ; they lost or damaged their packs ; and at the end of the first week eight of the men furnished by the Sultan ran away, taking with them all the remaining goats. Soon afterwards, Grant was seized with the inevitable African fever, which revisited him every fortnight during the whole journey ; while Speke, after some slight attacks the first year, remained exempt from it.

By the 23d of October, they had crossed the low tropical region and reached Zungomero. The reports of famine in the interior, as Speke had anticipated, were confirmed, and he decided to try the southern route across the mountains, (which Burton had followed on his return, two years before,) in the hope of finding more supplies. But, after four days' march, on reaching a station beyond the Mabruki Pass—the first range of mountains—he was informed by a travelling Arab that the whole of the fertile Maroro district had been laid waste by war, and was compelled to choose a middle route, and finally, since that proved to be impracticable, the northern or Rubeho Pass.

They soon reached a more elevated region, and marched over rolling ground, covered with groves of small trees. The scenery was most interesting, with every variety of hill, plateau, and ravine, wild and beautifully wooded; but they saw nothing of the people. At every village they approached, the inhabitants, accustomed only to brutal treatment from the traders, buried themselves in the jungles, carrying off their grain with them. Foraging parties were sent out, with strict orders to take nothing by force : the only result was, that the natives attributed this kindness to fear, and threatened to attack the caravan at night.

On the 17th of November they reached Inenge, at the foot of the Rubeho Pass. The country was so famished that nothing but the continual hunt of both Grant and Speke for elands, antelopes, and other wild game kept the caravan from starvation. The forced marches which they were compelled to make at least carried them more rapidly on their way. In three days more they arrived at Ugogi, where there was little more food than in the mountain region; the natives were already mixing their small stores of grain with the seeds of the monkey bread-tree. Water was so scarce in the wells that the travellers were obliged to purchase it at the usual price of beer, and cattle, sheep and fowls were both scarce and very expensive.

Continuing their march, at Kanyenye, two or

three stations before entering on the " Fiery Field,"
Speke was lucky enough to shoot a rhinoceros.
Having learned that they frequented a bitter pool
in the neighborhood, " I set forth with the guide and
two of the sheikh's boys," he says, " each carrying
a single rifle, and ensconced myself in the nullah,
to hide until our expected visitors should arrive,
and there remained until midnight. When the
hitherto noisy villagers turned into bed, the silvery
moon shed her light on the desolate scene, and the
Mgogo guide, taking fright, bolted. He had not,
however, gone long, when, looming above us, coming
over the horizon line, was the very animal we
wanted.

In a fidgety manner, the beast then descended, as
if he expected some danger in store—and he was
not wrong; for, attaching a bit of white paper to
the fly-sight of my Blissett, I approached him,
crawling under cover of the banks until within
eighty yards of him, when, finding that the moon
shone full on his flank, I raised myself upright and
planted a bullet behind his left shoulder. Thus died
my first rhinoceros.

" To make the most of the night, as I wanted
meat for my men to cook, as well as a stock to
carry with them, or barter with the villagers for
grain, I now retired to my old position, and waited
again.

" After two hours had elapsed, two more rhinoceros approached me in the same stealthy, fidgety
way as the first one. They came even closer than
the first, but, the moon having passed beyond their

meridian, I could not obtain so clear a mark. Still they were big marks, and I determined on doing my best before they had time to wind us; so, stepping out, with the sheikh's boys behind me carrying the second rifle to meet all emergencies, I planted a ball in the larger one, and brought him round with a roar and whooh-whooh, exactly to the best position I could wish for receiving a second shot; but, alas! on turning sharply round for the spare rifle, I had the mortification to see that both the black boys had made off, and were scrambling like monkeys up a tree. At the same time, the rhinoceros, fortunately for me, on second consideration turned to the right-about, and shuffled away, leaving, as is usually the case when conical bullets are used, no traces of blood.

"Thus ended the night's work. We now went home by dawn to apprise all the porters that we had flesh in store for them, when the two boys who had so shamelessly deserted me, instead of hiding their heads, described all the night's scenes with such capital mimicry as set the whole camp in a roar. We had all now to hurry back to the carcass before the Wagogo could find it; but, though this precaution was quickly taken, still, before the tough skin of the beast could be cut through, the Wagogo began assembling like vultures, and fighting with my men. A more savage, filthy, disgusting, but, at the same time, grotesque scene than that which followed cannot be conceived. All fell to work, armed with swords, spears, knives, and hatchets, cutting and slashing, thumping and bawling, fighting

and tearing, tumbling and wrestling up to their knees in filth and blood in the middle of the carcass. When a tempting morsel fell to the possession of any one, a stronger neighbor would seize and bear off the prize in triumph. All right was now a matter of pure might, and lucky it was that it did not end in a fight between our men and the villagers. These might be afterward seen, one by one, covered with blood, scampering home each with his spoil—a piece of tripe, or liver, or lights, or whatever else it might have been his fortune to get off with."

On the 6th of December the party entered the Fiery Field; the next day Speke shot another rhinoceros, and soon after came upon a herd of buffalo in the jungle. In a little while he shot two cows, and wounded a large bull, which, however, got away and hid in the bushes. When Speke approached the place, he sprang out of his ambush and made a sudden and furious charge upon the hunter.

" It was a most ridiculous scene. Suliman by my side, with the instinct of a monkey, made a violent spring and swung himself by a bough immediately over the beast, while Faraj bolted away and left me single-gunned to polish him off. There was only one course to pursue, for in one instant more he would have been into me ; so, quick as thought, I fired the gun, and, as luck would have it, my bullet, after passing through the edge of one of his horns, stuck in the spine of his neck, and rolled him over at my feet as dead as a rabbit. Now, having cut the beast's throat to make him 'hilal,' according to Mussulman usage, and thinking we had done enough if I could only return to the first wounded bull and settle him too, we commenced retracing our steps, and by accident came on Grant. He was passing by from another quarter, and became amused by the glowing description of my boys, who never omitted to narrate their own cowardice as an excellent tale. He begged us to go on in our course, while he would go back and send us some porters to carry home the game."

Tracking the herd further, Speke had an equally narrow escape from the charge of another wounded bull, lost his way in the jungle, and was obliged to pass the night there with his native attendants. The halt had given ten of his porters an opportunity to desert, and every day's delay, in the hope of supplying their places, added to the difficulty. The native chief demanded renewed black mail, threatening to attack the camp; the remaining porters began to be excited and mutinous, and in two or three days all the natives of Unyamwezi deserted, leaving Speke only half his men. He made desperate efforts to advance, leaving some of his assistants to keep guard over part of the property, while the remainder was carried forward by forced marches. This obliged the porters to go over the ground twice, and added to their discontent.

On the 15th of December two men were sent on to Kazeh as messengers, with letters to the Arab merchants, Muza and Snay, begging them to dispatch sixty men to the caravan, with grain and tobacco. In the meantime Speke endeavored to cross the Fiery Field by forced marches, constantly delayed by the rising of streams from the rains, in ravines which had been perfectly dry during the former journey. Every day or two, some more of the natives deserted, but on the 1st of January, 1861, the party reached Jiwe la Mkoa, the Round Rock, and the half-way station in the wilderness. The remainder of the porters and goods did not arrive until four days afterwards. The messengers returned from Kazeh, bringing a very little rice and tobacco, with the news that the whole country was half-starved. Since no new porters came with them, Speke determined to try the expedient of hiring the natives from village to village, and meantime sent on his man Bombay to Kazeh, for further help. The day after he left, there was a great excitement in the village : a fugitive native chief, named Manua Sera, appeared, with thirty armed followers, and requested an interview with Speke. This was granted : he began the conversation by stating that he had heard of Speke's trouble from the want of porters, and offered to assist him, provided he would mediate between himself and the Arab merchants at Kazeh. The latter, he said, had interfered with his authority, brought on a war, and finally driven him from his possessions. Manua Sera was a bold, handsome young man, and his story impressed Speke with its truth. Inasmuch as it is connected with a fragment of history which afterwards interfered with the progress of the expedition, we quote Speke's report of the chief's narrative :

" Shortly after you left Kazeh for England, my old father, the late chief Fundi Kira, died, and by his desire I became lawful chief ; for, though the son of a slave girl, and not of Fundi Kira's wife, such is the law of inheritance—a constitutional policy established to prevent any chance of intrigues between the sons born in legitimate wedlock. Well, after assuming the title of chief, I gave presents of ivory to all the Arabs with a liberal hand, but most so to Musa, which caused great jealousy among the other merchants. Then, after this, I established a property tax on all merchandise that entered my country. Fundi Kira had never done so, but I did not think that any reason why I should not, especially as the Arabs were the only people who lived in my country exempt from taxation. This measure, however, exasperated the Arabs, and induced them to send me hostile messages, to the effect that, if I ever meddled with them, they would dethrone me, and place Mkisiwa, another illegitimate son, on the throne in my stead. This," Manua Sera continued, " I could not stand ; the merchants were living on sufferance only in my country. I told them so, and defied them to interfere with my orders, for I was not a ' woman,' to be treated with contempt ; and this got up a quarrel. Mkisiwa, seizing at the opportunity of the prize held out to him by the Arabs, as his supporters, then commenced a system of bribery. Words led to blows ; we had a long and tough fight ; I killed many of their number, and they killed mine. Eventually they drove me from my palace, and placed Mkisiwa there as chief in my stead. My faithful followers, however, never deserted me; so I went to Bubuga, and put up with old Maula there. The Arabs followed—drove me to Nguru, and tried to kill Maula for having fostered me. He, however, escaped them; but they destroyed his country, and then followed me down to Nguru. There we fought for many months, until all provisions were exhausted, when I defied them to catch me, and forced my way through their ranks. It is needless to say I have been a wanderer since; and though I wish to make friends, they will not allow it, but do all they can to hunt me to death. Now, as you were a friend of my father, I do hope you will patch up this war for me, which you must think is unjust."

Speke assured the chief that he would do what was possible in the way of mediation, but at the same time advised him to give up the system of black-mail which he had endeavored to establish. Manua Sera agreed to this, and promised to join the caravan in few days. On the 9th of January (1861) the expedition left Jiwe la Mkoa, and with only half the supplies, leaving the remainder to be forwarded, but on reaching Zimbo, two days' marches further, Bombay appeared from Kazeh, bringing seventy porters, and once more the caravan was able to move on as a body. Nevertheless, as Speke was obliged to pay each of the seventy porters sixteen yards of cloth, it would have been a great saving of time and expense to him, had he left the ten loads behind him, at the station in Ugogo where the first desertion occurred.

The disheartening impediments which had attended their journey across the Fiery Field, now disappeared. The caravan pushed forward rapidly, and on the 16th reached Tura, the first station in the Land of the Moon. " The whole place, once so fertile," Speke writes, " was now almost depopulated and in a sad state of ruin, showing plainly the savage ravages of war ; for the Arabs and their slaves, when they take the field, think more of plunder and slavery than the object they started on, each man of the force looking out for himself. The incentives, too, are so great—a young woman might be caught (the greatest treasure on earth),or a boy or a girl, a cow or a goat—all of them fortunes, of themselves too irresistible to be overlooked when the future is doubtful. Here Sheikh Said broke down in health of a complaint which he had formerly suffered from, and from which I at once saw he would never recover sufficiently well to be ever effective again. It was a sad misfortune, as the men had great confidence in him, being the representative of their Zanzibar government ; still it could not be helped ; for as a sick man is, after all, the greatest possible impediment to a march, it was better to be rid of him than have the trouble of dragging him.

" On the third day from Tura, we reached the western extremity of the cultivated opening, where, after sleeping the night, we threaded through another forest to the little clearance Kigué, and in one more march through the forest arrived in the large and fertile district of Unyanyembe, the centre of Unyamwezi—the Land of the Moon—within five miles of Kazeh, which is the name of a well in in the village of Tabora, now constituted the great central slave and ivory merchants' depot. My loss - es up this date (23d) were as follows : one Hottentot dead and five returned ; one freeman sent back with the Hottentots, and one flogged and turned off ; twenty-five of Sultan Majid's gardeners deserted ; ninety-eight of the original Wanyamwezi porters deserted ; twelve mules and three donkeys dead. Besides which, more than half of my property had been stolen ; while the travelling expenses had been unprecedented, in consequence of the severity of the famine throughout the whole length of the march.

"On the 24th, we all, as many as were left of us, marched into the merchants' depot at Kazeh, lat. 5° S., long. 33° W., escorted by Musa, who advanced to meet us, and guided us into his tembe, where he begged we would reside with him until we could find men to carry our property on to Karagwe. He added that he would accompany us ; for he was on the point of going there when my first installment of property arrived, but deferred his intention out of respect to myself. He had been detained at Kazeh ever since I last left it, in consequence of the Arabs, having provoked a war with Manua Sera, to which he was adverse. For a long time also he had been a chained prisoner ; as the Arabs, jealous of the favor Manua Sera had shown to him in preference to themselves, basely accused him of supplying Manua Sera with gunpowder, and bound

him hand and foot " like a slave." It was delightful to see old Musa's face again, and the supremely
hospitable, kind, and courteous manner in which he
looked after us, constantly bringing in all kinds of
small delicacies, and seeing that nothing was wanting to make us happy. All the property I had
sent on in advance he had stored away ; or rather,
I should say, as much as had reached him, for the
road expenses had eaten a great hole in it.

CHAPTER XII.

A S soon as he was settled at Kazeh, Snay bin
Amir and the other Arab merchants came in
a body to call upon Speke. They said they had an
army of four hundred slaves, with muskets ready to
take the field at once to hunt down Manua Sera,
who was cutting their caravan road to pieces, and
had just seized, by their latest reports, a whole con-
voy of their ammunition. Speke begged them
strongly to listen to reason, and accept his advice
as an old soldier, not to carry on their guerrilla
warfare in such a headlong hurry, else they would
be led a dance by Manua Sera, as the English had
been by Tantia Topee in India. He advised them
to allow him to mediate between them, after telling
them what a favorable interview he had had with
Manua Sera and Maula, whose son was at that moment concealed in Musa's tembe. His advice, however, was not wanted. Snay knew better than any
one how to deal with savages, and determined on
setting out as soon as his army had " eaten their
beef-feast of war."

One of the merchants, named Abdullah, con-

firmed Speke's views of the Victoria Nyanza being
the source of the White Nile, but the latter, as it
afterwards proved, was confused by the general application of the word *nyanza*, which is used to describe any large body of water, whether lake or river. Speke was greatly surprised at the change
which had taken place in Unyanyembe since his
former visit. Instead of the Arabs appearing simply merchants, as they then did, they had rather
the air of large farmers, with huge stalls of cattle
attached to their houses, while the native villages
were all in ruins—so much so that, to obtain corn
for his men, he had to send out into the district several days' journey off, and even then had to pay the
most severe famine prices for what he got. The
Wanyamwezi, he was assured, were dying of starvation in all directions ; for, in addition to the war,
the last rainy season had been so light, all their
crops had failed.

"I next," says Speke, "went into a long inquiry
with Musa about our journey northward to Karagwe ; and as he said there were no men to be found
in or near Unyanyembe, for they were either all
killed or engaged in the war, it was settled he
should send some of his head men on to Rungua,
where he had formerly resided, trading for some
years, and was a great favorite with the chief of the
place, by name Kiringuana. He also settled that I
might take out of his establishment of slaves as
many men as I could induce to go with me, for he
thought them more trouble than profit, hired porters being more safe ; moreover, he said the plan

would be of great advantage to him, as I offered to pay both man and master each the same monthly stipend as I gave my present men. This was paying double, and all the heavier a burden, as the number I should require to complete my establishment to one hundred armed men would be sixty. He, however, very generously advised me not to take them, as they would give so much trouble, but finally gave way when I told him I felt I could not advance beyond Karagwe unless I was quite independent of the natives there—a view in which he concurred."

On the 7th of February, information was brought to Kazeh that while Manua Sera was on his way from Ugogo to keep his appointment with Speke, Sheikh Snay's army came on him at Tura, where he was ensconced in a tembe. Hearing this, Snay, instead of attacking the village at once, commenced negotiations with the chief of the place by demanding him to set free his guest, otherwise they, the Arabs, would storm the tembe. The chief, unfortunately, did not comply at once, but begged grace for one night, saying that if Manua Sera was found there in the morning they might do as they liked. Of course Manua bolted ; and the Arabs, seeing the Tura people all under arms ready to defend themselves the next morning, set at them in earnest and shot, murdered, or plundered the whole of the district. This news threw the place into a tumult of excitement ; and, seeing that nothing could then be done, Speke and Grant went off for a week's hunting, but without much success.

Meanwhile the days rolled on, all was still uncertainty; when suddenly, on the 13th of March,
Kazeh became a scene of mourning. Some slaves
came in that night, having made their way through
the woods from Ugogo, avoiding the track to save
themselves from detection, and gave information
that Snay, Jafu, and five other Arabs had been
killed, as well as a great number of slaves. The
expedition, they said, had been defeated, and the positions were so complicated nobody knew what to do.
At first the Arabs achieved two brilliant successes,
having recovered their ivory, made slaves of all
they could find, and taken a vast number of cattle;
then attacking Usekhé, they reduced that place to
submission by forcing a ransom out of its people.
At this period, however, they heard that a whole
caravan, carrying 5,000 dollars' worth of property,
had been cut up by the people of Mzanza, a small
district ten miles north of Usekhé; so, instead of
going on to Kanyenyé to relieve the caravans
which were waiting there for them, they foolishly
divided their forces into three parts. Of these they
sent one to take their plunder back to Kazeh, another to form a reserve force at Mdaburu, on the
east flank of the wilderness, and a third, headed by
Snay and Jafu, to attack Mzanza. At the first on-
set Snay and Jafu carried everything before them,
and became so excited over the amount of their
plunder that they lost all feelings of care or precaution.

" In this high exuberance of spirits, a sudden
surprise turned their momentary triumph into a

total defeat; for some Wahumba, having heard the cries of the Wagogo, joined in their cause, and both together fell on the Arab force with such impetuosity that the former victors were now scattered in all directions. Those who could run fast enough were saved; the rest were speared to death by the natives. Nobody knew how Jafu fell: but Snay, after running a short distance, called one of his slaves, and begged him to take his gun, saying, 'I am too old to keep up with you; keep this gun for my sake, for I will lie down here and take my chance.' He never was seen again. But this was not all their misfortunes; for the slaves who brought in this information had met the first detachment, sent with the Khoko plunder, at Kigua, where, they said, the detachment had been surprised by Manua Sera, who, having fortified a village with four hundred men, expecting this sort of thing, rushed out upon them, and cut them all up."

The other Arab merchants at Kazeh were now as desirous for Speke's mediation between them and Manua Sera, as they had formerly been swift in rejecting it, and besought him not to leave until some truce had been concluded. "On the 14th, however," he says, "thirty-nine porters were brought in by Musa's men, who said they had collected one hundred and twenty, and brought them to within ten miles of this, when some travellers frightened all but thirty-nine away by telling them, 'Are you such fools as to venture into Kazeh now? All the Arabs have been killed, or were being cut up and pursued by Manua Sera.' This sad disappointment threw me on my 'beam-ends.' For some reason or other, none of Musa's slaves would take service, and the Arabs prevented theirs from leaving the place, as it was already too short of hands. To do the best under these circumstances, I determined on going to Rungua with what kit could be carried, leaving Bombay behind with Musa until such time as I should arrive there, and, finding more men, could send them back for the rest. I then gave Musa the last of the gold watches the Indian government had given me; and, bidding Sheikh Said take all our letters and specimens back to the coast as soon as the road was found practicable, set out on the march northward with Grant and Baraka, and all the rest of the party."

Moving slowly onward through the northern provinces of Unyamwezi, Speke halted on the 24th of March at a town called Mininga, to collect the remaining porters and await the arrival of the merchant Musa, who had promised to accompany him with a trading caravan to the kingdom of Karagué, or Karagwe. Here the travellers employed themselves in making zoölogical collections until the 2nd of April, when Musa's men arrived, with 300 porters. They were immediately sent to Kazeh, with the collections, to be forwarded to Zanzibar, and with instructions to Musa and Bombay (who had been left there) to join the caravan without delay.

"While waiting for these men's return," Speke writes, "one of Sirboko's slaves, chained up by him, in the most piteous manner cried out to me, 'Hai Bana wangi, Bana wangi (Oh, my lord, my lord)

take pity on me! When I was a free man I saw
you at Uvira, on the Tanganyika Lake, when you
were there; but since then the Watuta, in a fight
at Ujiji, speared me all over and left me for dead,
when I was seized by the people, sold to the Arabs,
and have been in chains ever since. Oh, I say, Bana
wangi, if you would only liberate me I would never
run away, but would serve you faithfully all my
life.' This touching appeal was too strong for my
heart to withstand, so I called up Sirboko, and told
him, if he would liberate this one man to please me,
he should be no loser; and the release was effected.
He was then christened Farhan, (Joy,) and was en-
rolled in my service with the rest of my freed men.
I then inquired if it was true the Wabembé were
cannibals, and also circumcised. In one of their
slaves the latter statement was easily confirmed."

After waiting at Mininga until the 15th of April,
Bombay arrived with the remainder of Speke's
goods, and a large quantity of Musa's, but without
the latter. During this time the Arab forces in the
field had recovered their courage, defeated Manua
Sera, and forced him to fly. On returning to Kazeh,
they had prevented Musa's departure, on the ground
that it would weaken their strength. Speke waited
some days longer, and then dispatched his man
Baraka to Kazeh, promising a large payment for
fifty armed men. On the 30th of April word came
of more projected wars, but nothing about the escort. The remaining Hottentots were suffering so
much from the climate that Speke determined to
send them back to the coast, and then push onward

without waiting for Musa : so, on the 1st of May, he set out for Kazeh, to put an end to all these uncertainties.

No· sooner had he arrived than, as he writes, "the Arabs came flocking in to beg, nay, implore me to help them out of their difficulties. Many of them were absolutely ruined, they said ; others had their houses full of stores unemployed. At Ugogo those who wished to join them were unable to do so, for their porters, what few were left, were all dying of starvation ; and at that moment Manua Sera was hovering about, shooting, both night and day, all the poor villagers in the district, or driving them away. Would to God, they said, I would mediate for them with Manua Sera—they were sure I would be successful—and then they would give me as many armed men as I liked. Their folly in all their actions, I said, proved to me that anything I might attempt to do would be futile, for their alliance with the Watuta, when they were not prepared to act, at once damned them in my eyes as fools. This they in their terror acknowledged, but said it was not past remedy, if I would join them, to counteract what had been done in that matter. Suffice it now to say, after a long conversation, arguing all the pros and cons over, I settled I would write out all the articles of a treaty of peace, by which they should be liable to have all their property forfeited on the coast if they afterward broke faith ; and I begged them to call the next day and sign it."

At length the form of armistice was agreed upon, but as none of the Arabs or their men dared to go to Manua Sera to negotiate it, Speke was obliged to send his man Baraka, and await his return at Kazeh.

" On the 6th of May, the deputation, headed by Baraka, returned triumphantly into Kazeh, leading in two of Manua Sera's ministers—one of them a man with one eye, whom I called Cyclops—and two others, ministers of a chief called Kitambi, or Little Blue Cloth. After going a day's journey, they said they came to where Manua Sera was residing with Kitambi, and met with a most cheerful and kind reception from both potentates, who, on hearing of my proposition, warmly acceded to it, issued orders at once that hostilities should cease, and, with one voice, said they were convinced that, unless through my instrumentality, Manua Sera would never regain his possessions. Kitambi was quite beside himself, and wished my men to stop one night to enjoy his hospitality. Manua Sera, after reflecting seriously about the treacherous murder of old Maula, hesitated, but gave way when it had been explained away by my men, and said, ' No ; they shall go at once, for my kingdom depends on the issue, and Bana Mzungu (the White Lord) may get anxious if they do not return promptly.' One thing, however, he insisted on, and that was, the only place he would meet the Arabs in was Unyanyembe, as it would be beneath his dignity to settle matters anywhere else."

The negotiations gave the promise of a peaceable settlement, and an invitation was sent to Manua Sera to appear in person at Kazeh, in order that the peace might be concluded. It turned out, however, that the Arabs, who had been supporting Mkisiwa, Manu Sera's rival to the chieftaincy, had dexterously avoided mentioning the former's claims —probably with the secret intention of violating the treaty as soon as they felt strong enough.

"On the evening of the 12th of May," Speke continues, " my men returned again with Cyclops, who said, for his master, that Manua Sera desired nothing more than peace, and to make friends with the Arabs ; but as nothing was settled about deposing Mkisiwa, he could not come over here. Could the Arabs, was Manua Sera's rejoinder, suppose for a moment that he would voluntarily divide his dominion with one whom he regarded as his slave ! Death would be preferable ; and although he would trust his life in the Mzungu's hands if he called him again, he must know it was his intention to hunt Mkisiwa down like a wild animal, and would never rest satisfied until he was dead. The treaty thus broke down ; for the same night Cyclops decamped like a thief, after brandishing an arrow which Manua Sera had given him to throw down as a gauntlet of defiance to fight Mkisiwa to death. After this the Arabs were too much ashamed of themselves to come near me, though invited by letter, and Musa became so ill he would not take my advice and ride in a hammock, the best possible cure for his complaint ; so, after being humbugged so many times by his procrastinations, I gave Sheikh Said more letters and specimens, with orders to take the Tots down to the coast as soon as practicable, and started

once more for the north, expecting very shortly to
hear of Musa's death, though he promised to follow
me the very next day or die in the attempt; for I
was fully satisfied in my mind that he would have
marched with me then had he had the resolution to
do so at all."

On returning to Mininga, Speke found Grant in
much better health. With the exception of some
thefts by the natives, nothing of importance had
occurred. So much of the supplies had already
been consumed by reason of the continued delays,
that Speke determined to push onward without
waiting for Musa; which proved, in the end, to be
very fortunate, for the old Arab died at Kazeh a
few weeks afterwards. After many perplexities, he
succeeded in engaging a native caravan leader, by
name Ungurué (the Pig.) He had made several
trips to the kingdom of Karagwe, was acquainted
with the native dialects, but in all other respects
was well described by his name.

Notwithstanding Speke offered thrice the hire
usually paid by merchants, he had the greatest difficulty in engaging porters. The natives advised
him to stop where he was until the harvests were
over, but the diminution of his stores prevented
this. He therefore tried the plan of advancing in
detachments, sending Grant forward with a part of
the men to Ukulima's, on the northern frontier of
Unyamwezi. When this was done, he waited until
the 30th of May, and then, hopeless of obtaining
men, went on to the village of Nunda, the residence
of the chief Ukulima, where he found not only

Grant, but four or five Arab merchants, unable to proceed further. The latter informed him that they had already lost $5,000 by their porters running away with their loads.

Speke held a council with his men, Bombay and Baraka, both of whom were in favor of remaining ; but after explaining to them that he had already sent messages to King Rumanika in Karagwe, and King Suwarora in Usui, they agreed to his proposition that the party should be divided. Grant and Bombay were to form a camp and remain behind, waiting the better season for procuring porters, while Speke with Baraka, the most valuable part of the supplies and the men who had been already hired, were to go forward and break the way.

On the 8th of June, all preparations having been completed, the separation took place. Speke bade good-bye to Grant and Bombay, and advanced directly into the territory of a chief named Myonga, who was famous for his dishonesty and his great extortions from travellers. " On nearing Myonga's palace," says Speke, " we heard war-drums beat in every surrounding village, and the kirangozi (leader) would go no farther until permission was obtained from Myonga. This did not take long, as the chief said he was most desirous to see a white man, never having been to the coast, though his father-in-law had, and had told him that the Wazungu were even greater people than the sultan reigning there. On our drawing near the palace, a small, newly-constructed hut was shown for my residence ; but as I did not wish

to stop there, knowing how anxious Grant would
be to have his relief, I would not enter it, but
instead sent Baraka to pay the hongo (black-mail)
as quickly as possible, that we might move on
again ; at the same time ordering him to describe
the position both Grant and myself were in, and
explain that what I paid now was to frank both of
us, as the whole of the property was my own.

"Myonga did not wish to see me, because he did
not know the coast language. He was immensely
pleased with the present I had given him, and said
he was much and very unjustly abused by the
Arabs, who never came this way, saying he was a
bad man. He should be very glad to see Grant,
and would take nothing from him ; and, though he
did not see me in person, he would feel much
affronted if I did not stop the night there. In the
meanwhile he would have the two cows which had
been stolen by his people, the day before, brought
in, for he could not allow any one to leave his
country abused in any way.

"My men had greatly amused him by firing their
guns off and showing him the use of their sword-
bayonets. I knew, as a matter of course, that if I
stopped any longer I should be teased for more
cloths, and gave orders to my men to march the
same instant, saying, if they did not—for I saw them
hesitate—I would give the cows to the villagers,
since I knew that was the thing that weighed on
their minds. This raised a mutiny. No one would
go forward with the two cows behind ; besides

which, the day was far spent, and there was nothing but jungle, they said, beyond."

The next morning, however, Speke succeeded in quieting his men, and after paying a little more black-mail to satisfy the renewed demands of the rapacious chief, went on his way. For the first few miles there were villages, but after that a long tract of jungle, inhabited chiefly by antelopes and rhinoceros. In the midst of this jungle a dry ravine marked the boundary between the Land of the Moon and the unknown kingdom of Uzinza, on the north.

CHAPTER XIII.

UZINZA, which we now entered, is ruled by two
Wahuma chieftains of foreign blood, descended
from the Abyssinian stock, of whom we saw specimens scattered all over Unyamwezi. Travellers see
very little, however, of these Wahuma, because,
being pastorals, they roam about with their flocks
and build huts as far away as they can from cultivation. Most of the small district chiefs, too, are
the descendants of those who ruled in the same
places before the country was invaded, and with
them travellers put up and have their dealings. The
dress of the Wahuma is very simple, composed
chiefly of cowhide tanned black—a few magic ornaments and charms, brass or copper bracelets, and
immense numbers of sambo for stockings, which
looked very awkward on their long legs. They
smear themselves with rancid butter instead of
macassar, and are, in consequence, very offensive to
all but the negro, who seems, rather than otherwise,
to enjoy a good sharp nose-tickler. For arms, they
carry both bow and spear; more generally the lat-

ter. The Wazinza in the southern parts are so much
like the Wanyamwezi as not to require any especial
notice; but in the north, where the country is more
hilly, they are much more energetic and actively
built. All alike live in grass-hut villages, fenced
round by bomas in the south, but open in the north.
Their country rises in high rolls, increasing in altitude as it approaches the Mountains of the Moon,
and is generally well cultivated, being subjected to
more of the periodical rains than the regions we
have left, though springs are not so abundant, I believe, as they are in the Land of the Moon, where
they ooze out by the flanks of the little granitic hills."

The first village in Uzinza was governed by a
chief named Ruhe, whom Speke vainly endeavored
to pass without visiting. Since each invitation was
only the pretext for demanding presents, it was
highly desirable to avoid these petty native rulers,
each of whom was very difficult to satisfy, before
allowing the drums to be beaten, as a sign to his
people that the caravan had purchased the right to
depart. The next village, Mihambo, belonged to a
more notorious chief, named Makaka, and Speke
promised his new guide, the Pig, a large increase of
wages to conduct him past without stopping; but
the treacherous fellow led him directly into the
hands of a sub-chief, who at once reported his arrival to Makaka.

The result was a summons to halt: the people
were forbidden to sell food to the party, and the
demand for a visit was so imperative that Speke
thought it best to comply. He was terribly plun-

dered by Makaka, who insisted upon having a *deole*, or silk mantle, or else four times the value of one in other goods. The conclusion of the traveller's experience is thus described :

"The drums as yet had not beaten, for Makaka said he would not be satisfied until we had exchanged presents, to prove that we were the best of friends. To do this last act properly I was to get ready whatever I wished to give him, while he would come and visit me with a bullock ; but I was to give him a royal salute, or the drums would not beat. I never felt so degraded as when I complied, and gave orders to my men to fire a volley as he approached my tent ; but I ate the dirt with a good grace, and met the young chief as if nothing had happened. My men, however, could not fire the salute fast enough for him ; for he was one of those excitable, impulsive creatures who expect others to do everything in as great a hurry as their minds wander. The moment the first volley was fired, he said, ' Now fire again, fire again ; be quick, be quick ! What's the use of those things ?' (meaning the guns.) ' We could spear you all while you are loading : be quick, be quick, I tell you.' But Baraka, to give himself law, said, ' No ; I must ask Bana' (master) ' first, as we do everything by order ; this is not fighting at all.'.

"The men being ready, file-firing was ordered, and then the young chief came into my tent. I motioned him to take my chair, which, after he sat down upon it, I was very sorry for, as he stained the seat all black with the running color of one of the new barsati cloths he had got from me, which, to improve its appearance, he had saturated with stinking butter, and had tied round his loins. A fine-looking man of about thirty, he wore the butt-end of a large sea-shell cut in a circle, and tied on his forehead, for a coronet, and sundry small saltiana antelope horns, stuffed with magic powder, to keep off the evil eye. His attendants all fawned on him, and snapped their fingers whenever he sneezed."

He was so rapacious and insolent that Speke seriously deliberated whether he should not have him shot as an example and warning; but the circumstance that Grant was behind, with the fear that other chiefs on the way might afterwards meet him as enemies, compelled him to submit to both outrage and insult. After paying a second exaction the drums were finally beaten, and a march was ordered for the next morning. Immediately afterwards, however, Baraka came to Speke and informed him that dreadful news had arrived. The King of Usui, the next country beyond Uzinza, had detained an Arab caravan in his country, and threatened the men with death. Speke saw plainly that this was a device to prevent him from marching further, and repeated his order to start in the morning; but when the time arrived it was found that all the native porters hired by the Pig had absconded. The leader himself joined them in refusing to proceed.

The expedition now appeared to be doomed to failure. There was but one course left to pursue : Speke had his goods placed in a hut which could easily be defended, gave Baraka sufficient beads to pay for the daily rations of the few remaining servants, and demanded a few men as an escort back to Kazeh. At first no one would go; but, after a day's delay, he secured a sufficient number, and set out on this last desperate endeavor to reconstruct his caravan.

"Next day," he says, "I joined Grant once more, and found he had collected a few Sorombo men, hoping to follow after me. I then told him all my mishaps in Sorombo, as well as of the 'blue-devil' frights that had seized all my men. I felt greatly alarmed about the prospects of the expedition, scarcely knowing what I should do. I resolved at last, if everything else failed, to make up a raft at the southern end of the Nyanza, and try to go up to the Nile in that way. My cough daily grew worse. I could not lie or sleep on either side. Still my mind was so excited and anxious that, after remaining one day here to enjoy Grant's society, I pushed ahead again, taking Bombay with me, and had breakfast at Mchiméka's.

My cough still grew worse, and became so bad that, while mounting a hill on entering Ungugu's the second day after, I blew and grunted like a broken-winded horse, and it became so distressing I had to halt a day. In two more marches, however, I reached Kazeh, and put up with Musa's eldest son, Abdalla, on the second of July, who now was transformed from a drunken, slovenly boy into the appearance of a grand swell, squatting all day as his old father used to do. The house, however, did not feel the same ; no men respected him as they had done his father."

After much trouble and many disappointments, he engaged two men, Bui and Nasib, who had been as far as Uganda, and knew all the native languages. But it was impossible to procure any additional supplies, except at the most ruinous rates.

" Marching slowly," he continues, " as my men kept falling sick, I did not reach Grant again until the 11th.   His health had greatly improved, and he had been dancing with Ukulima.   So, as I was obliged to wait for a short time to get a native guide for Bui, Nasib, and Bombay, who would show them a jungle-path to Usui, we enjoyed our leisure hours in shooting Guinea-fowls for the pot.   A report then came to us that Suwarora had heard with displeasure that I had been endeavoring to see him, but was deterred because evil reports concerning him had been spread.   This unexpected good news delighted me exceedingly ; confirmed my belief that Baraka, after all, was a coward, and induced me to recommend Bombay to make his cowardice more indisputable by going on and doing what he had feared to do.   To which Bombay replied, ' Of course I will.   It is all folly pulling up for every ill wind that blows, because, until one actually *sees* there is something in it, you never can tell among these savages, ' *shaves* ' are so common in Africa.   Besides, a man has but one life, and God is the director of everything.'   ' Bravo !' said I ; ' we will get on as long as you keep to that way of thinking.' "

The favorable report from Usui induced Speke to believe that he could persuade the refractory porters to accompany him. He therefore parted again from Grant, pushed forward, and reached Mihambo on the 18th of July. He found that his man Baraka had in the meantime received a pressing invitation from Lumeresi, a chief living about ten miles to the eastward. After vainly endeavoring to persuade the men to go directly forward, disregarding this new device for plunder, he was compelled to march to the chieftain's village. By this time his physical condition was alarming. The racking cough and internal pains brought on a kind of semi-delirium, like that which had attacked him on the journey to Lake Tanganyika; and it was peculiarly unfortunate that he should be so prostrated at a time when he needed all his energy and patience.

During eight days, scarcely able to move or speak, he was delayed at Lumeresi's, each day being obliged to endure or resist the rapacity of the chief, whose demands increased in proportion as they were satisfied. Finally the latter declared that the additional gift of a red blanket would satisfy him. " I jumped at this concession," Speke writes, " with the greatest eagerness, paid down my cloths on the spot, and, thinking I was free at last, ordered a hammock to be slung on a pole, that I might leave the next day. Next morning, however, on seeing me actually preparing to start, Lumeresi found he could not let me go until he increased the tax by three more cloths, as some of his family complained that they had got nothing. After some badgering, I paid what he asked for, and ordered the men to carry me out of the palace before anything else was done, for I would not sleep another night where I was. Lumeresi then stood in my way, and said he would never allow a man of his country to give me any assistance until I was well, for he could not bear the idea of hearing it said that, after taking so many cloths from me, he had allowed me to die in the jungles, and dissuaded my men from obeying my orders."

For still another week Speke was detained by his own physical weakness. On the 6th of August, however, he was able to sit in a chair and smoke his pipe, and the men, who had expected his death, showed themselves more willing to advance. But it was not until three days afterwards that he succeeded in satisfying the chief Lumeresi, and having the drums beaten as the signal that he was free to depart. The two new guides, for whom he had walked all the way back to Kazeh, were then found wanting, and Speke declares that the shock of this new misfortune nearly killed him. There seemed to be no alternative but to sent or go to Kazeh once more. When the men heard this they mutinied, declaring they never would wait to be taken on to Karagwe and slaughtered there.

After sending an account of his miserable situation to Grant, Speke was greatly encouraged, on the 21st of August, by the arrival of a caravan from Karagwe, which reported that both Rumanika, the king of that country, and Suwarora, king of Usui, were expecting the travellers and wondering why they did not arrive. The latter, indeed, had sent four men as messengers, who arrived the next day. This occasioned a violent scene with Lumeresi, who was furious because Speke gave the Wasui (men of Usui) some small presents. A week afterwards, another caravan from Karagwe came in, and among its members was a half-caste Arab, named Saim, who had seen Burton and Speke at Kazeh, knew the native languages, and was willing to go back as guide and interpreter.

It was now only necessary to procure new porters and advise Grant of the prospect ahead. Although the latter was only two marches, or one good day's journey distant, it was very difficult to find men to convey a message; so, finally, Speke was forced to dispatch some of his own party and await their return. On the night of the 26th of September, he was aroused by the arrival of some native porters, who brought news that Grant had been attacked by an armed band, his men killed or dispersed, his goods stolen, and himself left standing alone, under a tree, with only a gun in his hand. Although convinced that the tale was greatly exaggerated, Speke was sure that some disaster had happened, and immediately sent off the last of his men, with a fresh supply of beads, for his unfortunate companion. The next day he received the following letter from Grant:

" IN THE JUNGLES, near Myonga's, 16th Sept., 1861.

" MY DEAR SPEKE : The caravan was attacked, plundered, and the men driven to the winds, while marching this morning, into Myonga's country.

"Awaking at cock-crow, I roused the camp, all anxious to rejoin you; and while the loads were being packed, my attention was drawn to an angry discussion between the head men and seven or eight armed fellows sent by Sultan Myonga, to insist on my putting up for the day in his village. They were summarily told that as *you* had already made him a present, he need not expect a visit from *me*. Adhering, I doubt not, to their master's instructions, they officiously constituted themselves our guides till we chose to strike off their path, when, quickly heading our party, they stopped the way, planted their spears, and *dared* our advance !

"This menace made us firmer in our determination, and we swept past the spears. After we had marched unmolested for some seven miles, a loud yelping from the woods excited our attention, and a sudden rush was made upon us by, say, two hundred men, who came down *seemingly* in great glee. In an instant, at the caravan's centre, they fastened upon the poor porters. The struggle was short; and with the threat of an arrow or spear at their breasts, men were robbed of their cloths and ornaments, loads were yielded and run away with before resistance could be organized ; only three men of a hundred stood by me ; the others, whose only *thought* was their lives, fled into the woods, where I went shouting for them. One man, little Rahan—rip as he is—stood with cocked gun, defending his load against five savages with uplifted spears. No one else could be seen. Two or three were reported killed ; some were wounded. Beads, boxes, cloths, etc., lay strewed about the woods. In fact, I felt wrecked. My attempt to go and demand redress from the sultan was resisted, and, in utter despair, I seated myself among a mass of rascals jeering round me, and insolent after the success of the day. Several were dressed in the very cloths, etc., they had stolen from my men.

"In the afternoon, about fifteen men and loads were brought me, with a message from the sultan that the attack had been a *mistake* of his subjects—that one man had had a hand cut off for it, and that all the property would be restored !

"Yours sincerely,　　　　　　J. W. GRANT.

"Now, judging from the message sent to Grant by Myonga," says Speke, " it appeared to me that his men had mistaken their chief's orders, and had gone one step beyond his intentions. It was obvious that the chief merely intended to prevent Grant from passing through or evading his district without paying a hongo, else he would not have sent his men to invite him to his palace, doubtless with instructions, if necessary, to use force. This appears the more evident from the fact of his subsequent contrition, and finding it necessary to send excuses when the property was in his hands ; for these chiefs, grasping as they are, know they must conform to some kind of system, to save themselves from a general war, or the avoidance of their territory by all travellers in future.

Next day, however, I had from Grant two very opposite accounts—one, in the morning, full of exultation, in which he said he hoped to reach Ruhe's this very day, as his complement of porters was then completed ; while by the other, which came in the evening, I was shocked to hear that Myonga, after returning all the loads, much reduced by rifling, had demanded as a hongo two guns, two boxes of ammunition, forty brass wires, and 160 yards of American sheeting, in default of which he, Grant, must lend Myonga ten Wanguana to build a boma on the west of his district, to enable him to fight some Wasonga who were invading his territory, otherwise he would not allow Grant to move from his palace. Grant knew not what to do."

Speke immediately sent Baraka to Grant, with orders not part with any guns or ammunition. In the meantime some of the robbers, who had innocently come to the former's camp with stolen articles, were seized and held captive. The prospects of the expedition improved a little, and this, with the constant excitement, had a favorable effect on Speke's health. He went out shooting birds for the scientific collection, and his strength increased from day to day. On the 24th of September he received a letter from Grant, giving a statement of his losses, which amounted to eight loads in all: and two days afterwards Grant himself walked into the camp, when all the long array of misfortunes was forgotten.

This, nevertheless, was not the end of the difficulty. The native porters again refused to go on, until, on the 4th of October, the chief Lumeresi consented to furnish a guide, after which about half the requisite number was procured. About the same time Suwarora, the king of Usui, again sent messengers, bearing his mace—a long rod of brass, bound with charms—as both an invitation and a command, and the expedition was free to advance. On the 6th, finally, they started, making very short marches: Speke was almost reduced to a skeleton by his illness. At the first halting-place he succeeded in engaging porters, at an exorbitant rate, to carry his stores as far as Usui.

" With at last a sufficiency of porters, we all set out together, walking over a new style of country. Instead of the constantly-recurring outcrops of granite, as in Unyamwezi, with valleys between, there were only two lines of little hills visible. one right

and one left of us, a good way off; while the ground
over which we were travelling, instead of being confined like a valley, rose in long high swells of sandstone formation, covered with small forest-trees,
among which flowers like primroses, only very much
larger, and mostly of a pink color, were frequently
met with. Indeed, we ought all to have been happy
together, for all my men were paid and rationed tre-
bly—far better than they would have been if they
had been travelling with any one else ; but I had
not paid all, as they thought, proportionably, and
therefore there were constant heart-burnings, with
strikes and rows every day."

On the 15th they reached the residence of a chief
named Pongo, where the customary tribute was exacted and paid. As soon as the drums were
beaten, the messengers from Usui dropped down
on their knees before the travellers, and congratulated them that now the payment of tribute was
over for them. The latter were obliged to halt a
day in Pongo's palace to hire more porters, half of
their men having left, but they had no intercourse
with the chief, who wrapped up his head whenever
they came near, to avoid their evil eyes.

On the 20th, after crossing a waste, uninhabited
tract, they came into the immediate dominion of
King Suwarora. "We were now in Usui," Speke
writes, "and so the mace-bearers, being on their
own ground, forgot their manners, and peremptorily
demanded their pay before they would allow us to
move one step farther. At first I tried to stave
the matter off, promising great rewards if they

took us quickly on to Suwarora ; but they would take no alternative—their rights were four wires each.   I could not afford such a sum, and tried to beat them down, but without effect ; for they said they had it in their power to detain us here a whole month, and they could get us bullied at every stage by the officers of the stations.   No threats of reporting them to their chief had any effect ; so, knowing that treachery in these countries was a powerful enemy, I ordered them to be paid."

After a delay of three days they got under way again ; the path wound through a long forest, and then entered the populous parts of Usui, a broken, convulsed-looking country, with rounded sandstone hills.   The villages of grass huts were surrounded by large orchards of plantains.   Cattle were numerous, but the people would not sell their milk to men who ate fowls.   On the 25th they reached a village called Vikora, where there was a cataract 70 feet high—a very unusual sight in these lands.   Here a messenger arrived from Suwarora, to say that they must come on at once, and his people should not molest them.   They resumed their march in high spirits, but on the summit of a lofty hill just beyond were stopped by a large body of men, who demanded tribute.   Speke therefore gave orders to form a camp, and sent off his interpreter, Nasib, (who had been returned to him from Kazeh,) and the mace-bearers to the king, to report the matter.

At sunset the natives were seen prowling in the jungle, in the hope of stealing from the caravan.   He

gave orders that any thief should be shot, and
" that night," he says, " one was hit, without any
mistake about it ; for the next morning we tracked
him by his blood, and afterward heard he had died
of his wound. The Wasui elders, contrary to my
expectation, then came and congratulated us on our
success. They thought us most wonderful men,
and possessed of supernatural powers ; for the thief
in question was a magician, who until now was
thought to be invulnerable. Indeed, they said Arabs
with enormous caravans had often been plundered
by these people ; but, though they had so many
more guns than ourselves, they never succeeded in
killing one.

" Nasib then returned to inform us that the king
had heard our complaint, and was sorry for it, but
said he could not interfere with the rights of his
officers. He did not wish himself to take anything
from us, and hoped we would come on to him as
soon as we had satisfied his officers with the trifle
they wanted."

Determined to resist this exaction, or at least
lessen its amount, Speke next sent his man Bombay
to the camp of an Arab trader named Masudi, to
solicit his favorable influence, and also to request
him, when he should reach Karagwe, to beg the
king to send his mace-bearers as a safe conduct.
The next morning Bombay returned, " flushed with
the excitement of a great success. He had been in
Masudi's camp, and had delivered my message.
Masudi, he said, had been there a fortnight unable
to settle his hongo, for the great Mkama had not

deigned to see him, though the Arab had been daily
to his palace requesting an interview. 'Well,' I
said, 'that is all very interesting, but what next?
will the big king see us?' 'Oh no; by the very
best good fortune in the world, on going into the
palace I saw Suwarora, and spoke to him at once;
but he was so tremendously drunk he could not understand me.' 'What luck was there in that?' I
asked. On which Bombay said, 'Oh, everybody in
the place congratulated me on my success in having
obtained an interview with that great monarch the
very first day, when Arabs had seldom that privilege
under one full month of squatting; even Masudi
had not yet seen him.' To which Nasib also added,
'Ah! yes—indeed it is so—a monstrous success!
there is great ceremony as well as business at these
courts; you will better see what I mean when you
get to Uganda. These Wahuma kings are not like
those you ever saw in Unyamwezi or anywhere else;
they have officers and soldiers like Said Majid, the
Sultan at Zanzibar.' 'Well,' said I to Bombay,
'what was Suwarora like?' 'Oh, he is a very fine
man—just as tall, and in the face very like Grant;
in fact, if Grant were black you would not know the
difference.' 'And were his officers drunk too?'
'Oh yes, they were all drunk together; men were
bringing in pombé all day.' 'And did you get
drunk?' 'Oh yes,' said Bombay, grinning, and
showing his whole row of sharp-pointed teeth,
'they *would* make me drink; and then they showed
me the place they assigned for your camp when you
came over there. It was not in the palace, but

>een dail
Well,' I
at next?
he very
nto the
t once;
ot un-
at?' I
dy in
aving
the
lege
udi
ed,
s!
se
u
э

NATIVES OF UZUI BRINGING PROVISIONS.

outside, without a tree near it—anything but a nice-looking residence."

On the 31st all difficulties were settled, and the party marched on to Suwarora's palace, in the Uthungu valley. It was a wild, picturesque spot, surrounded with mountains of sandstone. The mace-bearers would not allow them to halt in the neighborhood of the king's residence, but led them two miles further to the spot where the merchant, Masudi, was encamped. The latter had been detained nearly a year between Kazeh and the land of Usui, had been obliged to pay enormously, but was now free from the persecution, and ready to start for Karagwe the next morning.

In the evening Speke received a visit from a native of Uganda, the kingdom to the northward of Karagwe, where—according to the reports of traders—the Nile issued from the Victoria Nyanza. He was a handsome man of neat appearance and gentle manners, and willingly agreed to take a message from the travellers to Mtesa, the king of Uganda. The Usui people came to the camp with an abundance of provisions, but at the end of ten days Speke had not yet been permitted to see Suwarora, nor was there any sign of his being allowed to depart. It soon became evident that the chieftain was determined to exact a great deal of tribute, yet was superstitiously fearful of meeting the white men. The tedium of the delay was not agreeably relieved by a furious quarrel between the two men, Bombay and Baraka, a woman being the cause.

On the evening of November 13th, the subchiefs Virembo and Karambulé came to receive the tribute for Suwarora, " demanding," says Speke, " 60 wires, 160 yards of American domestics, 300 strings of mzizima, and 5,000 strings of white beads ; but they allowed themselves to be beaten down to 50 wires, 20 pretty cloths, 100 strings mzizima, and 4,000 kutuamnazi, or cocoa-nut leaf colored beads, my white being all done. It was too late, however, to count all the things out, so they came the next day and took them. They then said we might go as soon as we had settled with the Wahinda or Wanawami (the king's children,) for Suwarora could not see us this time, as he was so engaged with his army ; but he hoped to see us and pay us more respect when we returned from Uganda, little thinking I had sworn in my mind never to see him, or return that way again. I said to those men, I thought he was ashamed to see us, as he had robbed us so after inviting us into the country, else he was too superstitious, for he ought at least to have given us a place in his palace. They both rebutted the insinuation ; and to change the subject, commenced levying the remaining dues to the princes, which ended by my giving thirty-four wires and six pretty cloths in a lump.

" Early in the morning we were on foot again, only too thankful to have got off so cheaply. Then men were appointed as guides and protectors, to look after us as far as the border. What an honor ! We had come into the country drawn there by a combination of pride and avarice, and now we were leaving it in hot haste under the guidance of an escort of officers, who were in reality appointed to watch us as dangerous wizards and objects of terror. It was all the same to us, as we now only thought of the prospect of relief before us, and laughed at what we had gone through.

" Rising out of the Uthungu valley, we walked over rolling ground, drained in the dips by miry rush rivulets. The population was thinly scattered in small groups of grass huts, where the scrub jungle had been cleared away. On the road we passed cairns, to which every passer-by contributed a stone. Of the origin of the cairns I could not gain any information, though it struck me as curious I should find them in the first country we had entered governed by the Wahuma, as I formerly saw the same thing in the Somali country, which doubtless, in earlier days, was governed by a branch of the Abyssinians. Arrived at our camping, we were immediately pounced upon by a deputation of officers, who said they had been sent by Semamba, the officer of this district. He lived ten miles from the road ; but, hearing of our approach, he had sent these men to take his dues. At first I objected to pay, lest he should afterward treat me as Virembo had done ; but I gave way in the end, and paid nine wires, two chintz and two bandéra cloths, as the guides said they would stand my security against any farther molestation.

" Rattling on again as merry as larks, over the same red sandstone formation, we entered a fine forest, and trended on through it at a stiff pace until we arrived at the head of a deep valley called

Lohugati, which was so beautiful we instinctively pulled up to admire it. Deep down its well-wooded side below us was a stream, of most inviting aspect for a trout-fisher, flowing toward the Nyanza. Just beyond it the valley was clothed with fine trees and luxuriant vegetation of all descriptions, among which was conspicuous the pretty pandana palm, and rich gardens of plantains, while thistles of extraordinary size and wild indigo were the more common weeds. The land beyond that again rolled back in high undulations, over which, in the far distance, we could see a line of cones, red and bare on their tops, guttered down with white streaks, looking for all the world like recent volcanoes; and in the far background, rising higher than all, were the rich grassy hills of Karagwe and Kishakka.

"On resuming our march, a bird called khongota flew across our path; seeing which, old Nasib, beaming with joy, in his superstitious belief cried out with delight, 'Ali! look at that good omen! now our journey will be sure to be prosperous.' After fording the stream, we sat down to rest, and were visited by all the inhabitants, who were more naked than any people we had yet seen. All the maidens, even at the age of puberty, did not hesitate to stand boldly in front of us—for evil thoughts were not in their minds. From this we rose over a stony hill to the settlement of Vihembé, the last on the Usui frontier."

Beyond this, only a narrow strip of "neutral," that is, uninhabited territory, separated them from the famous and unknown kingdom of Karagwe.

CHAPTER XIV.

SPEKE.—THE KINGDOM OF KARAGWE.

AFTER crossing a broad, beautiful stretch of meadow-land, and threading a low pass between two dome-like hills, the travellers found themselves in the kingdom of Karagwe. The manner of their reception in this land differed so much from all their previous experiences that Speke's description of it must be quoted:

"On arriving in camp we pitched under some trees, and at once were greeted by an officer sent by Rumanika to help us out of Usui. This was Kachuchu, an old friend of Nasib's, who no sooner saw him than, beaming with delight, he said to us, 'Now, was I not right when I told you the birds flying about on Lohugati Hill were a good omen? Look here what this man says: Rumanika has ordered him to bring you on to his palace at once, and wherever you stop a day, the village officers are instructed to supply you with food at the king's expense, for there are no taxes gathered from strangers in the kingdom of Karagwe. Presents may be exchanged, but the name of tax is ignored.' Grant here shot a rhinoceros, which came well into play to mix with the day's flour we had carried on from Vihembé.

"Our day's march had been novel and very amusing. The hilly country surrounding us, together with the valley, brought back to recollection many happy days I had spent with the Tartars in the Thibetian valley of the Indus—only this was more picturesque ; for, though both countries are wild, and very thinly inhabited, this was greened over with grass, and dotted here and there on the higher slopes with thick bush of acacias, the haunts of rhinoceros, both white and black ; while in the flat of the valley, herds of hartebeest and fine cattle roamed about like the kiyang and tame yâk of Thibet. Then, to enhance all these pleasures, so different from our former experiences, we were treated like guests by the chief of the place, who, obeying the orders of his king, Rumanika, brought me presents, as soon as we arrived, of sheep, fowls, and sweet potatoes, and was very thankful for a few yards of red blanketing as a return, without begging for more.

"The farther we went in this country the better we liked it, as the people were all kept in good order ; and the village chiefs were so civil that we could do as we liked.

"After following down the left side of the valley and entering the village, the customary presents and returns were made. Wishing then to obtain a better view of the country, I strolled over the nearest hills, and found the less exposed slopes well covered with trees. Small antelopes occasionally sprang up from the grass. I shot a florikan for the pot; and as I had never before seen white rhinoceros, killed one now; though, as no one would eat him, I felt sorry rather than otherwise for what I had done. When I returned in the evening, small boys brought me sparrows for sale; and then I remembered the stories I had heard from Musa Mzuri, that in the whole of Karagwe these small birds were so numerous, the people, to save themselves from starvation, were obliged to grow a bitter corn which the birds disliked, and so I found it. At night, while observing for latitude, I was struck by surprise to see a long, noisy procession pass by where I sat, led by some men who carried on their shoulders a woman covered up in a blackened skin. On inquiry, however, I heard she was being taken to the hut of her espoused."

Travelling for a day or two along the valley of a stream called the Urigi, they passed over another range of sandstone hills, and entered the close, rich valley of Uthenga, bounded by mountains a thousand feet high, and covered with forests. In the bed of the valley there were not only magnificent trees of great height, but also an unusual amount of cultivation, plantations of bananas being most abundant. The change from former privations and troubles was so great that the weary explorers could hardly believe their good fortune.

" Leaving the valley of Uthenga," Speke says, " we rose over the spur of Nyamwara, where we found we had attained the delightful altitude of 5,000 odd feet. Oh, how we enjoyed it! every one feeling so happy at the prospect of meeting so soon the good king Rumanika. Tripping down the greensward, we now worked our way to the Rozoka valley, and pitched our tents in the village.

" Kachuchu here told us he had orders to precede us, and prepare Rumanika for our coming, as his king wished to know what place we would prefer to live at—the Arab depot at Kufro, on the direct line to Uganda, in his palace with himself, or outside his inclosures. Such politeness rather took us aback ; so, giving our friend a coil of copper wire to keep him in good spirits, I said all our pleasure rested in seeing the king ; whatever honors he liked to confer on us we should take with good grace, but one thing he must understand, we came not to trade, but to see him and great kings, and therefore the Arabs had no relations with us."

Another day's march brought them so near Rumanika's palace that it was considered proper to halt and await the return of the messenger. The latter soon arrived with an invitation to go on immediately, and a present of tobacco and pombé, or plantain beer, both very sweet and strong. The next morning, the 25th of November, 1861, they crossed a hill called Weranhanjé, the grassy top of which was 5,500 feet above the sea. Then descending a little they saw what appeared to be a rich clump of trees, but which proved to be the palace enclosure. About 500 feet below it there was a beautiful lake, in the bosom of the hills, to which Speke gave the name of the Little Windermere, on account of its resemblance to the English lake of

that name. Rumanika's palace was in lat. 1° 42'
S. and long. 31° 1' E. Speke thus describes his arrival :

"To do royal honors to the king of this charming
land, I ordered my men to put down their loads and
fire a volley. This was no sooner done than, as we
went to the palace gate, we received an invitation
to come in at once, for the king wished to see us
before attending to anything else. Now, leaving our
traps outside, both Grant and myself, attended by
Bombay and a few of the seniors of my Wanguana,
entered the vestibule, and, walking through extensive inclosures studded with huts of kingly dimensions, were escorted to a pent-roofed baraza, which
the Arabs had built as a sort of government office,
where the king might conduct his state affairs.

"Here, as we entered, we saw sitting cross-legged
on the ground Rumanika the king, and his brother
Nnanaji, both of them men of noble appearance and
size. The king was plainly dressed in an Arab's
black choga, and wore, for ornament, dress-stock-
ings of rich-colored beads, and neatly-worked wrist-
lets of copper. Nnanaji, being a doctor of very high
pretensions, in addition to a check cloth wrapped
round him, was covered with charms. At their
sides lay huge pipes of black clay. In their rear,
squatting quiet as mice, were all the king's sons,
some six or seven lads, who wore leather middle-
coverings, and little dream charms tied under their
chins. The first greetings of the king, delivered in
good Kisuahili, were warm and affecting, and in an
instant we both felt and saw we were in the com-

pany of men who were as unlike as they could be to
the common order of the natives of the surrounding
districts. They had fine oval faces, large eyes and
high noses, denoting the best blood of Abyssinia.
Having shaken hands in true English style, which is
the peculiar custom of the men in this country, the
ever-smiling Rumanika begged us to be seated on
the ground opposite to him, and at once wished to
know what we thought of Karagwe, for it had struck
him his mountains were the finest in the world;
and the lake, too, did we not admire it? Then
laughing, he inquired—for he knew all the story—
what we thought of Suwarora, and the reception we
had met with in Usui. When this was explained
to him, I showed him that it was for the interest of
his own kingdom to keep a check on Suwarora,
whose exorbitant taxations prevented the Arabs
from coming to see him and bringing things from
all parts of the world. He made inquiries for the
purpose of knowing how we found our way all over
the world; for on the former expedition a letter had
come to him for Musa, who no sooner read it than
he said I had called him and he must leave, as I was
bound for Ujiji.

"This of course led to a long story describing the
world, the proportions of land and water, and the
power of ships which conveyed even elephants and
rhinoceros—in fact, all the animals in the world—
to fill our menageries at home, etc., etc., as well as
the strange announcement that we lived to the northward, and had only come this way because his
friend Musa had assured me without doubt that he

TYPES OF NATIVES OF UZUI.

would give us the road on through Uganda. Time flew like magic, the king's mind was so quick and inquiring; but as the day was wasting away, he generously gave us our option to choose a place for our residence in or out of his palace, and allowed us time to select one. We found the view overlooking the lake to be so charming, that we preferred camping outside, and set our men at once to work cutting sticks and long grass to erect themselves sheds.

" One of the young princes—for the king had ordered them all to be constantly in attendance on us —happening to see me sit on an iron chair, rushed back to his father and told him about it. This set all the royals in the palace in a state of high wonder, and ended by my getting a summons to show off the white man sitting on his throne; for of course I could only be, as all of them called me, a king of great dignity, to indulge in such state. Rather reluctantly I did as I was bid, and allowed myself once more to be dragged into court. Rumanika, as gentle as ever, then burst into a fresh fit of merriment, and after making sundry enlightened remarks of inquiry, which of course were responded to with the greatest satisfaction, finished off by saying, with a very expressive shake of the head, ' Oh these Wazungu, these Wazungu! they know and do everything.'

" I then put in a word for myself. Since we had entered Karagwe we never could get one drop of milk either for love or for money, and I wished to know what motive the Wahuma had for withhold-

ing it. We had heard they held superstitious
dreads, that any one who ate the flesh of pigs, fish
or fowls, or the bean called maharagwe, if he tasted
the products of their cows, would destroy their cattle, and I hoped he did not labor under any such
absurd delusions.   To which he replied, it was only
the poor who thought so ; and as he now saw we
were in want, he would set apart one of his cows
expressly for our use.   On bidding adieu, the usual
formalities of hand-shaking were gone through ;
and on entering camp, I found the good, thought-
ful king had sent us some more of his excellent
beer.

"The Wanguana were now all in the highest of
good humor ; for time after time goats and fowls
were brought into camp by the officers of the
king, who had received orders from all parts of the
country to bring in supplies for his guests ; and
this kind of treatment went on for a month, though
it did not diminish my daily expenditure of beads,
as grain and plantains were not enough thought
of.   The cold winds, however, made the coast-men
all shiver, and suspect, in their ignorance, we must
be drawing close to England, the only cold place
they had heard of."

The details of Speke's interviews with the friendly monarch, in that hitherto unknown and unvisit-
ed kingdom, lying between the three great lakes of
Equatorial Africa—the Tanganyika, the Victoria
and Albert Nyanzas—are so interesting, and also
so agreeable after his long narrative of treachery

and hostility, that we give, in his own words, the main incidents of his stay at Rumanika's palace :

At the second visit, which took place on the 26th of November, "a long theological and historical discussion ensued, which so pleased the king that he said he would be delighted if I would take two of his sons to England, that they might bring him a knowledge of everything. Then turning again to the old point, his utter amazement that we should spend so much property in travelling, he wished to know what we did it for ; when men had such means they would surely sit down and enjoy it. 'Oh no,' was the reply ; 'we have had our fill of the luxuries of life ; eating, drinking, or sleeping have no charms for us now ; we are above trade, therefore require no profits, and seek for enjoyment the run of the world. To observe and admire the beauties of creation are worth much more than beads to us. But what led us this way we have told you before ; it was to see your majesty in particular, and the great kings of Africa, and at the same time to open another road to the north, whereby the best manufactures of Europe would find their way to Karagwe, and you would get so many more guests.' In the highest good-humor the king said, 'As you have come to see me and see sights, I will order some boats and show you over the lake, with musicians to play before you, or anything else that you like.' Then, after looking over our pictures with intensest delight, and admiring our beds, boxes, and outfit in general, he left for the day.

"In the afternoon, as I had heard from Musa

that the wives of the king and princes were fattened to such an extent that they could not stand upright, I paid my respect to Wazézéru, the king's eldest brother—who, having been born before his father ascended his throne, did not come in the line of succession—with the hope of being able to see for myself the truth of the story. There was no mistake about it. On entering the hut, I found the old man and his chief wife sitting side by side on a bench of earth strewed over with grass, and partioned like stalls for sleeping apartments, while in front of them were placed numerous wooden pots of milk, and, hanging from the poles that supported the beehive-shaped hut, a large collection of bows six feet in length, while below them were tied an even larger collection of spears, intermixed with a goodly assortment of heavy-handled assegais. I was struck with no small surprise at the way he received me, as well as with the extraordinary dimensions, yet pleasing beauty, of the immoderately fat fair one, his wife. She could not rise; and so large were her arms that between the joints the flesh hung down like large, loose-stuffed puddings. Then in came their children, all models of the Abyssinian type of beauty, and as polite in their manners as thorough-bred gentlemen. They had heard of my picture-books from the king, and all wished to see them; which they no sooner did, to their infinite delight, especially when they recognized any of the animals, than the subject was turned by my inquiring what they did with so many milk-pots. This was easily explained by Wazézéru himself, who, pointing to his wife, said, ' This is all the product of those pots : from early youth upward we keep those pots to their mouths, as it is the fashion at court to have very fat wives.'

" Ever anxious to push on with the journey, as I felt every day's delay only tended to diminish my means—that is, my beads and copper wire—I instructed Bombay to take the under-mentioned articles to Rumanika as a small sample of the products of my country ;* to say I felt quite ashamed of their being so few and so poor, but I hoped he would forgive my shortcomings, as he knew I had been so often robbed on the way to him ; and I trusted, in recollection of Musa, he would give me leave to go on to Uganda, for every day's delay was consuming my supplies. Nnanaji, however, it was said, should get something ; so, in addition to the king's present, I apportioned one out for him, and Bombay took both up to the palace. Everybody, I was pleased to hear, was surprised with both the quantity and quality of what I had been able to find for them ; for, after the plundering in Ugogo, the immense consumption caused by such long delays on the road, the fearful prices I had had to pay for my porters' wages, the enormous taxes I had been forced to give both in Msalala and Uzinza, besides the constant thievings in camp, all of which was

---

* *Rumanika's present.*—One block-tin box, one Raglan coat, five yards scarlet broadcloth, two coils copper wire, a hundred large blue egg-beads, five bundles best variegated beads, three bundles minute beads—pink, blue, and white.

made public by the constantly-recurring tales of my men, nobody thought had got anything left.

"Rumanika, above all, was as delighted as if he had come in for a fortune, and sent to say the Raglan coat was a marvel, and the scarlet broadcloth the finest thing he had ever seen. Nobody but Musa had ever given him such beautiful beads before, and none ever gave with such free liberality. Whatever I wanted I should have in return for it, as it was evident to him I had really done him a great honor in visiting him. Neither his father nor any of his forefathers had had such a great favor shown them. He was alarmed, he confessed, when he heard we were coming to visit him, thinking we might prove some fearful monsters that were not quite human, but now he was delighted beyond all measure with what he saw of us. A messenger should be sent at once to the king of Uganda to inform him of our intention to visit him, with his own favorable report of us. This was necessary according to the etiquette of the country. Without such a recommendation our progress would be stopped by the people, while with one word from him all would go straight; for was he not the gate-keeper, enjoying the full confidence of Uganda? A month, however, must elapse, as the distance to the palace of Uganda was great; but, in the meantime, he would give me leave to go about in his country to do and see what I liked, Nnanaji and his sons escorting me everywhere. Moreover, when the time came for my going on to Uganda, if I had not enough presents to give the king, he would fill up the complement from his own stores, and either go with me himself, or send his brother Nnanaji to conduct me as far as the boundary of Uganda.

" Returning home to the tents as the evening sky was illumined with the red glare of the sun, my attention was attracted by observing in the distance some bold sky-scraping cones situated in the country Ruanda, which at once brought back to recollection the ill-defined story I had heard from the Arabs of a wonderful hill always covered with clouds, on which snow or hail was constantly falling. This was a valuable discovery, for I found these hills to be the great turn-point of the Central African watershed. Without loss of time I set to work, and, gathering all the travellers I could in the country, protracted, from their descriptions, all the distant topographical features set down in the map, as far north as 3° of north latitude, as far east as 36°, and as far west as 26° of east longitude ; only afterward slightly corrected, as I was better able to connect and clear up some trifling but doubtful points.

" Indeed, I was not only surprised at the amount of information about distant places I was enabled to get here from these men, but also at the correctness of their vast and varied knowledge, as I afterword tested it by observation and the statements of others."

Speke estimated the height of Mount Mfumbiro at 10,000 feet, but he was undoubtedly wrong in calling this chain the " Mountains of the Moon." He seems to have been too ready to accept such native statements as tallied with his own preconceived theory, and many of the points which he laid down on his map were afterwards changed by Baker's discoveries.

While waiting the return of the messenger whom king Rumanika had dispatched to Uganda, he tried to replenish his almost exhausted stock of cloth, beads, and wire, from the Arab merchants.   There was a renewal of the old jealousy between Bombay and Baraka, which threw the whole camp into commotion. Meantime he had a chance of navigating the beautiful lake near the palace, of going on hunting expeditions, and securing some valuable specimens for his zoölogical collection.   Among the latter was a beautiful *nzoe*, or water antelope, which proved to be an entirely new species.

On the afternoon of December 5th the king invited the travellers to witness his New-moon Levée, a ceremony which takes place every month, with a view of ascertaining how many of his subjects are loyal. " On entering his palace enclosure," says Speke, " the first thing we saw was a blaue boc's horn stuffed full of magic powder, with very imposing effect, by Kyengo, and stuck in the ground, with its mouth pointed in the direction of Rogéro.   In the second court we found thirty-five drums ranged on the ground, with as many drummers standing behind them, and a knot of young princes and officers of high dignity waiting to escort us into the third inclosure, where, in his principal hut, we found Rumanika squatting on the ground, half concealed by the portal, but showing his smiling face to welcome us in. His head was got up with a tiara of beads, from the centre of which, directly over the forehead, stood a plume of red feathers, and encircling the lower face with a fine large white beard set in a stock or band of beads. We were beckoned to squat alongside Nnanaji, the master of ceremonies, and a large group of high officials outside the porch. Then the thirty-five drums all struck up together in very good harmony ; and when their deafening noise was over, a smaller band of hand-drums and reed instruments was ordered in to amuse us.

" This second performance over, from want of breath only, district officers, one by one, came advancing on tiptoe, then pausing, contorting and quivering their bodies, advancing again with a springing gait and outspread arms, which they moved as if they wished to force them out of their joints, in all of which actions they held drum-sticks or twigs in their hands, swore with a maniacal voice an oath of their loyalty and devotion to their king, backed by the expression of a hope that he would cut off their heads if they ever turned from his enemies, and then, kneeling before him, they held out their sticks that he might touch them. With a constant reiteration of these scenes —the saluting at one time, the music at another— interrupted only once by a number of girls dancing something like a good rough Highland fling while the little band played, the day's ceremonies ended."

A few days after this, Speke confirmed the impression he had made upon the king by shooting three rhinoceros. Now, when all aspects seemed to be so favorable, Grant was suddenly attacked with a disease in the leg, which rendered it evident that he would not be able to travel for some months, if, indeed, he should recover. On the 14th of December, Speke called upon one of the sisters-in-law of the king, who, according to the ideas of Karagwe, was a perfect beauty.

"She was another of those wonders of obesity, unable to stand excepting on all fours. I was desirous to obtain a good view of her, and actually to measure her, and induced her to give me facilities for doing so by offering in return to show her a bit of my naked legs and arms. The bait took as I wished it, and after getting her to sidle and wriggle into the middle of the hut, I did as I promised, and then took her dimensions, as noted below.* All of these are exact except the height, and I believe I could have obtained this more accurately if I could have had her laid on the floor. Not knowing. what difficulties I should have to contend with in such a piece of engineering, I tried to get her height by raising her up. This, after infinite exertions on the part of us both, was accomplished, when she sank down again, fainting, for her blood had rushed into her head. Meanwhile, the daughter, a lass of sixteen, sat stark-naked before us, sucking at a milk-pot, on which the father kept her at work by holding a rod in his hand ; for, as fattening is the first duty of fashion-

---

* Round the arm, 1 foot 11 inches ; chest, 4 feet 4 inches ; thigh, 2 feet 7 inches ; calf, 1 foot 8 inches ; height, 5 feet 8 inches.

able female life, it must be duly enforced by the rod if necessary. I got up a bit of a flirtation with missy, and induced her to rise and shake hands with me. Her features were lovely, but her body was as round as a ball.

" Of far more interest were the results of a conversation which I had with another of Kamrasi's servants, a man of Amara, as it threw some light upon certain statements made by Mr. Leon of the people of Amara being Christians. He said they bore single holes in the centres both of their upper and lower lips, as well as in the lobes of both of their ears, in which they wear small brass rings. They live near the Nyanza—where it is connected by a strait with a salt lake, and drained by a river to the northward—in comfortable houses, built like the tembes of Unyamwezi. When killing a cow, they kneel down in an attitude of prayer, with both hands together, held palm upward, and utter Zu, a word the meaning of which he did not know. I questioned him to try if the word had any trace of a Christian meaning—for instance, as a corruption of Jesu—but without success. Circumcision is not known among them, neither have they any knowledge of God or a soul. A tribe called Wakuavi, who are white, and described as not unlike myself, often came over the water-and made raids on their cattle, using the double-edged simé as their chief weapon of war. These attacks were as often resented, and sometimes led the Wamara in pursuit a long way into their enemy's country, where, at a place called Kisiguisi, they found men robed in red cloths."

On the 24th of December, a party of natives of Kidi (a country on the White Nile, in about lat. 2° N.) arrived. Their statement that traders came to them from the north created quite a sensation in Speke's camp, and strengthened the failing faith of some of his native attendants. " We all became transported with joy," he writes, " until Rumanika, reflecting on the sad state of Grant's leg, turned that joy into grief by saying that the rules of Uganda were so strict that no one who is sick could enter the country. ' To show,' he said, ' how absurd they are, your donkey would not be permitted because he has no trowsers ; and you even will have to put on a gown, as your unmentionables will be considered indecorous.' I now asked Rumanika if he would assist me in replenishing my fast-ebbing store of beads by selling tusks to the Arabs at Kufro, when for every 35 lb. weight I would give him $50 by orders on Zanzibar, and would insure him from being cheated by sending a letter of advice to our consul residing there. At first he demurred on the high-toned principle that he could not have any commercial dealings with myself ; but, at the instigation of Bombay and Baraka, who viewed it in its true character, as tending merely to assist my journey in the best manner he could, without any sacrifice to dignity, he eventually yielded, and, to prove his earnestness, sent me a large tusk, with a notice that his ivory was not kept in the palace, but with his officers, and as soon as they could collect it, so soon I should get it.

" Rumanika, on hearing that it was our custom to celebrate the birth of our Saviour with a good feast of beef, sent us an ox. I immediately paid him a visit to offer the compliments of the season, and at the same time regretted, much to his amusement, that he, as one of the old stock of Abyssinians, who are the oldest Christians on record, should have forgotten this rite ; but I hoped the time would come when, by making it known that his tribe had lapsed into a state of heathenism, white teachers would be induced to set it all to rights again."

On the 31st Speke gives the following account of his missionary labors.: " Ever proud of his history since I had traced his descent from Abyssinia and King David, whose hair was as straight as my own, Rumanika dwelt on my theological disclosures with the greatest delight, and wished to know what difference existed between the Arabs and ourselves ; to which Baraka replied, as the best means of making him understand, that while the Arabs had only one Book, we had two ; to which I added, Yes, that is true in a sense ; but the real merits lie in the fact that we have got the better *book*, as may be inferred from the obvious fact that we are more prosperous, and their superiors in all things, as I would prove to him if he would allow me to take one of his sons home to learn that *book ;* for then he would find his tribe, after a while, better off than the Arabs are. Much delighted, he said he would be very glad to give me two boys for that purpose.

" Then, changing the subject, I pressed Rumanika, as he said he had no idea of a God or future state, to tell me what advantage he expected from sacrificing a cow yearly at his father's grave. He laughingly replied he did not know, but he hoped he might be favored with better crops if he did so. He also placed pombé and grain, he said, for the same reason, before a large stone on the hill-side, although it could not eat, or make any use of it; but the coast-men were of the same belief as himself, and so were all the natives. No one in Africa, as far as he knew, doubted the power of magic and spells; and if a fox barked when he was leading an army to battle, he would retire at once, knowing that this prognosticated evil. There were many other animals, and lucky and unlucky birds, which all believed in.

" The new year, 1862, was ushered in by the most exciting intelligence, which drove us half wild with delight, for we fully believed Mr. Petherick was indeed on his road up the Nile, endeavoring to meet us. It was this : An officer of Rumanika's, who had been sent four years before on a mission to Kamrasi, had just then returned with a party of Kamrasi's who brought ivory for sale to the Arabs at Kufro, along with a vaunting commission to inform Rumanika that Kamrasi had foreign visitors as well as himself. They had not actually come into Unyoro, but were in his dependency, the country of Gani, coming up the Nile in vessels. They had been attacked by the Gani people, and driven back with considerable loss both of men and property, although they were in sailing vessels, and fired guns which even broke down the trees on the banks. Some of their property had been brought to him, and he, in return, had ordered his subjects not to molest them, but allow them to come on to him. Rumanika enjoyed this news as much as myself, especially when I told him of Petherick's promise to meet us, just as these men said he was doing.

" On the 10th of January we heard the familiar sound of the Uganda drum. Maula, a royal officer, with a large escort of smartly-dressed men, women, and boys, leading their dogs and playing their reeds, announced to our straining ears the welcome intelligence that their king had sent them to call us. Nyamgundu, who had seen us in Usui, had marched on to inform the king of our advance and desire to see him, and he, intensely delighted at the prospect of having white men for his guests, desired no time should be lost in our coming on. Maula told us that his officers had orders to supply us with everything we wanted while passing through his country, and that there would be nothing to pay.

" One thing only now embarrassed me—Grant was worse, without hope of recovery for at least one or two months. This large body of Waganda could not be kept waiting. To get on as fast as possible was the only chance of ever bringing the journey to a successful issue ; so, unable to help myself, with great remorse at another separation, on the following day I consigned my companion, with several Wanguana, to the care of my friend Rumamanika. I then separated ten loads of beads and thirty copper wires for my expenses in Uganda ; wrote a letter to Petherick, which I gave to Baraka ; and gave him and his companion beads to last as money for six months, and also a present both for Kamrasi and the Gani chief.

"This business concluded in camp, I started my men and went to the palace to bid adieu to Rumanika, who appointed Rozaro, one of his officers, to accompany me wherever I went in Uganda, and to bring me back safely again. At Rumanika's request, I then gave Mtesa's pages some ammunition to hurry on with to the great king of Uganda, as his majesty had ordered them to bring him, as quickly as possible, some strengthening powder, and also some powder for his gun. Then, finally, to Maula, also under Rumanika's instructions, I gave two copper wires and five bundles of beads ; and, when all was completed, set out on the march, perfectly sure in my mind that before very long I should settle the great Nile problem forever ; and, with this consciousness, only hoping that Grant would be able to join me before I should have to return again, for it was never supposed for a moment that it was possible I ever could go north from Uganda."

CHAPTER XV.

SPEKE'S journey to Uganda fairly commenced on the 11th of January, 1862. Crossing some spurs of the mountain country, by short marches, he descended on the third day into the valley of the Kitangulé, a considerable river, which flows into the Victoria Nyanza from the west. On the rich low-lands Rumanika kept a herd of cattle, many thousands in number: formerly there were great herds of elephants in the valley, but, since the ivory trade has increased, they have all been driven off. At the ferry over the Kitangulé, Speke had a long contest with the superstitious boatmen, who feared to let him cross in their canoe with his shoes on, lest it should upset, or the river suddenly dry up. The stream, which is sunk below the surface of the country like a huge ditch, is eighty yards in breadth, so deep that the canoes cannot be poled across, and the current runs at the rate of from three to four miles an hour.

The region on the northern bank, which is called Uddu, belongs to the kingdom of Uganda. Speke was accompanied by Maula, the Uganda officer, and there was, consequently, no hindrance to his journey except the whim or indolence of his conductor. The first village beyond the river, called Ndongo, was buried in a garden of plantains, and the whole region appeared surprisingly rich and fertile. On the 18th Speke reached a place called Ngambezi, which surprised him by its neat and well-arranged appearance, and the beauty of its surroundings. "No part of Bengal or Zanzibar," he says, "could excel it in either respect; and my men, with one voice, exclaimed, 'Ah! what people these Waganda are!' and passed other remarks, which may be abridged as follows: 'They build their huts and gardens just as well as we do at Unguja, with screens and enclosures for privacy, a clearance in front of their establishments, and a baraza or reception hut facing their buildings. Then, too, what a beautiful prospect it has! rich marshy plains studded with mounds, on each of which grow the umbrella cactus, or some other evergreen tree; and, beyond, again, another hillspur such as the one we have crossed over.' One of King Mtesa's uncles, who had not been burnt to death by the order of the late king Sunna on his ascension to the throne, was the proprietor of this place, but unfortunately he was from home. However, his substitute gave me his baraza to live in, and brought many presents of goats, fowls, sweet potatoes, yams, plantains, sugar-cane, and Indian corn, and apologized in the end for deficiency in hospitality. I, of course, gave him beads in return."

The Uganda officer, Maula, here took advantage of his home being at a village a little to the westward of the direct route, to pay his family a visit, and showed little disposition to leave. " On the 23rd," Speke writes, " another officer, named Maribu, came to me and said, Mtesa, having heard that Grant was left sick behind at Karagwe, had given him orders to go there and fetch him, whether sick or well, for Mtesa was most anxious to see white men. Hearing this, I at once wrote to Grant, begging him to come on if he could do so, and to bring with him all the best of my property, or as much as he could of it, as I now saw there was more cunning humbug than honesty in what Rumanika had told me about the impossibility of our going north from Uganda, as well as in his saying sick men could not go into Uganda, and donkeys without trowsers would not be admitted there because they were considered indecent.

" Maula now came again, after receiving repeated and angry messages, and I forced him to make a move. He led me straight up to his home, a very nice place, in which he gave me a very large, clean, and comfortable hut—had no end of plantains brought for me and my men—and said, " Now you have really entered the kingdom of Uganda, for the future you must buy no more food. At every place that you stop for the day, the officer in charge will bring you plantains, otherwise your men can help themselves in the gardens, for such are the laws of the land when a king's guest travels in it. Any one found selling anything to either yourself or your men would be punished.' Accordingly, I stopped the daily issue of beads ; but no sooner had I done so than all my men declared they could not eat plantains."

After a halt of three days, the departure being continually postponed on some frivolous pretext, Speke's patience gave way. He peremptorily ordered the caravan to move, and when Bombay refused to assist in striking the tent, gave him a sound beating. The Uganda officers and native attendants became alarmed at this outbreak of anger : the camp was broken up, and they went forward over low hills and rushy valleys, all draining to the eastward.

On the 28th, Speke writes : " Skirting the hills on the left, with a large low plain to the right, we soon came on one of those numerous rush-drains that appear to me to be the last waters left of the old bed of the Nyanza. This one in particular was rather large, being 150 yards wide. It was sunk where I crossed it, like a canal, 14 feet below the plain ; and what with mire and water combined, so deep, I was obliged to take off my trowsers while fording it. Once across, we sought for and put up in a village beneath a small hill, from the top of which I saw the Victoria Nyanza for the first time on the march.

" Next day, after crossing more of those abominable rush-drains, while in sight of the Victoria Nyanza, we ascended the most beautiful hills, covered with verdure of all descriptions. At Meruka, where I put up, there resided some grandees, the chief of whom was the king's aunt. She sent me a goat, a hen, a basket of eggs, and some plantains, in return for which I sent her a wire and some beads. I felt inclined to stop here a month, everything was so very pleasant. The temperature was perfect. The roads, as indeed they were everywhere, were as broad as our coach-roads, cut through the long grasses, straight over the hills and down through the woods in the dells—a strange contrast to the wretched tracks in all the adjacent countries. The huts were kept so clean and so neat, not a fault could be found with them—the gardens the same. Wherever I strolled I saw nothing but richness, and what ought to be wealth. The whole land was a picture of quiescent beauty, with a boundless sea in the back-ground. Looking over the hills, it struck the fancy at once that at one period the whole land must have been at a uniform level with their present tops, but that, by the constant denudation it was subjected to by frequent rains, it had been cut down and sloped into those beautiful hills and dales which now so much pleased the eye; for there were none of those quartz dikes I had seen protruding through the same kind of aqueous formations in Usui and Karagwe, nor were there any other sorts of volcanic disturbance to distort the calm, quiet aspect of the scene.''

For a few days longer Speke travelled on foot over a succession of hills, spurs of the interior table-land, from each of which there was a view eastward over the great Nyanza, with swampy bottoms between. The level of the table-lands of Uganda and Unyoro, lying between the Victoria and Albert Lakes, appears to be about 1,000 feet above the former. On the 7th of February he reached a village called Mbulé, at the northwestern corner of the Nyanza. Here he had reached the equator, and was just half-way, in latitude, between Kazeh, in the Land of the Moon, and Gondokoro, the last Egyptian trading-station on the White Nile.

At Mbulé he says : " Some little boys came who had all their hair shaved off excepting two round tufts on either side of the head. They were the king's pages ; and, producing three sticks, said they had brought them to me from their king, who wanted three charms or medicines. Then placing one stick on the ground before me, they said, ' This one is a head, which, being affected by dreams of a deceased relative, requires relief ;' the second symbolized the king's desire for the accomplishment of a phenomenon to which the old phallic worship was devoted ; ' and this third one,' they said, ' is a sign that the king wants a charm to keep all his subjects in awe of him.' I then promised I would do what I could when I reached the palace, but feared to do anything in the distance."

The path now led almost due eastward, a little further from the shores of the lake, which was seldom visible. The country was still very beautiful—a succession of hill and dale ; and Speke's reception by the natives was everywhere friendly. In five or six days more there were evidences of his approach to the residence of Mtesa ; but on the 13th of February he made a discovery of much greater importance than his approaching reception. " We came," he says, " on the Mwarango River, a broad rush-drain of three hundred yards' span, two thirds of which was bridged over. Until now I did not feel sure where the various rush-drains I had been crossing since leaving the Katonga valley all went to, but here my mind was made up, for I found a large volume of water going to the northward. I took off my clothes at the end of the bridge and jumped into the stream, which I found was twelve yards or so broad, and deeper than my height. I was delighted beyond measure at this very surprising fact, that I was indeed on the northern slopes of the continent, and had, to all appearance, found one of the branches of the Nile's exit from the Nyanza. I drew Bombay's attention to the current ; and, collecting all the men of the country, inquired of them where the river sprang from. Some of them said, in the hills to the southward ; but most of them said, from the lake. I argued the point with them ; for I felt quite sure so large a body of flowing water could not be collected together in any place but the lake. They then all agreed to this view, and farther assured me it went to Kamrasi's palace in Unyoro, where it joined the Nyanza, meaning the Nile."

Halting, the next day, a short march from the capital of Uganda, Speke gave each of his men a fez cap, and scarlet cloth to make military jackets, and taught Bombay the ceremonies in India, when a distinguished prince is presented at one of the native courts.   He made an attempt to reach the *exit* (as he believed it to be) of the Mwarango River from the lake, but did not succeed.   It is very doubtful whether he was correct in declaring this to be one of the arms of the Nile.

Speke's account of his reception by King Mtesa is so picturesque that it must be given entire :

" Next day, (17th,) in the evening, Nyamgundu returned full of smirks and smiles, dropped on his knees at my feet, and, in company with his ' children,' set to nyanzigging, according to the form of that state ceremonial already described.*   In his excitement he was hardly able to say all he had to communicate.   Bit by bit, however, I learned that he first went to the palace, and, finding the king had gone off yachting to the Murchison Creek, he followed him there.   The king for a long while would not believe his tale that I had come, but, being assured, he danced with delight, and swore he would not taste food until he had seen me.   ' Oh,' he said, over and over again and again, according to my informer, ' can this be true ?   Can the white man have come all this way to see me ?   What a

---

* Speke thus describes the ceremony of *nyanzigging* : " The lesser salutation, used by the people, consists of kneeling in the attitude of prayer, continually throwing open the hands, and repeating sundry words.   Among these the word ' nyanzig ' is the most frequent and conspicuous ; and hence these gesticulations receive the general name *nyanzig*, a term which will be frequently met with, and which I have found it necessary to use like an English verb.   In consequence of these salutations, there is always more ceremony in court than business. "

KIBUGA, OR RESIDENCE OF THE KING OF UGANDA.

strong man he must be too, to come so quickly!
Here are seven cows, four of them milch ones, as
you say he likes milk, which you will give him; and
there are three for yourself for having brought him
so quickly. Now hurry off as fast as you can, and
tell him I am more delighted at the prospect of
seeing him than he can be to see me. There is no
place here fit for his reception. I was on a pilgrimage which would have kept me here seven
days longer; but, as I am so impatient to see him,
I will go off to my palace at once, and will
send word for him to advance as soon as I arrive
there.

"About noon the succeeding day, some pages ran
in to say we were to come along without a moment's
delay, as their king had ordered it. He would not
taste food until he saw me, so that everybody might
know what great respect he felt for me.

"One march more, and we came in sight of the
king's kibuga or palace, in the province of Banda-
warogo, N. lat. 0° 21′ 19″, and E. long. 32° 44′ 30″.
It was a magnificent sight. A whole hill was covered with gigantic huts, such as I had never seen
in Africa before. I wished to go up to the palace at
once, but the officers said 'No, that would be considered indecent in Uganda; you must draw up
your men and fire your guns off, to let the king
know you are here; we will then show you your residence, and to-morrow you will doubtless be sent
for, as the king could not now hold a levee while it
is raining.' I made the men fire, and then was
shown into a lot of dirty huts, which, they said, were

built expressly for the king's visitors. The Arabs, when they came on their visits, always put up here, and I must do the same. At first I stuck out on my claims as a foreign prince, whose royal blood could not stand such an indignity. The palace was my sphere, and unless I could get a hut there, I would return without seeing the king.

" In a terrible fright at my blustering, Nyamgundu fell at my feet and implored me not to be hasty. I gave way to this good man's appeal, and cleaned my hut by firing the ground, for, like all the huts in this dog country, it was full of fleas. Once ensconced there, the king's pages darted in to see me, bearing a message from their master, who said he was sorry the rain prevented him from holding a levee that day, but the next he would be delighted to see me.

" On the 19th the king sent his pages to announce his intention of holding a levee in my honor. I prepared for my first presentation at court, attired in my best, though in it I cut a poor figure in comparison with the display of the dressy Waganda. They wore neat bark cloaks resembling the best yellow corduroy cloth, crimp and well set, as if stiffened with starch, and over that, as upper cloaks, a patchwork of small antelope skins, which I observed were sewn together as well as any English glovers could have pierced them ; while their head-dresses, generally, were abrus turbans, set off with highly-polished boar-tusks, stick-charms, seeds, beads, or shells, and on their necks, arms, and ankles they wore other charms of wood, or small horns stuffed with magic powder, and fastened on by strings generally covered with snakeskin. Nyamgundu and Maula demanded, as their official privilege, a first peep; and this being refused, they tried to persuade me that the articles comprising the present required to be covered with chintz, for it was considered indecorous to offer anything to his majesty in a naked state. This little interruption over, the articles enumerated below* were conveyed to the palace in solemn procession thus: With Nyamgundu, Maula, the pages, and myself on the flanks, the Union Jack, carried by the kirangozi guide, led the way, followed by twelve men as a guard of honor, dressed in red flannel cloaks, and carrying their arms sloped, with fixed bayonets; while in their rear were the rest of my men, each carrying some article as a present.

"On the march toward the palace, the admiring courtiers, wonder-struck at such an unusual display, exclaimed, in raptures of astonishment, some with both hands at their mouths, and others clasping their heads with their hands, ' Irungi! irungi!' which may be translated ' Beautiful! beautiful!' I thought myself everything was going on as well as could be wished; but, before entering the royal inclosures, I found, to my disagreeable surprise, that the men with Suwarora's hongo or offering, which

---

* 1 block-tin box, 4 rich silk cloths, 1 rifle, (Whitworth's,) 1 gold chronometer, 1 revolver pistol, 3 rifled carbines, 3 sword-bayonets, 1 box ammunition, 1 box bullets, 1 box gun-caps, 1 telescope, 1 iron chair, 10 bundles best beads, 1 set of table-knives, spoons, and forks.

consisted of more than a hundred coils of wire, were
ordered to lead the procession, and take precedence
of me.   There was something specially aggravating
in this precedence ; for it will be remembered that
these very brass wires which they saw I had myself
intended for Mtesa ; that they were taken from me
by Suwarora as far back as Usui ; and it would
never do, without remonstrance, to have them boast-
fully paraded before my eyes in this fashion.   My
protests, however, had no effect upon the escorting
wakungu.   Resolving to make them catch it, I
walked along as if ruminating in anger up the broad
high road into a cleared square, which divides Mtesa's
domain on the south from his kamraviona's, or com-
mander-in-chief, on the north, and then turned into
the court.   The palace or entrance quite surprised
me by its extraordinary dimensions, and the neatness with which it was kept.   The whole brow and
sides of the hill on which we stood were covered
with gigantic grass huts, thatched as neatly as so
many heads dressed by a London barber, and
fenced all round with the tall yellow reeds of the
common Uganda tiger-grass ; while within the inclosure the lines of huts were joined together, or
partitioned off into courts, with walls of the same
grass.   It is here most of Mtesa's three or four hundred women are kept, the rest being quartered
chiefly with his mother, known by the title of Nyam-
asore, or queen-dowager.   They stood in little
groups at the doors, looking at us, and evidently
passing their own remarks, and enjoying their own
jokes, on the triumphal procession.   At each gate

as we passed, officers on duty opened and shut it for us, jingling the big bells which are hung upon them, as they sometimes are at shop doors, to prevent silent, stealthy entrance.

" The first court passed, I was even more surprised to find the unusual ceremonies that awaited me. There courtiers of high dignity stepped forward to greet me, dressed in the most scrupulously neat fashions. Men, women, bulls, dogs, and goats were led about by strings ; cocks and hens were carried in men's arms ; and little pages, with rope turbans, rushed about, conveying messages, as if their lives depended on their swiftness, every one holding his skin cloak tightly round him lest his naked legs might by accident be shown.

" This, then, was the ante-reception court ; and I might have taken possession of the hut, in which musicians were playing and singing on large nine-stringed harps, like the Nubian tambira, accompanied by harmonicons. By the chief officers in waiting, however, who thought fit to treat us like Arab merchants, I was requested to sit on the ground outside in the sun with my servants. Now I had made up my mind never to sit upon the ground as the natives and Arabs are obliged to do, nor to make my obeisance in any other manner than is customary in England, though the Arabs had told me that from fear they had always complied with the manners of the court. I felt that if I did not stand up for my social position at once, I should be treated with contempt during the remainder of my visit, and thus lose the vantage-ground I had assumed of

appearing rather as a prince than a trader, for the
purpose of better gaining the confidence of the king.
To avert overhastiness, however—for my servants
began to be alarmed as I demurred against doing as
I was bid—I allowed five minutes to the court to
give me a proper reception, saying if it were not
conceded I would then walk away.

"Nothing, however, was done. My own men,
knowing me, feared for me, as they did not know
what a 'savage' king would do in case I carried out
my threat ; while the Waganda, lost in amazement
at what seemed little less than blasphemy, stood
still as posts. The affair ended by my walking
straight away home, giving Bombay orders to leave
the present on the ground, and to follow me.

" Although the king is said to be unapproachable
excepting when he chooses to attend court—a ceremony which rarely happens—intelligence of my hot
wrath and hasty departure reached him in an instant.
He first, it seems, thought of leaving his toilet-room
to follow me ; but, finding I was walking fast and
had gone far, changed his mind, and sent wakungu
running after me. Poor creatures ! they caught me
up, fell upon their knees, and implored I would return at once, for the king had not tasted food, and
would not until he saw me. I felt grieved at their
touching appeals ; but, as I did not understand all
they said, I simply replied by patting my heart and
shaking my head, walking, if anything, all the
faster.

" On my arrival at my hut, Bombay and others
came in, wet through with perspiration, saying the

king had heard of all my grievances. Suwarora's
hongo was turned out of court, and, if I desired it,
I might bring my own chair with me, for he was
very anxious to show me great respect, although
such a seat was exclusively the attribute of the king,
no one else in Uganda daring to sit on an artificial
seat.

" My point was gained, so I cooled myself with
coffee and a pipe, and returned rejoicing in my victory, especially over Suwarora. After returning to
the second tier of huts from which I had retired,
everybody appeared to be in a hurried, confused
state of excitement, not knowing what to make out
of so unprecedented an exhibition of temper. In
the most polite manner, the officers in waiting
begged me to be seated on my iron stool, which I
had brought with me, while others hurried in to announce my arrival. But for a few minutes only I
was kept in suspense, when a band of music, the
musicians wearing on their backs long-haired goatskins, passed me, dancing as they went along like
bears in a fair, and playing on reed instruments
worked over with pretty beads in various patterns,
from which depended leopard-cat skins, the time
being regulated by the beating of long hand-drums.

" The mighty king was now reported to be sitting
on his throne in the state hut of the third tier. I
advanced, hat in hand, with my guard of honor following, formed in ' open ranks,' who in their turn
were followed by the bearers carrying the present.
I did not walk straight up to him as if to shake
hands, but went outside the ranks of the three-

sided square of squatting wakungu, all habited in
skins, mostly cowskins ; some few of whom had, in
addition, leopard-cat skins girt round the waist, the
sign of royal blood.   Here I was desired to halt
and sit in the glaring sun ; so I donned my hat,
mounted my umbrella, a phenomenon which set
them all a wondering and laughing, ordered the
guard to close ranks, and sat gazing at the novel
spectacle.   A more theatrical sight I never saw.
The king, a good-looking, well-figured, tall young
man of twenty-five, was sitting on a red blanket
spread upon a square platform of royal grass, in-
cased in tiger-grass reeds, scrupulously well dressed
in a new mbugu.   The hair of his head was cut
short, excepting on the top, where it was combed up
into a high ridge, running from stem to stern like a
cock's comb.   On his neck was a very neat ornament
—a large ring, of beautifully-worked small beads,
forming elegant patterns by their various colors.
On one arm was another bead ornament, prettily
devised ; and on the other a wooden charm, tied
by a string covered with snakeskin.   On every finger and every toe he had alternate brass and copper rings ; and above the ankles, half way up to the
calf, a stocking of very pretty beads.   Everything
was light, neat, and elegant in its way ; not a fault
could be found with the taste of his ' getting up.'
For a handkerchief he held a well-folded piece of
bark, and a piece of gold-embroidered silk, which
he constantly employed to hide his large mouth when
laughing, or to wipe it after a drink of plantain wine,
of which he took constant and copious draughts

from neat little gourd-cups, administered by his ladies in waiting, who were at once his sisters and wives. A white dog, spear, shield, and woman—the Uganda cognizance—were by his side, as also a knot of staff officers, with whom he kept up a brisk conversation on one side; and on the other was a band of wichwezi, or lady-sorcerers, such as I have already described.

" I was now asked to draw nearer within the hollow square of squatters, where leopard-skins were strewed upon the ground, and a large copper kettle-drum, surmounted with brass bells on arching wires, along with two other smaller drums covered with cowrie-shells, and beads of color worked into patterns, were placed. I now longed to open conversation, but knew not the language, and no one near me dared speak, or even lift his head from fear of being accused of eying the women; so the king and myself sat staring at one another for full an hour—I mute, but he pointing and remarking with those around him on the novelty of my guard and general appearance, and even requiring to see my hat lifted, the umbrella shut and opened, and the guards face about and show off their red cloaks—for such wonders had never been seen in Uganda.

" Then, finding the day waning, he sent Maula on an embassy to ask me if I had seen him; and on receiving my reply, ' Yes, for full one hour,' I was glad to find him rise, spear in hand, lead his dog, and walk unceremoniously away through the inclosure into the fourth tier of huts; for this being a pure levée day, no business was transacted. The king's gait in retiring was intended to be very majestic, but did not succeed in conveying to me that impression. It was the traditional walk of his race, founded on the step of the lion; but the outward sweep of the legs, intended to represent the stride of the noble beast, appeared to me only to realize a very ludicrous kind of waddle, which made me ask Bombay if anything serious was the matter with the royal person.

" I had now to wait for some time, almost as an act of humanity; for I was told the state secret, that the king had retired to break his fast and eat for the first time since hearing of my arrival; but the repast was no sooner over than he prepared for the second act, to show off his splendor, and I was invited in, with all my men, to the exclusion of all his own officers, save my two guides. Entering as before, I found him standing on a red blanket, leaning against the right portal of the hut, talking and laughing, handkerchief in hand, to a hundred or more of his admiring wives, who, all squatting on the ground outside, in two groups, were dressed in new mbugus. My men dared not advance upright, nor look upon the women, but, stooping, with lowered heads and averted eyes, came cringing after me. Unconscious myself, I gave loud and impatient orders to my guard, rebuking them for moving like frightened geese, and, with hat in hand, stood gazing on the fair sex till directed to sit and cap.

" Mtesa then inquired what messages were brought from Rumanika; to which Maula, delighted with the favor of speaking to royalty, replied by saying

Rumanika had gained intelligence of Englishmen coming up the Nile to Gani and Kidi. The king acknowledged the truthfulness of their story, saying he had heard the same himself; and both wakungu, as is the custom in Uganda, thanked their lord in a very enthusiastic manner, kneeling on the ground— for no one can stand in the presence of his majesty —in an attitude of prayer, and throwing out their hands as they repeated the words, nyanzig, nyanzig, ai nyanzig mkahma wangi, etc., etc., for a considerable time; when, thinking they had done enough of this, and heated with exertion, they threw themselves flat upon their stomachs, and, floundering about like fish on land, repeated the same words over again and again, and rose doing the same, with their faces covered with earth; for majesty in Uganda is never satisfied till subjects have grovelled before it like the most abject worms. This conversation over, after gazing at me, and chatting with his women for a considerable time, the second scene ended. The third scene was more easily arranged, for the day was fast declining. He simply moved with his train of women to another hut, where, after seating himself upon his throne, with his women around him, he invited me to approach the nearest limits of propriety, and to sit as before. Again he asked me if I had seen him, evidently desirous of indulging in his regal pride; so I made the most of the opportunity thus afforded me of opening a conversation by telling him of those grand reports I had formerly heard about him, which induced me to come all this way to see him, and the trouble it had

cost me to reach the object of my desire ; at the
same time taking a gold ring from off my finger, and
presenting it to him, I said, ' This is a small token
of friendship ; if you will inspect it, it is made after
the fashion of a dog-collar, and, being the king of
metals, gold, is in every respect appropriate to your
illustrious race.'

" He said, in return, ' If friendship is your desire,
what would you say if I showed you a road by
which you might reach your home in one month ?'
Now everything had to be told to Bombay, then to
Nasib, my Kiganda interpreter, and then to either
Maula or Nyamgundu, before it was delivered to the
king, for it was considered indecorous to transmit
any message to his majesty excepting through the
medium of one of his officers.   Hence I could not
get an answer put in ; for as all Waganda are rapid
and impetuous in their conversation, the king, probably forgetting he had put a question, hastily
changed the conversation and said, ' What guns
have you got ?   Let me see the one you shoot with.'
I wished still to answer the first question first, as I
knew he referred to the direct line to Zanzibar
across the Masai, and was anxious, without delay, to
open the subject of Petherick and Grant ; but no one
dared to deliver my statement.   Much disappointed,
I then said, ' I had brought the best shooting-gun
in the world—Whitworth's rifle—which I begged
he would accept, with a few other trifles ; and, with
his permission, I would lay them upon a carpet at
his feet, as is the custom of my country when visiting sultans.'   He assented, sent all his women away,

and had an mbugu spread for the purpose, on which Bombay, obeying my order, first spread a red blanket, and then opened each article, one after the other, when Nasib, according to the usage already mentioned, smoothed them down with his dirty hands, or rubbed them against his sooty face, and handed them to the king to show there was no poison or witchcraft in them. Mtesa appeared quite confused with the various wonders as he handled them, made silly remarks, and pondered over them like a perfect child, until it was quite dark. Torches were then lit, and guns, pistols, powder, boxes, tools beads—the whole collection, in short—were tossed together topsy-turvy, bungled into mbugus, and carried away by the pages. Mtesa now said, ' It is late, and time to break up ; what provisions would you wish to have ?' I said, ' A little of everything, but no one thing constantly.' 'And would you like to see me to-morrow ?' ' Yes, every day.' ' Then you can't to-morrow, for I have business ; but the next day come if you like. You can now go away, and here are six pots of plantain wine for you ; my men will search for food to-morrow.

"21*st*. In the morning, while it rained, some pages drove in twenty cows and ten goats, with a polite metaphorical message from their king to the effect that I had pleased him much, and he hoped I would accept these few 'chickens' until he could send more ; when both Maula and Nyamgundu, charmed with their success in having brought a welcome guest to Uganda, never ceased showering eulogiums on me for my fortune in having gained the countenance of their king. The rain falling was considered at court a good omen, and everybody declared the king mad with delight.

CHAPTER XVI.

SPEKE.—FOUR MONTHS IN UGANDA.

HAVING thus safely reached, and been encouragingly received, at the capital of Uganda, on the northern shore of the great Nyanza. Speke's remaining object, while waiting for his companion, Grant, was to ascertain the point at which the White Nile issued from the lake, and also to decide whether it would be possible for him to return to the Eastern coast of Africa through the unknown region to the eastward. After escaping from the rapacity of the petty chiefs of Uzinza and Usui, his progress had been comparatively easy. The larger and better organized kingdoms of Karagwe and Uganda were easily traversed after he had gained the favor of the reigning monarch, and the influence of King Mtesa would no doubt be sufficient to procure him a safe conduct through the unknown country of Masai, east of the Victoria Nyanza. On the other hand, his stock of cloths, beads and wires, as well as of articles for presents, was almost exhausted, and could only be replenished by communicating with Petherick's expedition for his relief, which, he was firmly convinced, must be somewhere on the White Nile, endeavoring to reach him.

For a month or two nothing could be done, except to retain the good-will of the Uganda king, and at the same time defend himself against both the suspicion and the covetousness of the latter,—a task which required all his energy and watchfulness. Being recalled to court, four days after his arrival, he was requested to shoot four cows which were loose in the enclosure. The result is a striking illustration of the native barbarity. "Having no bullets for my gun," Speke writes, "I borrowed the revolving pistol I had given the king, and shot all four in a second of time ; but as the last one, only wounded, turned sharply upon me, I gave him the fifth and settled him. Great applause followed this *wonderful* feat, and the cows were given to my men. The king now loaded one of the carbines I had given him with his own hands, and giving it full-cock to a page, told him to go out and shoot a man in the outer court, which was no sooner accomplished than the little urchin returned to announce his success with a look of glee such as one would see in the face of a boy who had robbed a bird's nest, caught a trout, or done any other boyish trick. The king said to him, ' And did you do it well ?' ' Oh yes, capitally.' He spoke the truth, no doubt, for he dared not have trifled with the king ; but the affair created hardly any interest. I never heard, and there appeared no curiosity to know what individual human being the urchin had deprived of life."

The next morning the king's pages came to request that some of Speke's men would come to shoot cows. He sent Bombay, with instructions to excite Mtesa's cupidity with stories of supplies waiting for him farther down the Nile. The men shot seven cows, which were given to them for food. For his own part, Speke declared that he would only shoot elephants, rhinoceros, or buffaloes, which he was willing to hunt in company with the king. He was presently summoned to the palace, and asked to prescribe for the king's illness. " When only the interpreters and one confidential officer were left besides myself, he wished to know if I could apply the medicine without its touching the afflicted part. To give him confidence in my surgical skill, I moved my finger, and asked if he knew what gave it action ; and on his replying in the negative, I gave him an anatomical lecture, which so pleased him, he at once consented to be operated on, and I applied a blister to him accordingly. The whole operation was rather ridiculous ; for the blister, after being applied, had to be rubbed in turn on the hands and faces of both Bombay and Nasib, to show there was no evil spirit in the ' doctor.' "

At each interview, Speke endeavored to talk about his further journeys and secure the promise of assistance ; but the king always evaded the subject, saying he would speak of such things another time, and then, apparently forgetting all about it. By this time, the custom of the country required that he should call upon the queen-mother, and the visit, of course, must be preluded by a handsome present. He gives the following account of the interview :

"Her majesty—fat, fair, and forty-five—was sitting, plainly garbed in mbugu, upon a carpet spread upon the ground within a curtain of mbugu, her elbow resting on a pillow of the same bark material; the only ornaments on her person being an abrus necklace, and a piece of mbugu tied round her head, while a folding looking-glass, much the worse for wear, stood open by her side. An iron rod like a spit, with a cup on the top, charged with magic powder, and other magic wands, were placed before the entrance ; and within the room four Mabandwa sorceresses or devil-drivers, fantastically dressed as before described, and a mass of other women, formed the company. For a short while we sat at a distance, exchanging inquiring glances at another, when the women were dismissed, and a band of music, with a court full of wakungu, was ordered in to change the scene. I also got orders to draw near and sit fronting her within the hut. Pombé, the best in Uganda, was then drunk by the queen, and handed to me and to all the high officers about her, when she smoked her pipe, and bade me smoke mine. The musicians, dressed in long-haired Usoga goatskins, were now ordered to strike up, which they did, with their bodies swaying or dancing like bears in a fair. Different drums were then beat, and I was asked if I could distinguish their different tones.

"The queen, full of mirth, now suddenly rose,

leaving me sitting, while she went to another hut changed her mbugu for a deole, and came back again for us to admire her, which was no sooner done to her heart's content than a second time by her order, the court was cleared, and when only three or four confidential wakungu were left, she took up a small fagot of well-trimmed sticks, and selecting three, told me she had three complaints. 'This stick,' she says, 'represents my stomach, which gives me much uneasiness : this second stick my liver, which causes shooting pains all over my body; and this third one my heart, for I get constant dreams at night about Sunna, my late husband, and they are not pleasant.' "

On the 1st of March a letter came from Grant, saying that he had dispatched Bombay to Unyoro (the kingdom north of Uganda) to announce their coming to King Kamrasi, and that he himself expected to leave Karagwe before the end of February. The longer Speke remained in Uganda, the greater became his necessity for patience and cunning. King Mtesa was a spoiled child, in his whims and fancies, one day all friendship, the next cold and haughty, while the queen-mother, who had taken a strong fancy to the white stranger, intrigued to receive the greatest amount of attention, and, of course, the greatest share of presents. The king constantly importuned Speke to shoot birds for his amusement, and every attempt to introduce the former's real object was put aside by the wayward barbarian. Speke succeeded, by assuming an air of being offended with his treatment, in removing his quarters to a better part of the capital, but the supplies furnished to his men were so irregular and scanty that a new petition for food had to be made every few days.

This delay, at least, enabled him to witness the savage and violent way in which the king exercises his authority. On the 25th of March he writes : " I have now been for some time within the court precincts, and have consequently had an opportunity of witnessing court customs. Among these, nearly every day since I have changed my residence, incredible as it may appear to be, I have seen one, two, or three of the wretched palace women led away to execution, tied by the hand, and dragged along by one of the body-guard, crying out, as she went to premature death, ' Hai minangé !' (Oh, my lord!) ' Kbakka!' (My king!) ' Hai n'yawo!' (My mother!) at the top of her voice, in the utmost despair and lamentation ; and yet there was not a soul who dared lift hand to save any of them, though many might be heard privately commenting on their beauty."

On the 14th of April, while Speke was attending one of the king's childish and tiresome levees, the officers announced the startling fact that two white men had been seen at King Kamrasi's, in Unyoro ; one of them with a full beard, the other smooth-faced. Speke immediately exclaimed : " Of course they are there : let me sent a letter to them!" believing that it was Petherick and a companion who was to accompany him. The king, however, declared that the information was not perfect and he

would wait the return of certain messengers, whom he would sent to Unyoro. But, a week afterwards, Speke found that the messengers had not been sent. The king, like a child with a new toy, seemed determined to keep the white man at his court, as long as he was amused by his company. Speke persisted in his demand with so much energy that on the 22nd of April Budja, one of Mtesa's officers, was sent off with two men in search of Petherick, and another messenger with a letter to Grant.

The king then determined on a three days' trip to the Nyanza, for hippopotamus shooting. It was but a short march from his palace to the shore of the lake, through very rich and beautiful scenery. Speke thus describes the scene, after arriving at the place of embarcation: " Now for the Lake. Every body in a hurry falls into his place the best way he can—wakungu leading, and women behind. They rattle along, through plantains and shrubs, under large trees, seven, eight, and nine feet in diameter, till the beautiful waters are reached—a picture of the Rio scenery, barring that of the higher mountains in the background of that lovely place, which are here represented by the most beautiful little hills. A band of fifteen drums of all sizes, called the mazaguzo, playing with the regularity of a lot of factory engines at work, announced the king's arrival, and brought all the boats to the shore, but not as in England, where Jack with all the consequence of a lord at home, invites the ladies to be seated and enjoys the sight of so many pretty faces. Here every poor fellow, with his apprehensions written in his face, leaps over the gunwale into the water, ducking his head from fear of being accused of gazing on the fair sex, which is death, and bides patiently his time. They were dressed in plaintain leaves, looking like grotesque Neptunes. The king in his red coat and wideawake, conducted the arrangements, ordering all their proper places— the woman in certain boats, the wakungu and Wanguana in others, while I sat in the same boat with him at his feet, three women holding mbugus of pombé behind."

This excursion lasted five or six days, but it seems to have contributed little to Speke's knowledge of the lake. He gives, in fact, no distinct account of the outline or appearance of the shores and islands, describing, instead, the pranks of the king and his followers. The truth probably was that Speke, having arranged, as he supposed, for Grant's transportation from the Uganda frontier by water, relied upon the latter for a full report of the western shore of the lake. Grant, however, as Speke learned on the 1st of May, left Karagwe on a litter, and was obliged to make the journey by land.

The next letter from Grant stated that he expected to come by the lake from the mouth of the Kitangulé River. But on the 11th of May, Speke received letters from him, dated as late as the 2nd, which stated that the natives, afraid of undertaking the voyage on the lake, had deceived him about the route, and were bringing him on by the same road which Speke had already travelled. The next day,

GRANT ON HIS WAY FROM KARAGWE.

King Mtesa allowed ten of his men to go and help Grant along, and the messengers who had been sent to Unyoro returned, accompanied by a deputation from king Kamrasi, headed by an officer named Kidgwiga, who afterwards proved to be of great service to the expedition.

" Kidgwiga," says Speke, " said Petherick's party was not in Unyoro ; they had never reached there, but were lying at anchor off Gani. Two white men only had been seen—one, they said, a hairy man, the other smooth-faced ; they were as anxiously inquiring after us as we were after them ; they sat on chairs, dressed like myself, and had guns and everything precisely like those in my hut. On one occasion they sent up a necklace of beads to Kamrasi, and he, in return, gave them a number of women and tusks. If I wished to go that way, Kamrasi would forward me on to their position in boats ; for the land route, leading through Kidi, was a jungle of ten days, tenanted by a savage set of people, who hunt everybody, and seize everything they see."

On the 24th of May, word came that Grant was only one day's march distant, and Speke immediately sent him a shoulder of mutton. Three days elapsed, however, and Speke again attempted to make arrangements for going on to Unyoro, when his talk with the king was interrupted by the sound of guns announcing Grant's arrival, and he took leave to go and welcome his friend. " How we enjoyed ourselves," he says, " after so much anxiety and want of one another's company, I need not describe. For my part I was only too rejoiced to see that Grant could limp about a bit, and was able to laugh over the picturesque and amusing account he gave me of his own rough travels."

Another visit to the king, in company with Grant was equally fruitless in regard to their departure. Speke thus explains—and all explorers will appreciate his situation:

"It will be kept in view that the hanging about at this court, and all the perplexing and irritating negotiations here described, had always one end in view—that of reaching the Nile where it pours out of the Nyanza, as I was long certain that it did. Without the consent and even the aid of this capricious barbarian I was now talking to, such a project was hopeless. I naturally seized every opportunity for putting in a word in the direction of my great object, and here seemed to be an opportunity. We now ventured on a plump application for boats that we might feel our way to Gani by water, supposing the lake and river to be navigable all the way."

The negotiations were renewed from day to day, but, as it seemed, with increasing uncertainty. Speke at first requested leave to visit the Masai country, and see the reported salt lake at the northern corner of the Nyanza, while Grant returned to Karagwe by water, and brought on the stores which had been left there. This was immediately granted; but the orders and supplies were not forthcoming. One day the king desired the travellers to see him in European costume; another, he wanted a bird painted which he had shot, or the use of some new article explained, and each time their departure was mentioned, he pretended to be surprised, as if he had never heard of it before.

After several arrangements for further exploration had been made and prevented by the king's whims, Speke determined to confine himself to the task of pushing northward through the kingdom of Unyoro, and endeavoring to reach either Petherick's expedition, or the trading-station of Gondokoro, on the White Nile. Finally, a lucky fit of jealousy against Rumanika, the king of Karagwe, induced Mtesa to favor the travellers' design of going northward. He would show Rumanika, he said, that all the supplies for Uganda need not come through *his* country : if the white men would open a route of traffic for him to the north, he would send his officer, Budja, with· them to Unyoro, and have boats prepared, so that they could make the voyage on the Nile.

Speke now felt that his advance northward was assured. The king's mood fortunately lasted for a day or two, and all the necessary supplies were freely given. "Everything was granted without the slightest hesitation ; and then the king, turning to me, said, 'Well, Bana, so you really wish to go?' 'Yes, for I have not seen my home for four years and upward'—reckoning five months to the year, Uganda fashion. 'And you can give me no stimulants?' 'No.' 'Then you will send me some from Gani—brandy if you like ; it makes people sleep sound, and gives them strength.' Next we·went to the queen to bid farewell, but did not see her."

On the 6th of July Speke visited the king, and asked leave for the boats to go at once ; but a court-officer who held the post of fleet-admiral for the lake insisted that there were dangerous shallows along the shore, between the inlet on which the capital was situated and the exit of the Nile. He proposed that they should go to a station on the river, called Urondogani, leave their goods, and walk by land up the Nile bank, if a sight of the falls at the mouth of the lake was of such great importance to them. Of course the admiral carried his point, for there was no one able to contradict his assertions.

"Early the next morning the king bade us come to him to say farewell. Wishing to leave behind a favorable impression, I instantly complied. On the breast of my coat I suspended the necklace the queen had given me, as well as his knife and my medals. I talked with him in as friendly and flattering a manner as I could, dwelling on his shooting, the pleasant cruising on the lake, and our sundry picnics, as well as the grand prospect there was now of opening the country to trade, by which his guns, the best in the world, would be fed with powder, and other small matters of a like nature, to which he replied with great feeling and good taste. We then all rose with an English bow, placing the hand on the heart while saying adieu ; and there was a complete uniformity in the ceremonial, for, whatever I did, Mtesa, in an instant, mimicked with the instinct of a monkey.

"We had, however, scarcely quitted the palace

gate before the king issued himself, with his attendants and his brothers leading, and women bringing up the rear; here Kyengo and all the Wazinza joined in the procession with ourselves, they kneeling and clapping their hands after the fashion of their own country. Budja just then made me feel very anxious by pointing out the position of Urondogani, as I thought, too far north. I called the king's attention to it, and in a moment he said he would speak to Budja in such a manner that would leave no doubts in my mind, for he liked me much, and desired to please me in all things. As the procession now drew close to our camp, and Mtesa expressed a wish to have a final look at my men, I ordered them to turn out with their arms and nyanzig for the many favors they had received. Mtesa, much pleased, complimented them on their goodly appearance, remarking that with such a force I would have no difficulty in reaching Gani, and exhorted them to follow me through fire and water; then, exchanging adieus again, he walked ahead in gigantic strides up the hill, the pretty favorite of his harem, Lubuga—beckoning and waving with her little hands, and crying ' Bana ! Bana !'—trotting after him conspicuous among the rest, though all showed a little feeling at the severance. We saw them no more."

CHAPTER XVII.

SPEKE.—THE WHITE NILE AND THE KINGDOM OF UNYORO.

DURING the first five days after leaving the capital of Uganda, the expedition marched 30 miles in a northerly direction, through a fine hilly country, with jungles and rich cultivation alternating. They were then obliged to halt for some days at a small village until the cows given by the king should be driven together, and here one of Speke's men, going out on a private thieving expedition, was killed by the natives. The officer Budja insisted on the murder being reported to king Mtesa, from whom a satisfactory answer was received on the 15th. Next day the cows arrived, and inasmuch as considerable time had been lost, Speke determined to send Grant forward into Unyoro with the porters, goods, and cattle, while he made a rapid trip to the exit of the Nile from the Victoria Nyanza, and then followed the river down, until they should meet.

On the 19th they parted, Grant taking the high road northward to king Kamrasi's capital, while Speke marched eastward towards the White Nile.

He soon reached the Luajerri, a "rush-drain," three miles broad, with a current flowing northward; the natives declared that it also issued from the lake. The crossing occupied four hours, and the party lost their way so continually in the low, jungly country beyond, that they did not reach the station on the river where the boats had been ordered to await them, until the morning of the 21st.

"Here, at last," exclaims Speke, "I stood on the brink of the Nile. Most beautiful was the scene; nothing could surpass it! It was the very perfection of the kind of effect aimed at in a highly-kept park; with a magnificent stream from 600 to 700 yards wide, dotted with islets and rocks, the former occupied by fishermen's huts, the latter by sterns and crocodiles basking in the sun, flowing between fine high grassy banks, with rich trees and plantains in the background, where herds of the n'sunnu and hartebeest could be seen grazing, while the hippopotami were snorting in the water, and florikan and Guinea-fowl rising at our feet.

"We were now confronting Usoga, a country which may be said to be the very counterpart of Uganda in its richness and beauty. Here the people use such huge iron-headed spears with short handles, that, on seeing one to-day, my people remarked that they were better fitted for digging potatoes than piercing men. Elephants, as we had seen by their devastations during the last two marches, were very numerous in this neighborhood. Till lately, a party from Unyoro, ivory-hunting, had driven them away. Lions were also described as very numerous and destructive to human life."

It was two days before the boats arrived, and then the officer in charge of them refused to take Speke. The latter, however, succeeded in procuring a guide, marched up the west bank of the Nile, and after passing the Isamba rapids, where the stream was broken by beautiful islands, reached a district to which he gives the name of the "Church Estate." It is dedicated in some mysterious manner to Lubari, (the Almighty,) and although the king appeared to have authority over some of the inhabitants of it, yet others had apparently a sacred character, exempting them from the civil power, and the king had no right even to dispose of the land.

The next day after leaving this district—the 28th of July, 1862—the goal of so many struggles and dangers was attained. "With a good push for it, crossing hills and threading huge grasses, as well as extensive village plantations lately devastated by elephants—they had eaten all that was eatable, and what would not serve for food they had destroyed with their trunks, not one plantain nor one hut being left entire—we arrived at the extreme end of the journey, the farthest point ever visited by the expedition on the same parallel of latitude as king Mtesa's palace, and just forty miles east of it.

"We were well rewarded; for the 'stones,' as the Waganda call the falls, was by far the most interesting sight I had seen in Africa. Everybody ran to see them at once, though the march had been long and fatiguing, and even my sketch-block was called into play. Though beautiful, the scene was not exactly what I expected ; for the broad surface of the lake was shut out from view by a spur of hill, and the falls, about 12 feet deep, and 400 to 500 feet broad, were broken by rocks. Still it was a sight that attracted one to it for hours—the roar of the waters, the thousands of passenger-fish, leaping at the falls with all their might, the Wasoga and Waganda fishermen coming out in boats and taking post on all the rocks with rod and hook, hippopotami and crocodiles lying sleepily on the water, the ferry at work above the falls, and cattle driven down to drink at the margin of the lake, made, in all, with the pretty nature of the country—small hills, grassy-topped, with trees in the folds, and gardens on the lower slopes—as interesting a picture as one could wish to see.

" The expedition had now performed its functions. I saw that old Father Nile without any doubt rises in the Victoria Nyanza, and, as I had foretold, that lake is the great source of the holy river which cradled the first expounder of our religious belief. I mourned, however, when I thought how much I had lost by the delays in the journey having deprived me of the pleasure of going to look at the northeast corner of the Nyanza to see what connection there was, by the strait so often spoken of, with it and the other lake where the Waganda went to get their salt, and from which another river flowed to the north, making ' Usoga an island.' But I felt I ought to be content with what I had been spared to accomplish : for I had seen full half of the lake, and had infor-

mation given me of the other half, by means of
which I knew all about the lake, as far, at least, as
the chief objects of geographical importance were
concerned.

"Let us now sum up the whole and see what it is
worth. Comparative information assured me that
there was as much water on the eastern side of the
lake as there is on the western—if anything, rather
more. The most remote waters, *or top head of the
Nile,* is the southern end of the lake, situated close
on the third degree of south latitude, which gives to
the Nile the surprising length, in direct measure-
ment, rolling over thirty-four degrees of latitude, of
above 2,300 miles, or more than one eleventh of the
circumference of our globe."

Speke gave the name of Ripon Falls to the cataract. He remained two days at the spot, but was
not allowed either to enter the lake by boats, or to
climb the hills and get a last view of the broad sea-
horizon beyond the intervening cape. On the 1st
of August he started on his return, and in four days
reached Urondogani, the point where he first struck
the Nile. It was another week before the boats
and supplies were ready; but when they finally set
out, drifting slowly down the gentle current, the
weary explorer began to congratulate himself that
all his painful marches were over, and he would
easily reach the limits of exploration to the north.

It was but a few miles to the frontier of Unyoro,
and the native boatmen were afraid of crossing the
line, until assured of a friendly reception. Speke
took it for granted that Grant had already reached

RIPON FALLS.

Kamrasi's capital and arranged for his passage down the river; but to quiet his Waganda attendants, he sent Bombay in advance by land, and then resumed the voyage. At sunset they approached the first Unyoro village, governed by a chief named Nyamyonjo, and encountered an enormous canoe, full of armed men, which turned and fled as they drew near.

" The bank of the river, as we advanced," says Speke, " then rose higher, and was crowned with huts and plantations, before which stood groups and lines of men, all fully armed. Farther at this juncture, the canoe we had chased turned broadside on us, and joined in the threatening demonstrations of the people on shore. I could not believe them to be serious—thought they had mistaken us—and stood up in the boat to show myself, hat in hand. I said I was an Englishman going to Kamrasi's, and did all I could, but without creating the slightest impression. They had heard a drum beat, they said, and that was a signal of war, so war it should be ; and Kamrasi's drums rattled up both sides the river, preparing everybody to arm. This was serious. Farther, a second canoe full of armed men issued out from the rushes behind us, as if with a view to cut off our retreat, and the one in front advanced upon us, hemming us in. To retreat together seemed our only chance ; but it was getting dark, and my boats were badly manned. I gave the order to close together and retire, offering ammunition as an incentive, and all came to me but one boat, which seemed so paralyzed with fright it

kept spinning round and round like a crippled
duck."

Some of Speke's men fired and shot two of the
attacking party, which then retreated, and the
canoes returned up the river to their starting-point.
Soon afterwards Bombay arrived, having been driven
away from the same village. The boatmen refused
to undertake the voyage, and Speke was forced, to
his great disappointment, to set out for Unyoro by
land. On reaching the Luajerri branch of the Nile,
he was astounded by the intelligence that Grant was
encamped not far off, having returned from Kamrasi's capital. On the 19th, after two days' search,
he was found. He had waited many days in Unyoro, without receiving any answer to his requests,
and finally been ordered to leave the country.

On hearing this information, Budja, the Waganda
officer, who accompanied the expedition, refused to
go further; but in the midst of the debate, Kidgwiga, Kamrasi's officer, whom Speke had seen at
King Mtesa's court, suddenly made his appearance,
with a friendly invitation from Kamrasi himself, and
the news that the strangers were still waiting in
Gani, the country north of Unyoro. The way forward was again clear. On the 23rd of August
Speke writes: " To-day I felt very thankful to get
across the much-vexed boundary line and enter Unyoro, guided by Kamrasi's deputation of officers,
and so shake off the apprehensions which had
teased us for so many days. This first march was
a picture of all the country to its capital : an interminable forest of small trees, bush, and tall grass,

with scanty villages, low huts, and dirty-looking people clad in skins ; the plantain, sweet potato, sesamum, and ulezi (millet) forming the chief edibles, besides goats and fowls ; while the cows, which are reported to be numerous, being kept, as everywhere else where pasture-lands are good, by the wandering, unsociable Wahuma, are seldom seen. No hills, except a few scattered cones, disturb the level surface of the land, and no pretty views ever cheer the eye. Uganda is now entirely left behind ; we shall not see its like again ; for the farther one leaves the equator, and the rain-attracting influences of the Mountains of the Moon, vegetation decreases proportionately with the distance."

They had not travelled more than 25 miles, making very short marches, when Budja insisted on going back to Uganda, and taking the travellers with him. The latter positively refused, whereupon, on the 1st of September, he left them with all his men, and they trusted themselves entirely in Kidgwiga's hands. Their treatment was friendly, but the marches were very slow, and so many messages were sent in advance to king Kamrasi, that they were delayed more than a week, within a dozen miles of the capital. Finally, on the 9th of September, the order came and they hurried forwards. Issuing from the jungle they saw the mountains of Kidi, to the northward, and near at hand the great king's palace, on a low tongue of land, between the Kafue River and the White Nile, in lat. 1° 37' N., and long. 32° 19' E. The palace was a large, dumpy hut, surrounded by a number of smaller ones, and the worst royal residence they had seen since leaving Uzinza.

Instead of being received by the king, they were placed in some miserable huts, and presented with a small stock of flour. Five days more passed in tedious consultations, when Speke, tired and disgusted with the delay and with their wretched lodging, sent a messenger to say that if their residence was not changed at once, both Grant and himself had made up their minds to cut off their hair and blacken their faces, so that the king should have no more cause to fear them. Ignoring his claims to imperial rank, Speke asserted that Kamrasi's reasons for thus treating them must be fear: it could be nothing else. This message acted like magic: Kamrasi fully believed they would do as they said, and disappoint him altogether of the strange sight of white men.

He sent word at once that they must on no account change their complexion. They were conducted to much better quarters, and regaled with beer, fowls and plantains. Nevertheless, four days more elapsed before they were summoned to visit the king, who in the meantime prohibited any of his subjects from looking upon their faces. Crossing the Kafue River to the palace, they were surprised to find a new hut built for their reception, in a retired spot, out of sight of the multitude. " Within this," says Speke, " sitting on a low wooden stool placed upon a double matting of skins—cows' below and leopards' above—on an elevated platform of grass, was the great king Kamrasi, looking, en-

ANIMALS STARTLED WHILE DRINKING IN THE NILE

shrouded in his mbugu dress, for all the world like a pope in state—calm and actionless. One bracelet of fine-twisted brass wire adorned his left wrist, and his hair, half an inch long, was worked up into small peppercorn-like knobs by rubbing the hand circularly over the crown of the head. His eyes were long, face narrow, and nose prominent, after the true fashion of his breed ; and though a finely-made man, considerably above six feet high, he was not so large as Rumanika. A cowskin, stretched out and fastened to the roof, acted as a canopy to prevent dust falling, and a curtain of mbugu concealed the lower parts of the hut, in front of which, on both sides of the king, sat about a dozen head men."

The king's manner was friendly, and he interposed no objection to their request to be furnished with men to proceed to Gani. He received the presents with evident satisfaction, but Speke soon discovered that he was determined to obtain possession of his only remaining chronometer. Two days afterwards, fortunately, some natives of Gani arrived at the capital, and reported that there were strangers on the borders of their country, waiting for the arrival of white men from the south. Speke was convinced that this must be Petherick's relief expedition, and by sacrificing his chronometer, procured permission for Bombay to accompany the Gani men on ther return. He hoped by this means both to secure his own advance northwards, and to obtain a fresh stock of supplies. Bombay set out on the 22nd, expecting to be back in a fortnight.

More than a month passed away, however, and the explorers began to suffer seriously. Their anxiety on Bombay's account, the uncertainty of their situation, the unhealthy climate of the place, and the annoyances to which they were continually subjected by Kamrasi's endeavors to obtain every valuable object they possessed, were a severe trial both of strength and patience. Speke's diary of all these troubles contains many matters of interest, but we can only give his account of giving Kamrasi a Bible lesson. On the 29th of October he writes :

" To-day I met Kamrasi at his new reception-palace on this side the Kafue—taking a Bible to explain all I fancied I knew about the origin and present condition of the Wahuma branch of the Ethiopians, begining with Adam, to show how it was the king had heard by tradition that at one time the people of his race were half white and half black. Then, proceeding with the Flood, I pointed out that the Europeans remained white, retaining Japhet's blood ; while the Arabs are tawny, after Shem ; and the Africans black, after Ham. And, finally, to show the greatness of the tribe, I read the 14th chapter of 2d Chronicles, in which it is written how Zerah, the Ethiopean, with a host of a thousand thousand, met the Jew Asa with a large army, in the valley of Zephathah, near Mareshah ; adding to it that again, at a much later date, we find the Ethiopians battling with the Arabs in the Somali country and with the Arabs and Portuguese at Omwita (Mombas)—in all of which places they have taken possession of certain tracts of land, and left their sons to people it.

" To explain the way in which the type or physical features of people undergo great changes by interbreeding, Mtesa was instanced as having lost nearly every feature of his Mhuma blood by the kings of Uganda having been produced, probably for several generations running, of Wagandi mothers. This amused Kamrasi greatly, and induced me to inquire how his purity of blood was maintained : ' Was the King of Unyoro chosen, as in Uganda, haphazard by the chief men, or did the eldest son sit by succession on the throne?' The reply was, ' The brothers fought for it, and the best man gained the crown.'

" Kamrasi then began counting the leaves of the Bible, an amusement that every negro that gets hold of a book indulges in ; and, concluding in his mind that each page or leaf represented one year of time since the beginning of creation, continued his labor till one quarter of the way through the book, and then only shut it up on being told, if he desired to ascertain the number more closely, he had better count the words.

" On the 1st of November, Bombay at last arrived with Mabruki in high glee, dressed in cotton jumpers and drawers, presents given them by Petherick's outpost. Petherick himself was not there. The journey to and fro was performed in fourteen days' actual travelling, the rest of the time being frittered away by the guides. The jemadar of the guard said he commanded two hundred Turks, and had orders to wait for me, without any limits as to time, until I should arrive, when Petherick's name would be pointed out to me cut on a tree, but as no one in camp could read my letter, they were doubtful whether we were the party they were looking out for."

Kamrasi had now no reason for detaining them longer; but he endeavored, on various pretexts, to delay their departure. He must first send men, to make their journey safe through the intervening country of Kidi; he must ask them many more questions, and decide upon the presents they should send him; with much more, of the same character. Speke's patience finally gave way, and he refused to receive some spears which the king sent to him, unless immediate preparations were made for their departure. His determined attitude, together with the promise of sending more presents back from Gani, induced the king to give Kidwiga as a guide, and to allow them to leave, on the 9th of November. Two days before, they had an audience of leave.

The evening before starting, the king seemed entirely to disregard their comfort on the journey, they made a request for cows, butter, and coffee; in answer to which they only got ten cows, the other things not being procurable without delay. Twenty-four men were appointed to escort them and bring back their presents from Gani, which were to be—six carbines, with a magazine of ammunition, a large brass or iron water-pot, a hair-brush, lucifers a dinner-knife, and many other things procurable that had never been seen in Unyoro.

CHAPTER XVIII.

WE were now expected to march again," says Speke, "but, being anxious myself to see more of the river, before starting, I obtained leave to go by boat as far as the river was navigable, sending our cattle by land. To this concession was accompanied a request for a few more gun-caps, and liberty was given us to seize any pombé which might be found coming on the river in boats, for the supplies to the palace all come in this manner. We then took boat again, an immense canoe, and, after going a short distance, emerged from the Kafue, and found ourselves on what at first appeared a long lake, averaging from two hundred at first to one thousand yards broad, before the day's work was out ; but this was the Nile again, navigable in this way from Urondogani.

"Both sides were fringed with the huge papyrus rush. The left one was low and swampy, while the right one—in which the Kidi people and Wanyoro occasionally hunt—rose from the water in a gently sloping bank, covered with trees and beautiful con-

volvuli, which hung in festoons.   Floating islands,
composed of rush, grass, and ferns, were continually
in motion, working their way slowly down the stream,
and proving to us that the Nile was in full flood.
On one occasion we saw hippopotami, which our
men said came to the surface because we had do-
mestic fowls on board, supposing them to have an
antipathy to that bird.   Boats there were, which the
sailors gave chase to; but, as they had no liquor,
they were allowed to go their way, and the sailors,
instead, set to lifting baskets and taking fish from
the snares which fishermen, who live in small huts
among the rushes, had laid for themselves."

For eight days, Speke and Grant, in canoes,
slowly floated down the stream, passing through the
same beautiful but unchanging scenery, and being
obliged to keep pace with the porters and cattle on
the shore, which were conducted by the friendly
Kidgwiga.   Before reaching the Karuma Falls, they
were compelled to leave the canoes and join the
land party.   The country, they found, was highly
cultivated.   "The sand-paper tree, whose leaves resemble a cat's tongue in roughness, and which is
used in Uganda for polishing their clubs and spear-
handles, was conspicuous; but at the end of the
journey only was there anything of much interest to
be seen.   There suddenly, in a deep ravine one hundred yards below us, the formerly placid river, up
which vessels of moderate size might steam two or
three abreast, was now changed into a turbulent torrent.   Beyond lay the land of Kidi, a forest of mi-
mosa-trees, rising gently away from the water in

soft clouds of green. This the governor of the place, Kija, described as a sporting-field, where elephants, hippopotami, and buffalo are hunted by the occupants of both sides of the river."

At the Karuma Falls, or rather rapids, the White Nile is crossed by a chain of rocky islets, between which the water pours as through sluices, with a slanting fall of ten or twelve feet. Below them the river must be crossed, and as the country of Kidi, on the opposite shore, was represented to be an uninhabited wilderness, the party halted two days to lay in a stock of fish and flour. The crossing occupied another day, after which they formed a camp on the northern bank, and waited for the porters promised by Kamrasi. Only twenty-five arrived, but these, with the twenty free followers of Speke, and thirty-five of Kidgwiga's men, made a total of 78 souls in the caravan.

The wilderness of Kidi is a country of swamps, thickly overgrown with jungle and grasses so tall that they exclude the view. The only signs of man were in the caravan trail, which is frequently lost, and an occasional hut or two, the temporary quarters of the Kidi hunters. The marches did not average more than five or six miles a day; the weather was dull and rainy, and whenever Speke succeeded in shooting a buffalo, the native porters insisted on devouring the carcass before proceeding further.

On the seventh day the weather became fine, and the guides announced that they were approaching the village of Koki, in the country of Gani. "At

length," says Speke, " we reached the habitations of
men—a collection of conical huts on the ridge of a
small chain of granitic hills lying northwest.   As
we approached the southern extremity of this chain,
knots of naked men, perched like monkeys on the
granite blocks, were anxiously watching our arrival.
The guides, following the usages of the country, instead of allowing us to mount the hill and look out
for accommodation at once, desired us to halt, and
sent on a messenger to inform Chongi, the governor
general, that we were visitors from Kamrasi, who
desired he would take care of us and forward us to
our brothers.   This Mercury brought forth a hearty
welcome."

The chief received them with the greatest hospitality, the people were friendly, and they halted
three days to rest and recruit.   A guide was promised who would conduct them across the country,
in one long day's march to the camp of the "ele-
phant-hunters," which Speke understood to mean
Petherick's expedition.   Starting on the 2nd of December, the porters who had come through the
wilderness refused to carry any loads, and Speke
was obliged to hire natives from village to village.
This obliged him to stop at Mudua, a village in the
Madi country, that night.   The next day, a march
of two or three hours brought them to Faloro, the
chief of which insisted on their stopping to drink
beer with him, but Speke's haste to reach Petherick's
camp was all the greater now that the end appeared
to be so near.

"Half my men, however," he says, "did stop

there, but with the other half Grant and I went on ; and, as the sun was setting, we came in sight of what we thought was Petherick's outpost, N. lat. 3° 10′ 33″, and E. long. 31° 50′ 45″. My men, as happy as we were ourselves, now begged I would allow them to fire their guns, and prepare the Turks for our reception. Crack, bang, went their carbines, and in another instant crack, bang, was heard from the northerners' camp, when, like a swarm of bees, every height and other conspicuous place was covered with men. Our hearts leaped with an excitement of joy only known to those who have escaped from long-continued banishment among barbarians once more to meet with civilized people and join old friends. Every minute increased this excitement. We saw three large red flags heading a military procession, which marched out of the camp with drums and fifes playing. I halted and allowed them to draw near. When they did so, a very black man, named Mahamed, in full Egyptian regimentals, with a curved sword, ordered his regiment to halt, and threw himself into my arms, endeavoring to hug and kiss me. Rather staggered at this unexpected manifestation of affection, which was like a conjunction of the two hemispheres, I gave him a squeeze in return for his hug, but raised my head above the reach of his lips, and asked who was his master. 'Petrik,' was the reply. 'And where is Petherick now ?' 'Oh, he is coming.' 'How is it you have not got English colors, then ?' 'The colors are at Debono's.' 'Who is Debono ?' 'The same as Petrik ; but come along into my camp, and let us talk it out there ;' saying which Mahamed ordered his regiment (a ragamuffin mixture of Nubians, Egyptians, and slaves of all sorts, about two hundred in number) to rightabout, and we were guided by him, while his men kept up an incessant drumming and firing, presenting arms and firing, until we reached his huts, situated in a village kept exactly in the same order as that of the natives. Mahamed then gave us two beds to sit upon, and ordered his wives to advance on their knees and give us coffee, while other men brought pombé, and prepared us a dinner of bread and honey, and mutton."

In answer to Speke's eager inquiries, Mahamed assured him that Petherick was at Gondokoro, but that it was impossible for him now to reach that place, as no porters could be had. Speke determined to push on with Kidgwiga and his men, and guides were promised ; but at the end of four or five days, the former party deserted and partly refused to advance. No native guides would take service with the party : in short, Mahamed had determined that he would keep the travellers with him as an addition to his strength, until he had collected his ivory, and it was easy for him, with his knowledge of the natives, to accomplish his object.

Kidgwiga and his men therefore took their leave, bearing such presents as could be procured, for king Kamrasi, and Speke and Grant were obliged to content themselves with living in the Turkish camp, writing up their notes, adding to their scientific collections, and hunting game, until it should be possible to move northwards.   Speke proposed a trip to the westward, to visit the Nile ; but, although the river was within 30 miles of the camp, the Turks all declared that it was a journey of ten or twelve days through a dangerous country, and refused to furnish guides.

Finally, on the 11th of January, 1863, after a delay of more than a month, Speke and Grant started with their own men.   They walked over fine, rolling grassy plains, and on the third day reached a village called Paira, in sight of the Nile.   It was in appearance a noble stream, flowing on a flat bed from west to east, and immediately beyond it were the mountains of Kuku, rising to a height of 2,000 feet.   On the 15th they reached Apuddo, and at once went to see the tree, upon which, according to the natives, an Englishman had cut his name, some time before.   "There, sure enough," says Speke, " was a mark, something like the letters M. I., on its bark, but not distinct enough to be ascertained, because the bark had healed up.   In describing the individual who had done this, the Turks said he was exactly like myself, for he had a long beard, and a voice even much resembling mine.   He came thus far with Mahamed from Gondokoro two years ago, and then returned, because he was alarmed at the accounts the people gave of the countries to the southward, and he did not like the prospect of having to remain a whole rainy season with Mahamed at Faloro.   He knew we were endeavoring to come this way, and directed Mahamed to point out his name if we did so."

At Apuddo they were obliged to remain until the end of January, finding it impossible to go on without Mahamed's party. On the 1st of February they went ahead again, and in a few hours reached the Nile, at the point where it is joined by the Asua River, a tributary which comes down from the unknown eastern regions, in Lat. 3°, 42', North. Fording the latter river they kept on, over rolling country, covered in some places with bush-jungle, in others with villages, on the eastern bank of the Nile, and on the 11th reached the frontier of the Bari country, where the natives told them that three white men had just arrived in vessels at Gondokoro.

Mahamed's company of porters, with their own men, and the camp-followers, made a body of nearly a thousand persons, so that they were entirely secure against attacks from the hostile and warlike Bari tribe. Pushing on by degrees, on the 14th of February, they again came in sight of the Nile, and put up at a station called Doro, within a short distance of the Mountain of Rijeb, where the travellers up the White Nile from Egypt are in the habit of cutting their names. The country continued to be undulating and beautiful to the eye; but the grass was becoming shorter and finer every day, so much so that Speke's men all declared that it was a sign of their near approach to England.

That night there was an attack—or rather the menace of one—from the Bari, but the Turkish guards were vigilant, and the savages only howled, brandished their spears, and set fire to the dry

THE NILE ABOVE ASUA JUNCTION.

grass. " We slept the night out, nevertheless," writes Speke, " and next morning walked in to Gondokoro, N. lat. 4° 54' 5", and E. long. 31° 46' 9", where Mahamed, after firing a salute, took us in to see a Circassian merchant, named Kurshid Agha. Our first inquiry was, of course, for Petherick. A mysterious silence ensued ; we were informed that Mr. Debono was the man we had to thank for the assistance we had received in coming from Madi ; and then in hot haste, after warm exchanges of greeting with Mahamed's friend, who was Debono's agent here, we took leave, to hunt up Petherick. Walking down the bank of the river— where a line of vessels was moored, and on the right hand a few sheds, one half broken down, with a brick-built house representing the late Austrian Church Mission establishment—we saw hurrying on toward us the form of an Englishman, who for one moment we believed was the Simon Pure ; but the next moment my old friend Baker, famed for his sports in Ceylon, seized me by the hand. A little boy of his establishment had reported our arrival, and he in an instant came out to welcome us. What joy this was I can hardly tell. We could not talk fast enough, so overwhelmed were we both to meet again. Of course we were his guests in a moment, and learned everything that could be told. I now first heard of the death of H. R. H. the Prince Consort, which made me reflect on the inspiring words he made use of, in compliment to myself, when I was introduced to him by Sir Roderick Murchison a short while before leaving England. Then there was the terrible war in America, and other events of less startling nature, which came on us all by surprise, as years had now passed since we had received news from the civilized world.

"Baker then said he had come up with three vessels—one dyabir and two nuggers—fully equipped with armed men, camels, horses, donkeys, beads, brass wire, and everything necessary for a long journey, expressly to look after us, hoping, as he jokingly said, to find us on the equator in some terrible fix, that he might have the pleasure of helping us out of it. He had heard of Mahamed's party, and was actually waiting for him to come in, that he might have had the use of his return-men to start with comfortably. Three Dutch ladies,* also, with a view to assist us in the same was as Baker (God bless them) had come here in a steamer, but were driven back to Khartoum by sickness. Nobody had even dreamed for a moment it was possible we could come through. An Italian, named Miani, had gone farther up the Nile than any one else ; and he, it now transpired, was the man who had cut his name on the tree by Apuddo. But what had become of Petherick ? He was actually trading at Nyambara, seventy miles due west of this, though he had, since I left him in England, raised a subscription of £1,000 from those of my friends to whom this Journal is most

---

* The Baroness Miss A. van Capellan, and Mrs. and Miss Tinné.

respectfully dedicated as the smallest return a grateful heart can give for their attempt to succor me, when knowing the fate of the expedition was in great jeopardy."

Speke remained eleven days in Gondokoro, living with Baker, who, having come so far and prepared himself so thoroughly, was desirous of going on and adding something to the former's discoveries. Speke, therefore, suggested that he should explore the course of the White Nile between the Karuma Rapids and the point where himself and Grant had found it coming from the west, near the junction of the Asua, and especially to endeavor to reach the lake, or marsh, which the natives called Luta Uzigé. He gave Baker an account of his understanding with king Kamrasi, and an order for the property he had left there.

Two days before Speke and Grant left Gondokoro, Petherick arrived, having been collecting ivory in the country of the Nyam-Nyams, to the westward of the White Nile, instead of attempting to reach the explorers. On the 26th of February, 1863, the latter sailed for Khartoum in Baker's vessel, taking with them Bombay and the seventeen men who had faithfully followed them from Zanzibar, with four native women. They all reached Cairo in safety, in the summer, when the "Faithfuls," as they were now called, were sent by way of Aden back to Zanzibar, laden with presents ; while Speke and Grant hastened to England, to lay their reports before the Royal Geographical Society.

Shortly after the publication of the narrative of his extraordinary journey, Speke was accidentally killed in England by the discharge of his own musket, while hunting.

SIR SAMUEL AND LADY BAKER.

CHAPTER XIX.

IN March, 1861, Mr. Samuel White Baker under-
took an expedition into Central Africa, in the
hope of meeting Speke and Grant somewhere on the
head waters of the White Nile. He was an old
friend of the former, whom he had known in India;
like him he was a mighty hunter, and a residence of
eight years in Ceylon had inured his system to the
tropical climate. He set out on his journey, not
only without the support or encouragement of the
Royal Geographical Society, but without making his
intention publicly known.

In Cairo he made the acquaintance of a Swedish
lady, whose courage and enthusiasm were equal to
his own. They were married, and she became his
sole companion in all the dangers which followed.
" I weighed carefully the chances of the undertaking," he says, in the introduction to his narrative.
" Before me—untrodden Africa; against me—the
obstacles that had defeated the world since its creation; on my side—a somewhat tough constitution,
perfect independence, a long experience in savage

life, and both time and means which I intended to devote to the object without limit. England had never sent an expedition to the Nile sources previous to that under the command of Speke and Grant. Bruce, ninety years ago, had succeeded in tracing the source of the Blue or Lesser Nile : thus the honor of that discovery belonged to Great Britain ; Speke was on his road from the south ; and I felt confident that my gallant friend would leave his bones upon the path rather than submit to failure. I trusted that England would not be beaten ; and although I hardly dared to hope that I could succeed where others greater than I had failed, I determined to sacrifice all in the attempt. Had I been alone it would have been no hard lot to die upon the untrodden path before me, but there was one who, although my greatest comfort, was also my greatest care ; one whose life yet dawned at so early an age that womanhood was still a future. I shuddered at the prospect for her, should she be left alone in savage lands at my death ; and gladly would I have left her in the luxuries of home instead of exposing her to the miseries of Africa. It was in vain that I implored her to remain, and that I painted the difficulties and perils still blacker than I supposed they really would be ; she was resolved, with woman's constancy and devotion, to share all dangers and to follow me through each rough footstep of the wild life before me."

Thus, accompanied by his wife, Baker sailed up the Nile from Cairo, on the 15th of April, 1861. About the first of June he reached that large town of Berber in Ethiopia, within eight days' journey of Khartoum, at the junction of the Blue and White Niles. Here his plan of travel was changed. He says :

"From the slight experience I had gained in the journey to Berber, I felt convinced that success in my Nile expedition would be impossible with out a knowledge of Arabic. My dragoman had me completely in his power, and I resolved to become independent of all interpreters as soon as possible. I therefore arranged a plan of exploration for the first year, to embrace the affluents to the Nile from the Abyssinian range of mountains, intending to follow up the Atbara river from its junction with the Nile in lat. 17° 37' (twenty miles south of Berber,) and to examine all the Nile tributaries from the southeast as far as the Blue Nile, which river I hoped ultimately to descend to Khartoum. I imagined that twelve months would be sufficient to complete such an exploration, by which time I should have gained a sufficient knowledge of Arabic to enable me to start from Khartoum for my White Nile expedition."

This plan was successfully carried out, exactly as he had designed it. He explored the Atbara and its affluents, to the mountains of Abyssinia, acquired a good knowledge of Arabic, and arrived safely at Khartoum on the 11th of June, 1862. Here he was detained six months, partly by the necessity of waiting for the proper season for ascending the White Nile, and partly by the hostility of Moussa Pasha, the Egyptian Governor of Soudan, to his expedition. But the opposition of the government only stimulated Baker's energy ; his private means were ample, and in a few weeks he succeeded in manning and provisioning three large vessels. He had forty sailors and forty-five armed men as escort —with the servants, a party of ninety-six. As head man he engaged a German carpenter named Johann Schmidt, who was unfortunately far gone in consumption, and died in a few weeks.

Everything being finally in readiness, Baker started on the 18th of December, a Thursday, which is one of the most lucky days for a start, according to Arab superstition. " On passing the steamer belonging to the Dutch ladies, Madame van Capellan, and her charming daughter, Mademoiselle Tinné, we saluted them with a volley, and kept up a mutual waving of handkerchiefs until out of view ; little did we think that we should never meet those kind faces again, and that they should meet so dreadful a fate."*

Baker's voyage up the White Nile belongs to another field of travel, and his account of it need not be repeated here. His experiences of the native tribes, and his impressions of the scenery and climate, were very much the same as those of his predecessors. On the last day of the year, Schmidt died, and was buried on the shore, in the Shillook country. During the month of January, 1863,

---

* The entire party died of fever on the White Nile, excepting Mademoiselle Tinné. The victims to the fatal climate of Central Africa were Madame la Baronne van Capellan, her sister, two Dutch maid-servants, Dr. Steudner, and Signor Contarini.

Baker pushed southward, passing the Gazelle Lake, and the lands of the Nuehrs and Kyks, and on the 2nd of February arrived safely at the trading-post of Gondokoro. The horses and camels he brought with him were landed from the boats in excellent condition, and the supplies, which had been well husbanded, seemed ample for his purpose.

At this time nothing had been heard from Speke since he left Kazeh, two years before. " In conversing with the traders at Gondokoro," says Baker, " and assuring them that my object was entirely confined to a search for the Nile sources, and an inquiry for Speke and Grant, I heard a curious report that had been brought down by the natives from the interior, that at some great distance to the south there were two white men who had been for a long time prisoners of a sultan ; and that these had wonderful *fireworks ;* that both had been very ill, and that one had died. It was in vain that I endeavored to obtain some further clue to this exciting report. There was a rumor that some native had a piece of wood with marks upon it that had belonged to the white men ; but upon inquiry I found that this account was only a report given by some distant tribe. Nevertheless, I attached great importance to the rumor, as there was no white man south of Gondokoro engaged in the ivory trade ; therefore there was a strong probability that the report had some connection with the existence of Speke and Grant. I had heard, when at Khartoum, that the most advanced trading station was about fifteen days' march from Gondo-

koro, and my plan of operations had always projected a direct advance to that station, where I had
intended to leave all my heavy baggage in depot,
and to proceed from thence as a " point de départ "
to the south.   I now understood that the party
were expected to arrive at Gondokoro from that
station with ivory in a few days, and I determined
to wait for their arrival, and to return with them in
company.   Their ivory porters returning, might
carry my baggage, and thus save the backs of my
transport animals.

"I had been waiting at Gondokoro twelve days,
expecting the arrival of Debono's party from the
south, with whom I wished to return.   Suddenly,
on the 15th of February, I heard the rattle of musketry at a great distance, and a dropping fire from
the south.   To give an idea of the moment I must
extract *verbatim* from my journal as written at the
time.   ' Guns firing in the distance ; Debono's ivory
porters arriving, for whom I have waited.   My men
rushed madly to my boat, with the report that two
white men were with them who had come from the
sea !   Could they be Speke and Grant ?   Off I ran,
and soon met them in reality.   Hurrah for old England ! they had come from the Victoria Nyanza,
from which the Nile springs... The mystery of ages
solved.   With my pleasure of meeting them is
the one disappointment, that I had not met them
farther on the road in my search for them ; however, the satisfaction is, that my previous arrangements had been such as would have insured my
finding them had they been in a fix....My pro-

jected route would have brought me *vis-à-vis* with them, as they had come from the lake by the course I had proposed to take.... All my men perfectly mad with excitement : firing salutes as usual with ball cartridge, they shot one of my donkeys ; a melancholy sacrifice as an offering at the completion of this geographical discovery."

"When I first met them they were walking along the bank of the river towards my boats. At a distance of about a hundred yards I recognized my old friend Speke, and with a heart beating with joy I took off my cap and gave a welcome hurrah! as I ran towards him. For the moment he did not recognize me ; ten years' growth of beard and moustache had worked a change ; and as I was totally unexpected, my sudden appearance in the centre of Africa appeared to him incredible. I hardly required an introduction to his companion, as we felt already acquainted, and after the transports of this happy meeting we walked together to my diahbiah ; my men surrounding us with smoke and noise by keeping up an unremitting fire of musketry the whole way. We were shortly seated on deck under the awning, and such rough fare as could be hastily prepared was set before these two ragged, careworn specimens of African travel, whom I looked upon with feelings of pride as my own countrymen. As a good ship arrives in harbor, battered and torn by a long and stormy voyage, yet sound in her frame and seaworthy to the last, so both these gallant travellers arrived at Gondokoro. Speke appeared the more worn of the two ; he was excessively lean, but in reality he was in good tough condition ; he had walked the whole way from Zanzibar, never having once ridden during that wearying march.   Grant was in honorable rags ; his bare knees projecting through the remnants of trowsers that were an exhibition of rough industry in tailor's work.   He was looking tired and feverish, but both men had a fire in the eye that showed the spirit that had led them through.

" They wished to leave Gondokoro as soon as possible, *en route* for England, but delayed their departure until the moon should be in a position for an observation for determining the longitude.   My boats were fortunately engaged by me for five months, thus Speke and Grant could take charge of them to Khartoum.

" At the first blush on meeting them I had considered my expedition as terminated by having met them, and by their having accomplished the discovery of the Nile source ; but upon my congratulating them with all my heart, upon the honor they had so nobly earned, Speke and Grant with characteristic candor and generosity gave me a map of their route, showing that they had been unable to complete the actual exploration of the Nile, and that a most important portion still remained to be determined.   It appeared that in N. lat. 2° 17', they had crossed the Nile, which they had tracked from the Victoria Lake ; but the river, which from its exit from that lake had a northern course, turned suddenly to the *west* from Karuma Falls (the point at which they crossed it at lat. 2° 17').   They did not see the Nile again until they arrived in N. lat. 3° 32′, which was then flowing from the W.S.W. The natives and the King of Unyoro (Kamrasi) had assured them that the Nile from the Victoria Nyanza, which they had crossed at Karuma, flowed westward for several days' journey, and at length fell into a large lake called the Luta Nzige ; that this lake came from the south, and that the Nile on entering the northern extremity almost immediately made its exit, and as a navigable river continued its course to the north, through the Koshi and Madi countries. Both Speke and Grant attached great importance to this lake Luta Nzige, and the former was much annoyed that it had been impossible for them to carry out the exploration. He foresaw that stay-at-home geographers, who, with a comfortable arm-chair to sit in, travel so easily with their fingers on a map, would ask him why he had not gone from such a place to such a place ? why he had not followed the Nile to the Luta Nzige lake, and from the lake to Gondokoro ? As it happened, it was impossible for Speke and Grant to follow the Nile from Karuma :—the tribes were fighting with Kamrasi, and no strangers could have got through the country. Accordingly they procured their information most carefully, completed their map, and laid down the reported lake in its supposed position, showing the Nile as both influent and effluent precisely as had been explained by the natives.

"Speke expressed his conviction that the Luta Nzige must be a second source of the Nile, and that geographers would be dissatisfied that he had not explored it. To me this was most gratifying. I had been much disheartened at the idea that the great work was accomplished, and that nothing remained for exploration; I even said to Speke, ' Does not one leaf of the laurel remain for me?' I now heard that the field was not only open, but that an additional interest was given to the exploration by the proof that the Nile flowed out of one great lake, the Victoria, but that it evidently must derive an additional supply from an unknown lake as it entered it at the *northern* extremity, while the body of the lake came from the south. The fact of a great body of water such as the Luta Nzige extending in a direct line from south to north, while the general system of drainage of the Nile was from the same direction, showed most conclusively, that the Luta Nzige, if it existed in the form assumed, must have an important position in the basin of the Nile.

" My expedition had naturally been rather costly, and being in excellent order it would have been heartbreaking to have returned fruitlessly. I therefore arranged immediately for my departure, and Speke most kindly wrote in my journal such instructions as might be useful.

" We were now all ready to start. Speke and Grant, and their party of twenty-two people, for Egypt, and I in the opposite direction. At this season there were many boats at Gondokoro belonging to the traders' parties, among which were four belonging to Mr. Petherick, three of which were open cargo boats, and one remarkably nice diahbiah, named the 'Kathleen,' that was waiting for Mrs. Petherick and her husband, who were supposed to be at their trading station, the Niambara, about seventy miles west of Gondokoro ; but no accounts had been heard of them. On the 20th of February they suddenly arrived from the Niambara, with their people and ivory, and were surprised at seeing so large a party of English in so desolate a spot. It is a curious circumstance, that although many Europeans had been as far south as Gondokoro, I was the first Englishman that had ever reached it. We now formed a party of four.

"On the 26th of February, Speke and Grant sailed from Gondokoro. Our hearts were too full to say more than a short 'God bless you !' They had won their victory ; my work lay all before me. I watched their boat until it turned the corner, and wished them in my heart all honor for their great achievement. I trusted to sustain the name they had won for English perseverance, and I looked forward to meeting them again in dear old England, when I should have completed the work we had so warmly planned together."

CHAPTER XX.

BAKER made immediate preparations for returning on the line of Speke's and Grant's march. On weighing his supplies, he found that they amounted to fifty-four hundred weight. He therefore applied to Mahamed, the *vakeel* or agent of the trader Debono, who had escorted the two explorers from his camp in Faloro, to Gondokoro, and begged his coöperation in the expedition. "These people," Baker writes, "had brought down a large quantity of ivory from the interior, and had therefore a number of porters who would return empty-handed; I accordingly arranged with Mahamed for fifty porters, who would much relieve the backs of my animals from Gondokoro to the station at Faloro, about twelve days' march. At Faloro I intended to leave my heavy baggage in depot, and to proceed direct to Kamrasi's country. I promised Mahamed that I would use my influence in all new countries that I might discover, to open a road for his ivory trade, provided that he would agree to conduct it by legitimate purchase, and I gave him a list of the quality of beads most desirable for Kamrasi's country, according to the description I had received from Speke.

" Mahamed promised to accompany me, not only to his camp at Faloro, but throughout the whole of my expedition, provided that I would assist him in procuring ivory, and that I would give him a handsome present. All was agreed upon, and my own men appeared in high spirits at the prospect of joining so large a party as that of Mahamed, which mustered about two hundred men.

" At that time I really placed dependence upon the professions of Mahamed and his people ; they had just brought Speke and Grant with them, and had received from them presents of a first-class double-barrelled gun and several valuable rifles. I had promised not only to assist them in their ivory expeditions, but to give them something very handsome in addition, and the fact of my having upwards of forty men as escort was also an introduction, as they would be an addition to the force, which is a great advantage in hostile countries. Everything appeared to be in good train, but I little knew the duplicity of these Arab scoundrels. At the very moment that they were most friendly, they were plotting to deceive me, and to prevent me from entering the country. They knew, that should I penetrate the interior, the *ivory trade* of the White Nile would be no longer a mystery, and that the atrocities of the slave trade would be exposed, and most likely be terminated by the intervention of European Powers ; accordingly they combined to prevent my advance, and to overthrow my expedition completely. The whole of the men belonging to the various traders were determined that no Englishman should penetrate into the country ; accordingly they fraternized with my escort, and persuaded them that I was a Christian dog, that it was a disgrace for a Mohammedan to serve ; that they would be starved in my service, as I would not allow them to steal cattle ; that they would have no slaves ; and that I should lead them—God knew where—to the sea, from whence Speke and Grant had started ; that they had left Zanzibar with two hundred men, and had only arrived at Gondokoro with eighteen, thus the remainder must have been killed by the natives on the road ; that if they followed me, and arrived at Zanzibar, I should find a ship waiting to take me to England, and I should leave them to die in a strange country. Such were the reports circulated to prevent my men from accompanying me, and it was agreed that Mahamed should fix a day for our pretended start *in company,* but that he would in reality start a few days before the time appointed ; and that my men should mutiny, and join his party in cattle-stealing and slave-hunting. This was the substance of the plot thus carefully concocted.

"Among my people were two blacks : one, ' Richarn,' already described as having been brought up by the Austrian Mission at Khartoum ; the other, a boy of twelve years old, ' Saat.' As these were the only really faithful members of the expedition, it is my duty to describe them. Richarn was an habit-nal drunkard, but he had his good points; he was honest, and much attached to both master and mistress. He had been with me for some months, and was a fair sportsman, and being of an entirely different race to the Arabs, he kept himself apart from them, and fraternized with the boy Saat.

"Not only was the latter boy trustworthy, but he had an extraordinary amount of moral in addition to physical courage. If any complaint were made, and Saat was called as a witness—far from the shyness too often evinced when the accuser is brought face to face with the accused—such was Saat's proudest moment; and, no matter who the man might be, the boy would challenge him, regardless of all consequences. We were very fond of this boy; he was thoroughly good; and in that land of iniquity, thousands of miles away from all except what was evil, there was a comfort in having some one innocent and faithful, in whom to trust.

"One morning I had returned to the tent after having, as usual, inspected the transport animals, when I observed Mrs. Baker looking extraordinarily pale, and immediately upon my arrival she gave orders for the presence of the vakeel (headman). There was something in her manner, so different to her usual calm, that I was utterly bewildered when I heard her question the vakeel, 'Whether the men were willing to march?' Perfectly ready, was the reply. 'Then order them to strike the tent, and load the animals; we start this moment.' The man appeared confused, but not more so than I. Something was evidently on foot, but what I could not

conjecture.   The vakeel wavered, and to my astonishment I heard the accusation made against him,
that, ' during the night, the whole of the escort had
mutinously conspired to desert me, with my arms
and ammunition that were in their hands, and to
fire simultaneously at me should I attempt to dis-
arm them.'   At first this charge was indignantly de-
nied until the boy Saat manfully stepped forward,
and declared that the conspiracy was entered into
by the whole of the escort, and that both he and
Richarn, knowing that mutiny was intended, had
listened purposely to the conversation during the
night ; at daybreak the boy reported the fact to his
mistress.   Mutiny, robbery, and murder were thus
deliberately determined."

Baker immediately called out the escort, confronted
them with a loaded rifle, and ordered them to lay
down their arms.   There was some wavering among
the ringleaders ; but his determined attitude over-
awed them, and they finally obeyed.   They then
demanded their discharge, which he gave, writing
the word "mutineer" in English on each of the
papers, that they might be afterwards identified in
Khartoum.   The same day, the sound of drums and
muskets announced that Mahamed's party was
leaving for Faloro, sending Baker word that if he
followed on their road, they would fire upon him.

The next day Koorshid, a Circassian trader, who
was friendly to Baker and had promised to assist
him, called and stated that he was utterly unable to
do so, since every man refused.   The slave-traders
had done their work well ; all the native mercenaries

were convinced that Baker was a spy, who would report everything to the Government, and finally ruin the whole commerce of the region. Baker's answer was, that he had enough of stores and provisions for a year; he would not return, and only asked to be furnished with an interpreter, as he had no means of communicating with the natives. This Koorshid promised to provide.

"After Koorshid's departure," says Baker, "we sat silently for some minutes, both my wife and I occupied by the same thoughts. No expedition had ever been more carefully planned; everything had been well arranged to insure success. My transport animals were in good condition; their saddles and pads had been made under my own inspection; my arms, ammunition, and supplies were abundant, and I was ready to march at five minutes' notice to any part of Africa; but the expedition, so costly, and so carefully organized, was completely ruined by the very people whom I had engaged to protect it."

After vainly trying various expedients to go onwards, Baker's plans were suddenly favored by chance. Some of Koorshid's people arrived with ivory from the Latooka country, an unknown region lying some seventy or eighty miles eastward of Gondokoro. They brought with them, as porters, a number of the Latooka tribe, remarkably handsome men, wearing curious helmets of brass beads. The chief of the party came to Baker's tent, with some of his men, gave much information concerning the country, and begged him to visit it. Koorshid's

men, however, declared that they would prevent
Baker from accompanying them. He nevertheless
made his preparations, not believing they would
dare to use force.

There was an intervening region called Ellyria,
inhabited by a fierce and warlike tribe, the chief
of which was in league with Koorshid's party ; and
the road to Latooka led through a narrow defile in
the mountains, where Baker's small band of seventeen would surely be waylaid. After a rapid deli-
beration, the intrepid traveller resolved to start
after the party, pass them by rapid marches, get
through the defile before them and push on to Latooka. Soon the day arrived for the departure of
Koorshid's party ; the drums beat, and at 2 P.M.
they marched off, sending a message *daring* Baker
to follow them.

But he was equal to the emergency. He says :
" I immediately ordered the tent to be struck, the
luggage to be arranged, the animals to be collected,
and everything to be ready for the march. Richarn
and Saat were in high spirits, even my unwilling
men were obliged to work, and by 7 P.M. we were
all ready. The camels were too heavily loaded,
carrying about seven hundred pounds each. The
donkeys were also overloaded, but there was no help
for it. Mrs. Baker was well mounted on my good
old Abyssinian hunter, *Tetel*, carrying several leather
bags slung to the pommel, while I was equally
loaded on my horse, *Tilfil*. We had neither guide
nor interpreter ; and, perfectly hopeless, commenced
the desperate journey about an hour after sunset.

"'Where shall we go?' said the men, just as the order was given to start. 'Who can travel without a guide? No one knows the road.' The moon was up, and the mountain of Belignan was distinctly visible about nine miles distant. Knowing that the route lay on the east side of that mountain, I led the way, Mrs. Baker riding by my side, and the British flag following close behind us as a guide for the caravan of heavily laden camels and donkeys. We shook hands warmly with Dr. Murie, who had come to see us off, and thus we started on our march in Central Africa on the 26th of March, 1863.

"The country was park-like, but much parched by the dry weather. The ground was sandy, but firm, and interspersed with numerous villages, all of which were surrounded with a strong fence of euphorbia. The country was well wooded, being free from bush or jungle, but numerous trees, all evergreens, were scattered over the landscape. No natives were to be seen, but the sound of their drums and singing in chorus was heard in the far distance. Whenever it is moonlight the nights are passed in singing and dancing, beating drums, blowing horns, and the population of whole villages thus congregate together.

"After a silent march of two hours we saw watch-fires blazing in the distance, and upon nearer approach we perceived the trader's party bivouacked. Their custom is to march only two or three hours on the first day of their departure, to allow stragglers who may have lagged behind in Gondokoro to rejoin the party before morning."

After camping in the neighborhood of the Turks, Baker and his little party pushed forward in the early morning. His great object was to keep in advance and get through the mountain pass before his enemies could communicate with the chief of Ellyria. He accordingly gave orders for an *immediate* start. "Load the camels, my brothers!" he exclaimed, to the sullen ruffians around him ; but not a man stirred except Richarn and a fellow named Sali, who began to show signs of improvement. Seeing that the men intended to disobey, he immediately set to work himself loading the animals, requesting his men not to trouble themselves, and begging them to lie down and smoke their pipes while he did the work. A few rose from the ground ashamed, and assisted to load the camels, while the others declared the impossibility of camels travelling by the road they were about to take, as the Turks had informed them that not even the donkeys could march through the thick jungles between Belignan and Ellyria.

"All right my brothers!" Baker replied ; "then we'll march as far as the donkeys can go, and leave both them and the baggage on the road when they can go no farther ; but *I go forward.*"

The road was crossed by many dry beds of torrents, where each animal had to be assisted over by the men, and the camels invariably fell. The delay was consequently great, and the anxiety of the explorer increased, from the fear that the Turks would overtake him. "My wife and I," he says, "rode about a quarter of a mile at the head of the party as an advance guard, to warn the caravan of any difficulty. The very nature of the country declared that it must be full of ravines, and yet I could not help hoping against hope that we might have a clear mile of road without a break. The evening had passed, and the light faded. What had been difficult and tedious during the day, now became most serious—we could not see the branches of hooked thorns that overhung the broken path ; I rode in advance, my face and arms bleeding with countless scratches, while at each rip of a thorn I gave a warning shout—' Thorn !' for those behind, and a cry of ' Hole !' for any deep rut that lay in the path. It was fortunately moonlight, but the jungle was so thick that the narrow track was barely perceptible: thus both camels and donkeys ran against the trunks of trees, smashing the luggage, and breaking all that could be broken ; nevertheless, the case was urgent ; march we must, at all hazards.''

By this time he had been joined by two natives of Latooka, whom he had seen in Gondokoro, and who had deserted from the Turks on account of having been beaten. These men knew the way, and, after a short sleep, hurried the party forward at dawn for three hours, when they were obliged to rest again until afternoon. Then, after ascending a mile further through jungle, they suddenly emerged upon an eminence, and looked down upon a valley called Tollogo. This was extremely picturesque. An abrupt wall of grey granite rose on the east side of the valley to a height of about a thousand feet : from this perpendicular wall huge blocks had fallen, strewing the base with a confused mass of granite lumps ten to forty feet in diameter; and among these natural fortresses of disjointed masses were numerous villages. The bottom of the valley was a meadow, in which grew several enormous fig-trees by the side of a sluggish, and in some places stagnant, brook. The valley was not more than half a mile wide, and was also walled in by mountains on the west, having, the appearance of a vast street.

No sooner had they reached the valley than the natives flocked around them in great numbers, much excited by the appearance of the horses, which they had never before seen. Finally a humpback who spoke some Arabic came forward, and Baker requested him to keep off the crowd, which now numbered five or six hundred, and were menacingly pressing upon the party.

"In reply to a question of the humpback, he asked me, 'Who I was?' I explained that I was a traveller. 'You want ivory?' he said. 'No,' I answered, 'it is of no use to me.' 'Ah, you want slaves!' he replied. 'Neither do I want slaves,' I answered. This was followed by a burst of laughter from the crowd, and the humpback continued his examination. 'Have you got plenty of cows?' 'Not one; but plenty of beads and copper.' 'Plenty? Where are they?' 'Not far off; they will be here presently with my men;' and I pointed to the direction from which they would arrive. 'What countryman are you?' 'An Englishman.' He had never heard of such people. 'You are a Turk?' 'All right,' I replied; 'I am anything you

like.' 'And that is your son?' (pointing at Mrs.
Baker). 'No, she is my wife.' 'Your wife! What
a lie! He is a boy.' 'Not a bit of it,' I replied;
'she is my wife, who has come with me to see the
women of this country.' 'What a lie!' he again
politely rejoined in the one expressive Arabic word,
'Katab.'

"After this charmingly frank conversation he addressed the crowd, explaining, I suppose, that I was
endeavoring to pass off a boy for a woman. Mrs.
Baker was dressed similarly to myself, in a pair of
loose trowsers and gaiters, with a blouse and belt—
the only difference being that she wore long sleeves,
while my arms were bare from a few inches below
the shoulder. I always kept my arms bare, as being
cooler than if covered."

Presently the chief arrived and made order. The
party rested there quietly for the night, being then
only six miles from Ellyria. Starting early in the
morning, they made for the famous pass, which was
destined to decide the fate of the expedition. Baker
had three men as an advance guard, and five or six
in the rear, while the remainder drove the animals.
Mrs. Baker and himself rode on horseback at the
head of the party. The mountain of Ellyria, between two and three thousand feet high, rose abrupt
on the left, while the base was entirely choked with
enormous fragments of grey granite that, fallen from
the face of the mountain, had completely blocked
the pass. Even the horses had great difficulty in
threading their way through narrow alleys formed

of opposing blocks, and it appeared impossible for loaded camels to proceed.

Baker and his wife rode on, " accompanied only by one of the Latookas as a guide. After turning a sharp angle of the mountain, leaving the cliff abruptly rising to the left from the narrow path, we descended a ravine worse than any place we had previously encountered, and we were obliged to dismount, in order to lead our horses up the steep rocks on the opposite side. On arrival on the summit, a lovely view burst upon us. The valley of Ellyria was about four hundred feet below, at about a mile distant. Beautiful mountains, some two or three thousand feet high, of grey granite, walled in the narrow vale ; while the landscape of forest and plain was bounded at about fifty or sixty miles' distance to the east by the blue mountains of Latooka. The mountain of Ellyria was the commencement of the fine range that continued indefinitely to the south. We were now in the very gorge of that chain. Below us, in the valley, I observed some prodigious trees growing close to a Hor, (ravine,) in which was running water, and the sides of the valley under the mountains being as usual a mass of *débris* of huge detached rocks, were thronged with villages, all strongly fortified with thick bamboo palisades. The whole country was a series of natural forts, occupied by a large population.

" Tying our horses to a bush, we sat upon a rock beneath the shade of a small tree within ten paces of the path, and considered the best course to pursue. I hardly liked to risk an advance into Ellyria alone, before the arrival of my whole party, as we had been very rudely received by the Tollogo people on the previous evening;—nevertheless I thought it might be good policy to ride unattended into Ellyria, and thus to court an introduction to the chief. However, our consultation ended in a determination to wait where we then were, until the caravan should have accomplished the last difficulty by crossing the ravine; when we would all march into Ellyria in company. For a long time we sat gazing at the valley before us in which our fate lay hidden, feeling thankful that we had thus checkmated the brutal Turks. Not a sound was heard of our approaching camels: the delay was most irksome. There were many difficult places that we had passed through, and each would be a source of serious delay to the animals.

"At length we heard them in the distance. We could distinctly hear the men's voices; and we rejoiced that they were approaching the last remaining obstacle;—that one ravine passed through, and all before would be easy. I heard the rattling of the stones as they drew nearer; and, looking towards the ravine, I saw emerge from the dark foliage of the trees within fifty yards of us the hated *red flag and crescent, leading the Turks' party!* We were outmarched!

" One by one, with scowling looks, the insolent scoundrels filed by us within a few feet, without making the customary salaam; neither noticing us in any way, except by threatening to shoot the Latooka, our guide, who had formerly accompanied them. At length their leader, Ibrahim, appeared in the rear of the party. He was riding on a donkey, being the last of the line, behind the flag that closed the march.

"I never saw a 'more atrocious countenance than that exhibited in this man. A mixed breed, between a Turk sire and Arab mother, he had the good features and bad qualities of either race. The fine, sharp, high-arched nose and large nostril ; the pointed and projecting chin ; rather high cheek-bones and prominent brow, overhanging a pair of immense black eyes full expression of all evil. As he approached he took no notice of us, but studiously looked straight before him with the most determined insolence.

"The fate of the expedition was, at this critical moment, retrieved by Mrs. Baker. She implored me to call him, to insist upon a personal explanation, and to offer him some present in the event of establishing amicable relations. I could not condescend to address the sullen scoundrel. He was in the act of passing us, and success depended upon that instant. Mrs. Baker herself called him. For the moment he made no reply ; but, upon my repeating the call in a loud key, he turned his donkey towards us and dismounted. I ordered him to sit down, as his men were ahead and we were alone.

"The following dialogue passed between us after the usual Arab mode of greeting. I said, 'Ibrahim, why should we be enemies in the midst of this hostile country ? We believe in the same God, why should we quarrel in this land of heathens, who believe in no God? You have your work to perform; I have mine. You want ivory; I am a simple traveller; why should we clash? If I were offered the whole ivory of the country, I would not accept a single tusk, nor interfere with you in any way. Transact your business, and don't interfere with me: the country is wide enough for us both. I have a task before me, to reach a great lake— the head of the Nile. Reach it *I will* (Inshallah). No power shall drive me back. If you are hostile, I will imprison you in Khartoum; if you assist me, I will reward you far beyond any reward you have ever received. Should I be killed in this country, you will be suspected; you know the result; the Government would hang you on the bare suspicion. On the contrary, if you are friendly, I will use my influence in any country that I discover, that you may procure its ivory for the sake of your master Koorshid, who was generous to Captains Speke and Grant, and kind to me. Should you be hostile, I shall hold your master responsible as your employer. Should you assist me, I will befriend you both. Choose your course frankly, like a man— friend or enemy?'

"Before he had time to reply, Mrs. Baker addressed him much in the same strain, telling him that he did not know what Englishmen were; that nothing would drive them back; that the British Government watched over them wherever they might be, and that no outrage could be committed with impunity upon a British subject. That I would not deceive him in any way; that I was not a trader; and that I should be able to assist him materially by discovering new countries rich in ivory, and that he would benefit himself personally by civil conduct.

"He seemed confused, and wavered. I immediately promised him a new double-barrelled gun and some gold, when my party should arrive, as an earnest of the future.

"He replied, 'That he did not himself wish to be hostile, but that all the trading parties, without one exception, were against me, and that the men were convinced that I was a consul in disguise, who would report to the authorities at Khartoum all the proceedings of the traders.' He continued, 'That he believed me, but that his men would not; that all people told lies in their country, therefore no one was credited for the truth. However,' said he, 'do not associate with my people, or they may insult you, but go and take possession of that tree (pointing to one in the valley of Ellyria) for yourself and people, and I will come there and speak with you. I will now join my men, as I do not wish them to know that I have been conversing with you.' He then made a salaam, mounted his donkey, and rode off.

"I had won him. I knew the Arab character so thoroughly that I was convinced that the tree he had pointed out, followed by the words, 'I will come there and speak to you,' was to be the rendezvous for the receipt of the promised gun and money.

"I did not wait for the arrival of my men, but

mounting our horses, my wife and I rode down the hillside with lighter spirits than we had enjoyed for some time past. I gave her the entire credit of the ' ruse.' Had I been alone, I should have been too proud to have sought the friendship of the sullen trader, and the moment on which success depended would have been lost."

That evening Baker's small party encamped in the valley of Ellyria, near the Turks, and were not molested by the natives. They were not able to procure provisions, but, fortunately, they had a good supply on hand. Baker's men, as he well knew, were still resolved upon mutiny,—perhaps murder ; but his alliance with Ibrahim gave him a new feeling of security. He thus describes the next day's march towards Latooka :

" Ibrahim, my new ally, was now riding in front of the line, carrying on his saddle a pretty little girl, his daughter, a child of a year and a half old ; her mother, a remarkably pretty Bari girl, one of his numerous wives, was riding behind him on an ox. We soon got into conversation ;—a few pieces of sugar given to the child and mother by Mrs. Baker was a sweet commencement ; and Ibrahim then told me to beware of my own men, as he knew that they did not intend to remain with me ; that they were a different tribe from his men, and they would join Chenooda's people and desert me on our arrival at their station in Latooka. This was a corroboration of all I had heard previous to leaving Gondokoro, therefore I had the promised mutiny in perspective. I had noticed that my men were even more sullen than usual since I had joined Ibrahim ; however, I succeeded in convincing him that he would benefit so decidedly by an alliance with me, that he now frankly told me that I should receive no opposition from his party.   So far all had prospered beyond my most sanguine expectations.   We were fairly launched upon our voyage, and now that we were in the wild interior, I determined to crush the mutiny with an iron hand should the rascals attempt to carry their murderous threats into execution.   Two or three of the men appeared willing, but the original ringleader, 'Bellaal,' would literally do nothing, not even assisting at loading the animals ; but swaggering about with the greatest insolence."

After two days' journey due east, without particular incident, they reached the boundaries of the Latooka country.   On approaching the first village, about a hundred men of the Turkish caravan, who were in league with Baker's mutinous escort, fired off a volley of welcome, evidently for the purpose of allaying his suspicions.   He was not deceived ; his two faithful attendants advised him that the decisive moment was at hand.   The next morning, when the Turkish drums beat the signal for starting, Baker's *vakeel* (head man) was not to be found ; the men lay as they had been sleeping, and not a man obeyed the order, except Richarn and a native named Sali.   Finally, the man named Bellaal rose, gun in hand, and faced Baker insolently, while he appeared to be making signs to the others.   It was evident that the time had arrived.   Baker himself must describe the occurrence ;

"Pretending not to notice Bellaal, who was now as I had expected once more the ringleader, for the third time I ordered the men to rise immediately, and to load the camels. Not a man moved, but the fellow Bellaal marched up to me, and looking me straight in the face dashed the butt-end of his gun in defiance on the ground, and led the mutiny. 'Not a man shall go with you!—go where you like with Ibrahim, but we won't follow you nor move a step farther. The men shall not load the camels; you may employ the "niggers" to do it, but not us.'

"I looked at this mutinous rascal for a moment; this was the burst of the conspiracy, and the threats and insolence that I had been forced to pass over for the sake of the expedition all rushed before me. 'Lay down your gun!' I thundered, 'and load the camels!' . . . . 'I won't'—was his reply. 'Then stop here!' I answered; at the same time lashing out as quick as lightning with my right hand upon his jaw.

"He rolled over in a heap, his gun flying some yards from his hand; and the late ringleader lay apparently insensible among the luggage, while several of his friends ran to him, and did the good Samaritan. Following up on the moment the advantage I had gained by establishing a panic, I seized my rifle and rushed into the midst of the wavering men, catching first one by the throat, and then another, and dragging them to the camels, which I insisted upon their immediately loading. All except three, who attended to the ruined ringleader, mechanically obeyed. Richarn and Sali both shouted to them to 'hurry;' and the vakeel arriving at this moment and seeing how matters stood, himself assisted, and urged the men to obey."

This was the end of the conspiracy. Baker's party marched on without the mutinous escort, and the vakeel, who had kept purposely away from the scene, reappeared in the course of the day. The country of Latooka, which they entered, was a broad, beautiful valley, twenty miles in length, bounded on the north by mountains 3,000 feet in height, while a peak of 5,000 feet closed the vista to the east.

We now quote Baker's account of his arrival at Tarrangòllé, the capital of the country, and his description of the natives and their mode of living :

"On the arrival of my vakeel he told me, in the face of the men, that so many had deserted, and that the others had refused to assist him in taking the guns from them ; thus my arms and ammunition had been forcibly stolen. I abused both the vakeel and the men most thoroughly ; and 'as for the mutineers who have joined the slave-hunters, Inshallah, the vultures shall pick their bones !'

"This charitable wish—which, I believe, I expressed with intense hatred—was never forgotten either by my own men or by the Turks. Believing firmly in the evil eye, their superstitious fears were immediately excited.

" Continuing the march along the same style of country we shortly came in view of Tarrangollé, the chief town of Latooka, at which point was the station of Ibrahim. We had marched thirteen miles from Latomé, the station of Mahommed Her, at which place my men had deserted, and we were now 101 miles from Gondokoro by dead reckoning.

" There were some superb trees situated close to the town, under which we camped until the natives could prepare a hut for our reception. Crowds of people now surrounded us, amazed at the two great objects of interest—the camels, and a white woman. They did not think me very peculiar, as I was nearly as brown as an Arab.

" The Latookas are the finest savages I have ever seen. I measured a number of them as they happened to enter my tent, and allowing two inches for the thickness of their felt helmets, the average height was 5 ft. 11½ in. Not only are they tall, but they possess a wonderful muscular development, having beautifully proportioned legs and arms ; and although extremely powerful, they are never fleshy or corpulent. The formation of head and general physiognomy is totally different from all other tribes that I have met with in the neighborhood of the White Nile. They have high foreheads, large eyes, rather high cheek-bones, mouths not very large, well-shaped, and the lips rather full. They all have a remarkably pleasing cast of countenance, and are a great contrast to other tribes in civility of manner.

" There is little difficulty in describing the toilette of the natives,—that of the men being simplified by the sole covering of the head, the body being entirely nude. It is curious to observe among these savages the consummate vanity displayed in their head-dresses. Every tribe has a distinct and un-changing fashion for dressing the hair; and so elaborate is the *coiffure* that hair-dressing is reduced to a science. European ladies would be startled at the fact, that to perfect the *coiffure* of a man requires a period of from eight to ten years! However tedious the operation, the result is extraordinary. The Latookas wear most exquisite helmets, all of which are formed of their own hair; and are, of course, fixtures. At first sight it appears incredible, but a minute examination shows the wonderful per-severance of years in producing what must be highly inconvenient. The thick, crisp wool is woven with fine twine, formed from the bark of a tree, until it presents a thick network of felt. As the hair grows through this matted substance it is subjected to the same process, until, in the course of years, a compact substance is formed like a strong felt, about an inch and a half thick, that has been trained into the shape of a helmet. A strong rim, of about two inches deep, is formed by sewing it together with thread; and the front part of the helmet is protected by a piece of polished copper; while a piece of the same metal, shaped like the half of a bishop's mitre and about a foot in length, forms the crest.

" Although the men devote so much attention to their head-dress, the women are extremely simple. It is a curious fact, that while the men are remark-ably handsome, the women are exceedingly plain; —they are immense creatures, few being under five feet seven in height, with prodigious limbs. Their

TÉTEL IN DANGER.

superior strength to that of other tribes may be seen in the size of their water jars, which are nearly double as large as any I have seen elsewhere, containing about ten gallons; in these they fetch water from the stream about a mile distant from the town. They wear exceedingly long tails, precisely like those of horses, but made of fine twine and rubbed with red ochre and grease. They are very convenient when they creep into their huts on hands and knees. In addition to the tails, they wear a large flap of tanned leather in front. Should I ever visit that country again, I should take a great number of ' Freemasons' ' aprons for the women; these would create a perfect *furor*.

" The houses of the Latookas are generally bell-shaped, while others are precisely like huge candle-extinguishers, about twenty-five feet high. The roofs are neatly thatched, at an angle of about 75°, resting upon a circular wall about four feet high; thus the roof forms a cap descending to within two feet and a half of the ground. The doorway is only two feet two inches high, thus an entrance must be effected upon all-fours. The interior is remarkably clean, but dark, as the architects have no idea of windows. It is a curious fact that the circular form of hut is the only style of architecture adopted among all the tribes of Central Africa, and also among the Arabs of Upper Egypt; and that, although these differ more or less in the form of the roof, no tribe has ever yet sufficiently advanced to construct a window. The town of Tarrangollé is arranged with several entrances, in the shape of low archways through the palisades ; these are closed at night by large branches of the hooked thorn of the kittur bush (a species of mimosa). The main street is broad, but all others are studiously arranged to admit of only one cow, in single file, between high stockades ; thus, in the event of an attack, these narrow passages could be easily defended, and it would be impossible to drive off their vast herds of cattle unless by the main street."

A short time before this there occurred a little adventure which nearly resulted in the death of the horse Tétel. Baker had ridden to the top of a hill in order to get a view of the surrounding country, when he perceived two rhinoceroses at the base of the elevation. He at once ordered Tétel to be tied to a tree at the bottom of the hill and sent a messenger to the camp for the other horses. Scarcely was Tétel secured to the tree when the rhinoceroses were disturbed by two pigs, and at once began to walk away in a direct line towards Tétel. Suddenly one of them sighted the horse and rushed at him. Baker hurried toward the scene and when about six hundred feet off, fired. The shot missed, and just as it seemed as though Tétel must surely die he reared and breaking his bridle was out of danger in an instant. The messenger returning with the horses just at this point the party began the hunt which terminated in the death of both the rhinoceroses.

BOKIE, WIFE OF MOY.

CHAPTER XXI.

BAKER.—RESIDENCE IN LATOOKA AND OBBO.

HAVING gained the friendship of Moy, the chief of Latooka, by a few presents, Baker established himself in one of the native huts, to await his chance of pushing southward. The region he had reached was not only unknown to European explorers, but even its name had never been heard before. But a few days after his arrival, an event took place, which undoubtedly was one cause of the consideration which he secured in his later journeys. One afternoon a number of Ibrahim's men, together with the mutineers who had left Baker, set out from the village under circumstances of great mystery. A number of them returned at midnight, still silent and mysterious, and another day elapsed before the truth became known.

They had started to attack a village in the mountains, for the purpose of capturing slaves. Succeeding in this, they descended the mountains with their booty, when the news of a large herd of cattle which they had failed to discover, induced them to return.   Meanwhile the Latookas had rallied, began a fierce attack, and soon succeeded in driving the Turks down the pass.

"It was in vain that they fought; every bullet aimed at a Latooka struck a rock, behind which the enemy was hidden.   Rocks, stones, and lances were hurled at them from all sides and from above; they were forced to retreat.   The retreat ended in a panic and precipitate flight.   Hemmed in on all sides, amidst a shower of lances and stones thrown from the mountain above, the Turks fled *pêle-mêle* down the rocky and precipitous ravines.   Mistaking their route, they came to a precipice from which there was no retreat.   The screaming and yelling savages closed round them.   Fighting was useless; the natives, under cover of the numerous detached rocks, offered no mark for an aim; while the crowd of armed savages thrust them forward with wild yells to the very verge of the great precipice about five hundred feet below.   Down they fell! hurled to utter destruction by the mass of Latookas pressing onward!   A few fought to the last; but one and all were at length forced, by sheer pressure, over the edge of the cliff, and met a just reward for their atrocities.

"My men were almost green with awe, when I asked them solemnly, 'Where were the men who had deserted from me?'   Without answering a word they brought two of my guns and laid them at my feet.   They were covered with clotted blood mixed with sand, which had hardened like cement over the locks and various portions of the barrels.

My guns were all marked. As I looked at the numbers upon the stocks, I repeated aloud the names of the owners. 'Are they all dead?' I asked. 'None of the bodies can be recovered,' faltered my vakeel. 'The two guns were brought from the spot by some natives who escaped, and who saw the men fall. They are all killed.' 'Better for them had they remained with me and done their duty. The hand of God is heavy,' I replied. My men slunk away abashed, leaving the gory witnesses of defeat and death on the ground. I called Saat and ordered him to give the two guns to Richarn to clean.

"Not only my own men but the whole of Ibrahim's party were of opinion that I had some mysterious connection with the disaster that had befallen my mutineers. All remembered the bitterness of my prophecy, 'The vultures will pick their bones,' and this terrible mishap having occurred so immediately afterwards took a strong hold upon their superstitious minds. As I passed through the camp, the men would quietly exclaim, 'Wah Illahi Hawaga!' (My God Master.) To which I simply replied, 'Robiné fe!' (There is a God.) From that moment I observed an extraordinary change in the manner of both my people and those of Ibrahim, all of whom now paid us the greatest respect."

After this disaster Ibrahim was obliged to return to Gondokoro for more ammunition. During his absence the conduct of the Turks provoked an attack from the natives, but Baker avoided any serious trouble by showing his own neutrality, and having a strict watch kept at night. As there seemed to be no chance of advancing southward, he prepared a garden and sowed many seeds, and also endeavored to procure a better supply of animal food by hunting in the neighborhood.

He finally secured an interpreter, a boy of the Bari tribe, and interested himself in long conversations with the chief, Commoro, a brother of Moy. One of these dialogues is very curious, as an illustration of the mode of thinking among the Latookas. " I asked him, " says Baker, " why those slain in battle were allowed to remain unburied. He said it had always been the custom, but that he could not explain it.

" ' But,' I replied, ' why should you disturb the bones of those whom you have already buried, and expose them on the outskirts of the town?'

" ' It was the custom of our forefathers,' he answered, ' therefore we continue to observe it.'

" ' Have you no belief in a future existence after death? Is not some idea expressed in the act of exhuming the bones after the flesh is decayed?'

" *Commoro.*—' Existence *after* death! How can that be? Can a dead man get out of his grave, unless we dig him out?'

" ' Do you think man is like a beast, that dies and is ended?'

" *Commoro.*—' Certainly; an ox is stronger than a man; but he dies, and his bones last longer; they are bigger. A man's bones break quickly—he is weak.'

" ' Is not a man superior in sense to an ox? Has he not a mind to direct his actions?'

" *Commoro.*—' Some men are not so clever as an ox. Men must sow corn to obtain food, but the ox and wild animals can procure it without sowing.'

" ' Do you not know that there is a spirit within you more than flesh ? Do you not dream and wander in thought to distant places in your sleep ? Nevertheless, your body rests in one spot. How do you account for this ?'

" *Commoro* (laughing).—' Well, how do *you* account for it ? It is a thing I cannot understand ; it occurs to me every night.'

" ' The mind is independent of the body ;—the actual body can be fettered, but the mind is uncontrollable ; the body will die and will become dust, or be eaten by vultures, but the spirit will exist forever.'

" *Commoro.*—' Where will the spirit live ?'

" ' Where does fire live ? Cannot you produce a fire * by rubbing two sticks together, yet you *see* not the fire in the wood. Has not that fire, that lies harmless and unseen in the sticks, the power to consume the whole country ? Which is the stronger, the small stick that first *produces* the fire, or the fire itself ? So is the spirit the element within the body, as the element of fire exists in the stick ; the element being superior to the substance.'

" *Commoro.*—' Ha ! Can you explain what we frequently see at night when lost in the wilderness ? I have myself been lost, and wandering in the dark,

---

* The natives always produce fire by rubbing two sticks together.

I have seen a distant fire; upon approaching, the fire has vanished, and I have been unable to trace the cause—nor could I find the spot.'

" ' Have you no idea of the existence of spirits superior to either man or beast? Have you no fear of evil except from bodily causes?'

" *Commoro.*—' I am afraid of elephants and other animals when in the jungle at night, but of nothing else.'

" ' Then you believe in nothing; neither in a good nor evil spirit! And you believe that when you die it will be the end of body and spirit; that you are like other animals; and that there is no distinction between man and beast; both disappear, and end at death?'

" *Commoro.*—' Of course they do.'

" ' Do you see no difference in good and bad actions?'

" *Commoro.*—' Yes, there are good and bad in men and beasts.'

" ' Do you think that a good man and a bad must share the same fate, and alike die, and end?'

" *Commoro.*—' Yes; what else can they do? How can they help dying? Good and bad all die.'

" ' Their bodies perish, but their spirits remain; the good in happiness, the bad in misery. If you have no belief in a future state, *why should a man be good?* Why should he not be bad, if he can prosper by wickedness?

" *Commoro.*—' Most people are bad; if they are strong they take from the weak. The good people are all weak; they are good because they are not strong enough to be bad.'

" Some corn had been taken out of a sack for the horses, and a few grains lying scattered on the ground, I tried the beautiful metaphor of St. Paul as an example of a future state. Making a small hole with my finger in the ground, I placed a grain within it : ' That,' I said, ' represents you when you· die.' Covering it with earth, I continued, ' That grain will decay, but from it will rise the plant that will produce a reappearance of the original form.'

" *Commoro.*—' Exactly so ; that I understand. But the *original* grain does *not* rise again ; it rots like the dead man, and is ended ; the fruit produced is not the same grain that we buried, but the *production* of that grain : so it is with man—I die, and decay, and am ended ; but my children grow up like the fruit of the grain. Some men have no children, and some grains perish without fruit ; then all are ended.'

" I was obliged to change the subject of conversation. In this wild, naked savage there was not even a superstition upon which to found a religious feeling ; there was a belief in matter ; and to his understanding everything was *material.* It was extraordinary to find so much clearness of perception combined with such complete obtuseness to anything ideal."

Thus, with an occasional elephant-hunt, the days passed away. Ibrahim returned from Gondokoro, fell sick, and was cured by Baker's prescriptions—a circumstance which increased the latter's influence.

But troubles between the Turks and Latookas became frequent, and the explorer's situation was very precarious. Finally some natives arrived from a country named Obbo, lying to the southwest, exactly in the direction which Baker wished to pursue. He determined to accompany Ibrahim thither, as the people were said to be friendly; and set out on the 2nd of May, leaving the greater part of his stores behind, in the charge of a few men, and under the protection of the chief.

After two days' march across valleys and over rugged granite hills, they reached a high mountain chain which bounds the Latooka country on the south. Here an entirely new region unfolded itself as they advanced. "Winding through the very bosom of the mountains, well covered with forest until the bare granite peaks towered above all vegetation to the height of about 5,000 feet, we continued through narrow valleys bordered by abrupt spurs of the mountains from 1,500 to 2,000 feet high. On the peak of each was a village; evidently these impregnable positions were chosen for security. At length the great ascent was to be made, and for two hours we toiled up a steep zigzag pass. The air was most invigorating; beautiful wild flowers, some of which were highly scented, ornamented the route, and innumerable wild grape-vines hung in festoons from tree to tree. We were now in an elevated country on the range of mountains dividing the lower lands of Latooka from the high lands of Obbo. We arrived at the summit of the pass about 2,500 feet above the Latooka valley. In addition to the

wild flowers were numerous fruits, all good ; especially a variety of custard apple, and a full-flavored
yellow plum. The grapes were in most promising
bunches, but unripe. The scenery was very fine ;
to the east and southeast, masses of high mountains,
while to the west and south were vast tracts of park-
like country of intense green."

Twelve miles beyond the pass was the village
of Obbo, in Lat. 4° N., the general elevation of the
country being 3,674 feet above the sea, and the
average temperature 76°. It would be a healthy
country, were the population sufficiently large to
keep the jungles cleared ; but they form a damp,
almost impenetrable wilderness, inhabited by elephants, rhinoceros and buffaloes.

" The chief of Obbo," he relates, " came to meet
us with several of his head men. He was an extra-
ordinary-looking man, about fifty-eight or sixty
years of age ; but, far from possessing the dignity
usually belonging to a grey head, he acted the
buffoon for our amusement, and might have been a
clown in a pantomime.

" The Obbo natives were a great and agreeable
change after the Latookas, as they never asked for
presents. Although the old chief, Katchiba, be-
haved more like a clown than a king, he was
much respected by his people. He holds his authority over his subjects as general rain-maker and
sorcerer. Should a subject displease him, or refuse
him a gift, he curses his goats and fowls, or threat-
ens to wither his crops, and the fear of these inflic-
tions reduces the discontented. There are no spe-

cific taxes, but he occasionally makes a call upon the country for a certain number of goats and supplies. These are generally given, as Katchiba is a knowing old diplomatist, and he times his demands with great judgment.

"Notwithstanding his magic, Katchiba was not a bad man : he was remarkably civil, and very proud at my having paid him a visit. He gave me much information regarding the country, but assured me that I should not be able to travel south for many months, as it would be quite impossible to cross the Asua River during the rainy season ; he therefore proposed that I should form a camp at Obbo, and reside there until the rains should cease. It was now May, thus I was invited to postpone my advance south until December.

"I determined to make a reconnaissance south towards the dreaded Asua, or, as the Obbo people pronounced it, the Achua River, and to return to my fixed camp. Accordingly I arranged to leave Mrs. Baker at Obbo with a guard of eight men, while I should proceed south without baggage, excepting a change of clothes and a cooking pot. Katchiba promised to take the greatest care of her, and to supply her with all she might require ; offering to become personally responsible for her safety ; he agreed to place a spell upon the door of our hut, that nothing evil should enter it during my absence. It was a snug little dwelling, about nine feet in diameter, and perfectly round ; the floor well cemented with cow-dung and clay, and the walls about four feet six inches in height, formed of mud and sticks, likewise polished off with cow-dung. The door had enlarged, and it was now a very imposing entrance of about four feet high, and a great contrast to the surrounding hut or dog-kennel with two feet height of doorway.

"On the 7th of May I started with three men, and taking a course south, I rode through a most lovely country, within five miles of the base, and parallel with the chain of the Madi Mountains. There was abundance of beautiful flowers, especially of orchidaceous plants ; the country was exceedingly park-like and well wooded, but generally overgrown with grass then about six feet high.

"I reached the Atabbi River about eighteen miles from Obbo. This is a fine perennial stream flowing from the Madi Mountains towards the west, forming an affluent of the Asua River. There was a good ford, with a hard gravel and rocky bottom, over which the horse partly waded and occasionally swam. There were fresh tracks of immense herds of elephants with which the country abounded, and I heard them trumpeting in the distance. Ascending rising ground in perfectly open prairie on the opposite side of Atabbi, I saw a dense herd of about two hundred elephants—they were about a mile distant, and were moving slowly through the high grass.

"On the following morning I started at daybreak, and after a march of about thirteen miles through the same park-like and uninhabited country as that of the preceding day, I reached the country of Farajoke, and arrived at the foot of a rocky hill, upon the summit of which was a large village. I was met by the chief and several of his people leading a goat, which was presented to me, and killed immediately as an offering, close to the feet of my horse. The chief carried a fowl, holding it by the legs, with its head downwards; he approached my horse, and stroked his fore-feet with the fowl, and then made a circle around him by dragging it upon the ground; my feet were then stroked with the fowl in the same manner as those of the horse, and I was requested to stoop, so as to enable him to wave the bird around my head; this completed, it was also waved round my horse's head, who showed his appreciation of the ceremony by rearing and lashing out behind.

"I was now conducted to the village. It was defended by a high bamboo fence, and was miserably dirty, forming a great contrast to the clean dwellings of the Bari and Latooka tribes. The hill upon which the village was built was about eighty feet above the general level of the country, and afforded a fine view of the surrounding landscape. On the east was the chain of Madi Mountains, the base well wooded, while to the south all was fine open pasturage of sweet herbage, about a foot high, a totally different grass to the rank vegetation we had passed through. The country was undulating, and every rise was crowned by a village. Although the name of the district is Farajoke, it is comprised in the extensive country of Sooli, together with the Shoggo and Madi tribes, all towns being under the command of petty chiefs.

" The general elevation of the country was 3,966 feet above the sea-level, 292 feet higher than Obbo."

Finding it impossible to cross the Asua River, on account of high water, Baker returned to Obbo, where his wife had, in the meantime, been kindly treated by the old chief. " The rains," he says, " were terrific; the mornings were invariably fine, but the clouds gathered upon the mountains soon after noon and ended daily in a perfect deluge. Not being able to proceed south, I determined to return to my head-quarters at Latooka, and to wait for the dry season. I had made the reconnaissance to Farajoke, in latitude 3° 32', and I saw my way clear for the future, provided my animals should remain in good condition. Accordingly, on the 21st of May we started for Latooka in company with Ibrahim and his men, who were thoroughly sick of the Obbo climate.

" Before parting, a ceremony had to be performed by Katchiba. His brother was to be our guide, and he was to receive power to control the elements as deputy-magician during the journey, lest we should be wetted by the storms, and the torrents should be so swollen as to be impassable.

" With great solemnity Katchiba broke a branch from a tree, upon the leaves of which he spat in several places. This branch, thus blessed with holy water, was laid upon the ground, and a fowl was dragged around it by the chief; and our horses were then operated on precisely in the same manner as had been enacted at Farajoke. This ceremony completed, he handed the branch to his bro ther (our guide), who received it with much gravity, in addition to a magic whistle of antelope's horn that he suspended from his neck. All the natives wore whistles similar in appearance, being simply small horns in which they blew, the sound of which was considered either to attract or to drive away rain, at the option of the whistler. No whistle was supposed to be effective unless it had been blessed by the great magician Katchiba. The ceremony being over, all commenced whistling with all their might; and taking leave of Katchiba, with an assurance that we should again return, we started amidst a din of " toot too too-ing " upon our journey."

They returned to Latooka without adventure, found their stores in good condition, and prepared themselves to endure the monotony of a long residence there during the rainy season, varied only by the deaths of horses and camels, attacks of fever, and quarrels between the Turks and natives, which always more or less disturbed their security. A month of this life was enough, and on the 23rd of June Baker started again with his men and supplies for the more peaceable country of Obbo. Mrs. Baker was so prostrated by the fever that she was obliged to be carried in a litter. We extract from his journal the following notes of his arrival there, and experiences during the succeeding six months :

"On arrival at my former hut I found a great change ; the grass was at least ten feet high, and my little camp was concealed in the rank vegetation. Old Katchiba came to meet us, but brought nothing, as he said the Turks had eaten up the country. An extract from my journal, dated July 1st, explains the misery of our position.

" 'This Obbo country is now a land of starvation. The natives refuse to supply provision for beads ; nor will they barter anything unless in exchange for flesh. This is the curse that the Turks have brought upon the country by stealing cattle and throwing them away wholesale. We have literally nothing to eat except tullaboon, a small bitter grain used in lieu of corn by the natives : there is no game ; if it existed, shooting would be impossible, as the grass is impenetrable.'

" The wet herbage disagreed with my baggage animals. Innumerable flies appeared, including the Tsetse, and in a few weeks the donkeys had no hair left, either on their ears or legs ; they dropped and died one by one. It was in vain that I erected sheds and lighted fires ; nothing would protect them from the flies. The moment the fires were lit, the animals would rush wildly into the smoke, from which nothing would drive them, and in the clouds of imaginary protection they would remain all day, refusing food. On the 16th of July my last horse, Mouse, died ; he had a very long tail, for which I obtained *a cow in exchange.* Nothing was prized so highly as horses' tails, the hairs being used for stringing beads, and also for making tufts as ornaments, to be suspended from the elbows. It was highly fashionable in Obbo for the men to wear such tufts, formed of the bushy ends of cow's-tails.

It was also ' the thing ' to wear six or eight polished rings of iron, fastened so tightly round the throat as to almost choke the wearer, somewhat resembling dog-collars.

"*Aug.* 13*th.*—I had a long examination of a slave woman, Bacheeta, belonging to one of Koorshid's men. She had been sent two years ago by the king, Kamrasi, from Unyoro, as a spy among the traders, with orders to attract them to the country if appearances were favorable, but to return with a report should they be dangerous people.

"On her arrival at Faloro, Debono's people captured her, and she was eventually sold to her present owner. She speaks Aarbic, having learnt it from the traders' people. She declares that Magungo, the place of which I have heard so much, is only four days' hard marching for a native, direct from Faloro, but eight days' for the Turks : and that it is equi-distant from Faloro and from Kamrasi's capital in Unyoro. She had heard of the Luta Nzige, as reported to Speke, but she knew it only by the name of ' Kara-wootan-Nzige.'

" She corroborated the accounts I had formerly received, of large boats arriving with Arabs at Magungo, and she described the lake as a ' white sheet as far as the eye could reach.' She particularized it as a peculiar water, that was unlike other waters, as it would ' come up to a water-jar, if put upon the shore, and carry it away and break it.' By this description I understood ' waves.' She also described the ' Gondokoro River,' or While Nile, as flowing

into and out of the lake, and she spoke of a ' great roar of water, that fell from the sky.'

" *Aug.* 23*rd.*—My last camel died to-day ; thus all my horses and camels are dead, and only eight donkeys remain out of twenty-one ; most of these will die, if not all. There can be no doubt that the excessive wet in all the food, owing to the constant rain and dew, is the principal cause of disease. The camels, horses, and donkeys of the Soudan, all thrive in the hot dry air of that country, and are unsuited for this damp climate.

" Had I been without transport animals, my expedition could not have left Gondokoro, as there was no possibility for procuring porters. I had always expected that my animals would die, but I had hoped they would have carried me to the equator : this they would have accomplished during the two months of comparative dry weather following my arrival at Gondokoro, had not the mutiny thwarted all my plans, and thrown me into the wet season. My animals have delivered me at Obbo, and have died in inaction, instead of wearing out upon the road. Had I been able to start direct from Gondokoro, as I had intended, my animals would have delivered me in Kamrasi's country before the arrival of the heavy rains.

" *Oct.* 6*th.*—I have examined my only remaining donkey ; he is a picture of misery—eyes and nose running, coat staring, and he is about to start to join his departed comrades ; he has packed up for his last journey. With his loose skin hanging to his withered frame he looked like the British lion on the shield over the door of the Khartoum consulate. In that artistic effort the lion was equally lean and ragged, having perhaps been thus represented by the artist as a pictorial allusion to the smallness of the Consul's pay ; the illustration over the shabby gateway utters, ' Behold my leanness ! £150 per annum !'

"I feel a touch of the poetic stealing over me when I look at my departing donkey. 'I never loved a dear gazelle,' etc.; but the practical question, ' Who is to carry the portmanteau ?' remains unanswered. I do not believe the Turks have any intention of going to Kamrasi's country ; they are afraid, as they have heard that he is a powerful king, and they fear the restrictions that power will place upon their felonious propensities. In that case I shall go on without them ; but they have deceived me, by borrowing 165 lbs. of beads which they cannot repay ; this puts me to much inconvenience. The Asua River is still impassable, according to native reports ; this will prevent a general advance south. Should the rains cease, the river will fall rapidly, and I shall make a forward move and escape this prison of high grass and inaction.

"For months we dragged on a miserable existence at Obbo, wrecked by fever ; the quinine exhausted ; thus the disease worried me almost to death, returning at intervals of a few days. Fortunately my wife did not suffer so much as I did. I had nevertheless prepared for the journey south; and as travelling on foot would have been

impossible in our weak state, I had purchased and
trained three oxen in lieu of horses. They were
named ' Beef,' ' Steaks,' and ' Suet.' ' Beef ' was a
magnificent animal, but having been bitten by the
flies, he so lost his condition that I changed his
name to ' Bones.' We were ready to start, and the
natives reported that early in January the Asua
would be fordable. I had arranged with Ibrahim
that he should supply me with porters for payment
in copper bracelets, and that he should accompany
me with one hundred men to Kamrasi's country,
(Unyoro,) on condition that he would restrain his
people from all misdemeanors, and that they should
be entirely subservient to me. It was the month of
December, and during the nine months that I
had been in correspondence with his party, I had
succeeded in acquiring an extraordinary influence.
Although my camp was nearly three quarters of a
mile from their zareeba, I had been besieged daily
for many months, for everything that was wanted ;
my camp was a kind of general store that appeared
to be inexhaustible. I gave all that I had with a
good grace, and thereby gained the goodwill of the
robbers, especially as my large medicine-chest contained a supply of drugs that rendered me in their
eyes a physician of the first importance. I had
been very successful with my patients ; and the medicines that I generally used being those which
produced a very decided effect, both the Turks and
natives considered them with perfect faith. There
was seldom any difficulty in prognosticating the effect of tartar emetic, and this became the favorite

drug that was almost daily applied for; a dose of three grains enchanting the patient, who always advertised my fame by saying, 'He told me I should be sick, and, by Allah! there was no mistake about it.' "

Some little time before this Baker witnessed a very exciting hippopotamus hunt conducted by the natives. A herd was found enjoying themselves in the water, and the negroes at once proceeded to attack it. Two of them swimming out to the herd unperceived, as closely as possible, hurled their harpoons at the animals. One missed, but the other became deeply imbedded in the flesh of a large bull. With some difficulty, on account of the frantic struggles of the beast, the other blacks of the party succeeded in attaching a strong rope to the float which is always connected with the harpoon in this kind of hunting, and proceeded to drag him to the shore. It was a tremendous pull, and when they had brought him to shallow water he suddenly changed his tactics and rushed on shore at the men. A dozen lances cast into his open jaws had little effect, but sand thrown into his eyes compelled him to retreat. Six times more this was repeated, when Baker, at the request of the natives, finished the struggle by a shot from his favorite rifle.

SCENE AT THE CLOSE OF A HIPPOPOTAMUS HUNT.

CHAPTER XXII.

BAKER.—THE MARCH TO KAMRASI'S COUNTRY.

AT length, after six months of tedious waiting at Obbo, the rainy season ceased. Ibrahim, who had finally resolved to accompany Baker to Unyoro, the country of king Kamrasi, prepared his caravan for the start, and there was apparently no obstacle in the way. As far as Farajoke, Baker was already familiar with the country. He thus describes the start from Obbo, and the journey into the regions beyond :

" A bad attack of fever laid me up until the 31st of December. On the first day of January, 1864, I was hardly able to stand, and was nearly worn out at the very time that I required my strength, as we were to start south in a few days.

" Although my quinine had been long since exhausted, I had reserved ten grains to enable me to start in case the fever should attack me at the time of departure. I now swallowed my last dose, and on 3rd January I find the following note in my journal : 'All ready for a start to-morrow. I trust the year 1864 will bring better luck than the past, that having been the most annoying that I have ever experienced, and full of fever. I hope now to reach Kamrasi's country in a fortnight, and to obtain guides from him direct to the lake. My Latooka, to whom I have been very kind, has absconded; there is no difference in any of these savages; if hungry, they will fawn upon you, and when filled, they will desert. I believe that ten years' residence in the Soudan and this country would spoil an Angel, and would turn the best heart to stone.'

"It was difficult to procure porters, therefore I left all my effects at my camp in charge of two of my men, and I determined to travel light, without the tent, and to take little beyond ammunition and cooking utensils. Ibrahim left forty-five men in his zareeba, and on the 5th of January we started. Mrs. Baker rode her ox, but my animal being very shy, I ordered him to be driven for about a mile with the others to accustom him to the crowd; not approving of the expedition, he bolted into the high grass with my English saddle, and I never saw him again. In my weak state I had to walk. We had not gone far when a large fly fastened upon Mrs. Baker's ox, just by his tail, the effect of which was to produce so sudden a kick and plunge, that he threw her to the ground and hurt her considerably; she accordingly changed the animal, and rode a splendid ox that Ibrahim very civilly offered.

"In three days' march from this point through beautiful park-like country, we arrived at the Asua River. The entire route from Farajoke had been a gentle descent, and I found this point of the Asua in lat. N. 3° 12′ to be 2,875 feet above the sea-level, 1,091 feet lower than Farajoke. The river was a hundred and twenty paces broad, and from the bed to the top of the perpendicular banks was about fifteen feet. At this season it was almost dry, and a narrow channel of about six inches deep flowed through the centre of the otherwise exhausted river. The bed was much obstructed by rocks, and the inclination was so rapid that I could readily conceive the impossibility of crossing it during the rains. It formed the great drain of the country, all its waters flowing to the Nile, but during the dry months it was most insignificant. The country between Farajoke and the Asua, although lovely, was very thinly populated, and the only villages that I saw were built upon low hills of bare granite, which lay in huge piles of disjointed fragments.

" After a delay of a few days, we started at daybreak on 13th January, and, ascending the whole way, we reached Shooa, in latitude 3° 4′. The route throughout had been of the same park-like character, interspersed with occasional hills of fine granite, piled in the enormous blocks so characteristic of that stone.

" Shooa was a lovely place. A fine granite mountain ascended in one block in a sheer precipice for about 800 feet from its base, perfectly abrupt on the eastern side, while the other portions of the mountain were covered with fine forest trees, and picturesquely dotted over with villages. This country formed a natural park, remarkably well watered by numerous rivulets, ornamented with fine timber, and interspersed with numerous high rocks of granite, which from a distance produced the effect of ruined castles.

"By Casella's thermometer, I determined the altitude of Shooa to be 3,877 feet—1,002 feet above the Asua River, and 89 feet lower than Farajoke. These observations of the thermometer agreed with the natural appearance of the country, the Asua River forming the main drain in a deep valley, into which innumerable rivulets convey the drainage from both north and south. Accordingly, the Asua, receiving the Atabbi River, which is the main drain of the western face of the Madi Mountains, and the entire drainage of the Madi and Shooa countries, together with that of extensive countries to the east of Shooa, including the rivers Chombi and Udat, from Lira and Umiro, it becomes a tremendous torrent so long as the rains continue, and conveys a grand volume of water to the Nile; but the inclination of all these countries tending rapidly to the northwest, the bed of the Asua River partakes of the general incline, and so quickly empties after the cessation of the rains that it becomes *nil* as a river. By the mean of several observations I determined the latitude of Shooa 3° 04', longitude 32° 04' E. We were now about twelve miles south of Debono's outpost, Faloro.

"Two days after our arrival at Shooa, the whole of our Obbo porters absconded: they had heard that we were bound for Kamrasi's country, and having received exaggerated accounts of his power from the Shooa people, they had determined upon retreat : thus we were at once unable to proceed unless we could procure porters from Shooa. This was exceedingly difficult, as Kamrasi was well known here, and was not loved. His country was known as 'Quanda,' and I at once recognized the corruption of Speke's 'Uganda.' The slave woman, 'Bacheeta,' who had formerly given me in Obbo so much information concerning Kamrasi's country, was to be our interpreter ; but we also had the luck to discover a lad who had formerly been employed by Mahamed in Faloro, who also spoke the language of Quanda, and had learnt a little Arabic. I now discovered that the slave woman Bacheeta had formerly been in the service of a chief named Sali, who had been killed by Kamrasi. Sali was a friend of Rionga, (Kamrasi's greatest enemy,) and I had been warned by Speke not to set foot upon Rionga's territory, or all travelling in Unyoro would be cut off. I plainly saw that Bacheeta was in favor of Rionga, as a friend of the murdered Sali, by whom she had had two children, and that she would most likely tamper with the guide, and that we should be led to Rionga instead of to Kamrasi. There were ' wheels within wheels.' "

There were signs that Ibrahim's men would also rebel or desert ; whereupon Baker guaranteed that Ibrahim should receive at least 10,000 pounds of ivory, if he would march at once to Kamrasi's country. The latter, who was now entirely friendly to the expedition, agreed, and thenceforth acted in good faith. " On the 18th of January, 1864," says Baker, " we left Shooa. The pure air of that country had invigorated us, and I was so improved in strength that I enjoyed the excitement of the launch into unknown lands. The Turks knew nothing of the route south, and I accordingly took the lead of the entire party. I had come to a distinct understanding with Ibrahim that Kamrasi's country should belong to *me;* not an act of felony would be permitted ; all were to be under my government, and I would insure him at least 100 cantars of tusks.

" Eight miles of agreeable march through the usual park-like country brought us to the village of Fatiko, situated upon a splendid plateau of rock upon elevated ground with beautiful granite cliffs, bordering a level table-land of fine grass that would have formed a race-course. The high rocks were covered with natives, perched upon the outline like a flock of ravens.

" We halted to rest under some fine trees growing among large isolated blocks of granite and gneiss.

" In a short time the natives assembled around us : they were wonderfully friendly, and insisted upon a personal introduction to both myself and Mrs. Baker. We were thus compelled to hold a levee ; not the passive and cold ceremony of Europe, but a most active undertaking, as each native that was introduced performed the salaam of his country, by seizing both my hands and raising my arms three times to their full stretch above my head. After about one hundred Fatikos had been thus gratified by our submission to this infliction, and our arms had been subjected to at least three hundred stretches each, I gave the order to saddle

A LION HUNT.

the oxen immediately, and we escaped a further proof of Fatiko affection that was already preparing, as masses of natives were streaming down the rocks hurrying to be introduced. Notwithstanding the fatigue of the ceremony, I took a great fancy to these poor people : they had prepared a quantity of merissa and a sheep for our lunch, which they begged us to remain and enjoy before we started ; but the pumping action of half a village not yet gratified by a presentation was too much ; and, mounting our oxen, with aching shoulders we bade adieu to Fatiko.

"Descending the picturesque rocky hill of Fatiko, we entered upon a totally distinct country. We had now before us an interminable sea of prairies, covering to the horizon a series of gentle undulations inclining from east to west.

"I led the way on foot from the hour we left Fatiko, as, the country being uninhabited for five days' march between that place and Kamrasi's, the men had more faith in my steering by the compass than they had in the native guide. I felt sure that we were being deceived, and that the woman Bacheeta had directed the guide to take us to Rionga's. Accordingly on the fourth night, when Canopus was in the meridian, I asked our conductor to point by a star in the direction of Karuma Falls. He immediately pointed to Canopus, which I knew by Speke's map should be the direction of Rionga's islands, and I charged him with the deceit. He appeared very much astonished, and asked me 'why I wanted a guide if I knew the way?' confessing that Karuma

Falls were 'a little to the east of the star.' I
I thanked Speke and Grant at that moment, and
upon many other occasions, for the map they had so
generously given me!"

At length, on the morning of the 22nd of January,
a fog hanging over a distant valley, announced the
vicinity of the White Nile, and the same day the
caravan reached the banks of the stream, which
they found to be about 150 yards wide, flowing
rapidly between rocky islands.

"The slave woman, Bacheeta, secretly instructed
the guide to lead us to Rionga instead of Kamrasi,
precisely as I had suspected. The Karuma Falls are
a day's march east of this, at which point we must
cross the river. Obtained a clear observation of
Capella, meridian altitude showing latitude 2° 18'
N.

"We could get no supplies from Rionga's people,
who returned to their island after their conference
with Bacheeta, promising to send us some plantains
and a basket of flour; but upon gaining their secure retreat they shouted, ' that we might go to
Kamrasi if we liked, but that we should receive no
assistance from them.'

"Early in the morning we started for Karuma.
This part of the forest was perfectly open, as the
grass had been burnt by the natives about three
weeks ago, and the young shoots of the vines were
appearing from the scorched roots; among other
plants was an abundance of the prickly asparagus,
of which I collected a basketful. Nothing could
exceed the beauty of the march. Our course

through the noble forest was parallel with the river, that roared beneath us on our right in a succession of rapids and falls between high cliffs covered with groves of bananas and varieties of palms, including the graceful wild date—the certain sign of either marsh or river. The Victoria Nile or Somerset River was about 150 yards wide ; the cliffs on the south side were higher than those upon the north, being 150 feet above the river. These heights were thronged with natives, who had collected from the numerous villages that ornamented the cliffs situated among groves of plantains ; they were armed with spears and shields ; the population ran parallel to our line of march, shouting and gesticulating as though daring us to cross the river.

" After a most enjoyable march through the exciting scene of the glorious river crashing over innumerable falls—and in many places ornamented with rocky islands, upon which were villages and plantain groves—we at length approached the Karuma Falls, close to the village of Atada above the ferry. The heights were crowded with natives, and a canoe was sent across to within parleying distance of our side, as the roar of the rapids prevented our voices from being heard except at a short distance. Bacheeta now explained, that ' *Speke's brother* had arrived from his country to pay Kamrasi a visit, and had brought him valuable presents.'

" ' Why has he brought so many men with him ?' inquired the people from the canoe.

" ' There are so many presents for the M'Kamma

(King) that he has many men to carry them,' shouted Bacheeta.

" ' Let us look at him!' cried the head man in the boat : having prepared for the introduction by changing my clothes in a grove of plantains for my dressing-room, and altering my costume to a tweed suit, something similar to that worn by Speke, I climbed up a high and almost perpendicular rock that formed a natural pinnacle on the face of the cliff, and, waving my cap to the crowd on the opposite side, I looked almost as imposing as Nelson in Trafalgar Square.

" I instructed Bacheeta, who climbed up the giddy height after me, to shout to the people that an English lady, my wife, had also arrived and that we wished immediately to be presented to the king and his family, as we had come to thank him for his kind treatment of Speke and Grant, who had arrived safe in their own country. Upon this being explained and repeated several times, the canoe approached the shore.

" I ordered all our people to retire, and to conceal themselves among the plantains, that the natives might not be startled by so imposing a force, while Mrs. Baker and I advanced alone to meet Kamrasi's people, who were men of some importance. Upon landing through the high reeds, they immediately recognized the similarity of my beard and general complexion to that of Speke ; and their welcome was at once displayed by the most extravagant dancing and gesticulating with lances and shields, as though intending to attack, rushing at

me with the points of their lances thrust close to
my face, and shouting and singing in great excitement.

Nevertheless, these Unyoro hesitated to permit
Baker to cross the river, fearing some treachery, on
account of his Turkish companions. He thereupon
showed them the magnificent presents he had
brought for King Kamrasi, and they begged him
not to return, promising to obtain permission from
the king. Late in the evening, the native messengers returned and agreed to take Baker with his
wife and servants, Ibrahim being temporarily included among the latter.

" It was quite dark when we started. The canoe
was formed of a large hollow tree, capable of holding twenty people, and the natives paddled us
across the rapid current just below the falls. A
large fire was blazing upon the opposite shore, on a
level with the river, to guide us to the landing-place.
Gliding through a narrow passage in the reeds, we
touched the shore and landed upon a slippery rock,
close to the fire, amidst a crowd of people, who immediately struck up a deafening welcome with horns
and flageolets, and marched us up the steep face of
the rocky cliff through a dark grove of bananas.
Torches led the way, followed by a long file of
spearmen ; then came the noisy band and ourselves
—I towing my wife up the precipitous path, while
my few attendants followed behind with a number
of natives who had volunteered to carry the luggage.

" On arrival at the top of the cliff, we were

about 180 feet above the river, and after a walk
of about a quarter of a mile, we were triumphantly led into the heart of the village, and halted in
a small courtyard in front of the head man's residence.

"A bundle of straw was laid on the ground for
Mrs. Baker and myself, and, in lieu of other beds,
the ground was our resting-place. It was bitterly
cold that night, as the guns were packed up in the
large blanket, and, not wishing to expose them, we
were contented with a Scotch plaid each. Ibrahim, Saat, and Richarn watched by turns.

"On the following morning an immense crowd of
natives thronged to see us. There was a very beautiful tree about a hundred yards from the village, capable of shading upwards of a thousand men, and I
proposed that we should sit beneath this protection
and hold a conference. The head man of the village gave us a large hut with a grand doorway of
about seven feet high, of which my wife took possession, while I joined the crowd at the tree.
There were about six hundred men seated respectfully on the ground around me, while I sat with
my back to the huge knotty trunk, with Ibrahim
and Richarn at a few paces distant.

"Hardly had the few boatmen departed, than
some one shouted suddenly, and the entire crowd
sprang to their feet and rushed towards the hut
where I had left Mrs. Baker. For the moment I
thought that the hut was on fire, and I joined the
crowd and arrived at the doorway, where I found a
tremendous press to see some extraordinary sight.

Every one was squeezing for the best place; and, driving them on one side, I found the wonder that had excited their curiosity. The hut being very dark, my wife had employed her solitude during my conference with the natives in dressing her hair at the doorway, which, being very long and blonde, was suddenly noticed by some natives—a shout was given, the rush described had taken place, and the hut was literally mobbed by the crowd of savages eager to see the extraordinary novelty. The Gorilla would not make a greater stir in London streets than we appeared to create at Atada.

"By astronomical observation I determined the latitude of Atada at Karuma Falls, 2° 15'; and by Casella's thermometer, the altitude of the river level above the sea 3,996 feet.

"After the disgusting naked tribes that we had been travelling amongst for more than twelve months, it was a delightful change to find ourselves in comparative civilization; this was evinced not only in the decency of clothing, but also in the manufactures of the country. The blacksmiths were exceedingly clever, and used iron hammers instead of stone; they drew fine wire from the thick copper and brass wire that they received from Zanzibar; their bellows were the same as those used by the more savage tribes—but the greatest proof of their superior civilization was exhibited in their pottery."

After a delay of a week, a message was received from Kamrasi, inviting Baker to his capital, and on the 29th of January the deputation arrived at the falls.   Baker continues :

" I received them standing ; and after thorough inspection I was pronounced to be ' Speke's own brother,' and all were satisfied.   However, the business was not yet over ; plenty of talk, and another delay of four days, was declared necessary until the king should reply to the satisfactory message about to be sent.   Losing all patience, I stormed, declaring Kamrasi to be mere dust ; while a white man was a king in comparison.   I ordered all my luggage to be conveyed immediately to the canoe, and declared that I would return immediately to my own country ; that I did not wish to see any one so utterly devoid of manners as Kamrasi, and that no other white man would ever visit his kingdom.

. " The effect was magical !   I rose hastily to depart.   The chiefs implored, declaring that Kamrasi would kill them all if I retreated ; to prevent which misfortune they secretly instructed the canoe to be removed.   I was in a great rage ; and about 400 natives, who were present, scattered in all quarters, thinking that there would be a serious quarrel.   I told the chiefs that nothing should stop me, and that I would seize the canoe by force unless my whole party should be brought over from the opposite side that instant.   This was agreed upon.   One of Ibrahim's men exchanged and drank blood from the arm of Speke's deserter, who was Kamrasi's representative ; and peace thus firmly established, several canoes were at once employed, and sixty of our men were brought across the river before sun-

set. The natives had nevertheless taken the precaution to send all their women away from the village."

Entrance into the country having been thus successfully effected, the caravan was only delayed by
the illness of Baker and his wife, who were prostrated with fever. The march was very slow, but
on the 10th of February they arrived at Mrooli,
Kamrasi's capital, at the junction of the Nile with
the Kafue or Kafoor River. Baker's description of
the place corresponds exactly with that given by
Speke, and his experience of the cunning and rapacity of the savage monarch resembled that received by the latter. He thus describes his reception : he was suffering from fever at the time, and
unable to walk :

" Upon my approach, the crowd gave way, and I
was shortly laid on a mat at the king's feet. He
was a fine-looking man, but with a peculiar expression of countenance, owing to his extremely prominent eyes ; he was about six feet high, beautifully
clean, and was dressed in a long robe of bark cloth
most gracefully folded. The nails of his hands and
feet were carefully attended, and his complexion
was about as dark a brown as that of an Abyssinian.
He sat upon a copper stool placed upon a carpet of
leopard skins, and he was surrounded by about ten
of his principal chiefs.

" Our interpreter, Bacheeta, now informed him
who I was, and what were my intentions. He said
that he was sorry I had been so long on the road,
but that he had been obliged to be cautious, having

been deceived by Debono's people.   I replied that
I was an Englishman, a friend of Speke and Grant
—that they had described the reception they had
met with from him, and that I had come to thank
him, and to offer him a few presents in return for
his kindness, and to request him to give me a guide
to the Lake Luta Nzige.   He laughed at the name,
and repeated it several times with his chiefs,—he
then said, it was not *Luta*, but *M-wootan* Nzige—
but that it was *six months'* journey from Mrooli, and
that in my weak condition I could not possibly
reach it ; that I should die upon the road, and that
the king of my country would perhaps imagine that
I had been murdered, and might invade his territory.
I replied, that I was weak with the toil of years in
the hot countries of Africa, but that I was in search
of the great lake, and should not return until I had
succeeded ;   that I had no king, but a powerful
Queen who watched over all her subjects, and that
no Englishman could be murdered with impunity ;
therefore he should send me to the lake without delay, and there would be the lesser chance of my
dying in his country.

"I explained that the river Nile flowed for a distance of two years' journey through wonderful countries, and reached the sea, from which many valuable articles would be sent to him in exchange for
ivory, could I only discover the great lake.   As a
proof of this, I had brought him a few curiosities
that I trusted he would accept, and I regretted that
the impossibility of procuring porters had necessi-

A RHINOCEROS AT BAY.

tated the abandonment of others that had been better intended for him.

"I ordered the men to unpack a Persian carpet, which was spread upon the ground before him. I then gave him an Abbia, (large white Cashmere mantle,) a red silk netted sash, a pair of scarlet Turkish shoes, several pairs of socks, a double-barrelled gun and ammunition, and a great heap of first-class beads made up into gorgeous necklaces and girdles. He took very little notice of the presents, but requested that the gun might be fired off. This was done to the utter confusion of the crowd, who rushed away in such haste, that they tumbled over each other like so many rabbits ; this delighted the king, who, although himself startled, now roared with laughter. He told me that I must be hungry and thirsty, therefore he hoped I would accept something to eat and drink : accordingly he presented me with seventeen cows, twenty pots of sour plantain cider, and many loads of unripe plantains. I inquired whether Speke had left a medicine-chest with him. He replied that it was a very feverish country, and that he and his people had used all the medicine. Thus my last hope of quinine was cut off. I had always trusted to receive a supply from the king, as Speke had told me that he had left a bottle with him. It was quite impossible to obtain any information from him, and I was carried back to my hut, where I found Mrs. Baker lying down with fever, and neither could render assistance to the other."

During the following twelve days Baker endeavored to procure men and guides for the journey to the lake. Present after present was demanded by the king, and given, but the assistance required was still delayed. Finally, on the 22nd of February, Baker writes:

" Kamrasi promised to send me porters, and that we should start for the lake to-day, but there is no sign of preparation; thus am I delayed when every day is so precious. Added to this trouble, the woman that I have as an interpreter *will not speak*, being the most sulky individual I ever encountered. In the evening Kamrasi sent to say he would give a guide and porters to-morrow morning. It is impossible to depend upon him."

" After some delay we were at length honored by a visit from Kamrasi, accompanied by a number of his people, and he promised that we should start on the following day. He pointed out a chief and a guide who were to have us in their charge, and who were to see that we obtained all that we should require. He concluded, as usual, by asking for my watch and for a number of beads; the latter I gave him, together with a quantity of ammunition for his guns. He showed me a beautiful double-barrelled rifle by Blissett, that Speke had given him. I wished to secure this to give to Speke on my return to England, as he had told me, when at Gondokoro, how he had been obliged to part with that and many other articles solely against his will. I therefore offered to give him three common double-barrelled guns in exchange for the rifle. This he declined, as he was quite aware of the difference in

ESCAPE OF TWO RHINOCEROSES.

quality. He then produced a large silver chronometer that he had received from Speke. 'It was
dead,' he said, 'and he wished me to repair it.'
This I declared to be impossible. He then confessed to having explained its construction, and the
cause of the 'ticking,' to his people, by the aid of
a needle, and that it had never ticked since that occasion. I regretted to see such 'pearls cast before
swine,' as the rifle and chronometer in the hands of
Kamrasi. Thus he had plundered Speke and Grant
of all they possessed before he would allow them to
proceed."

About this time Baker had several exciting rhinoceros hunts, though he was not always successful.
In one instance, after chasing two rhinoceroses a
long way, the animals escaped into the jungle. In
another case the rhinoceros was chased for a considerable distance, though badly wounded in the
shoulder, and then turned and charged at Tétel. A
shot from Baker's rifle, however, finished it.

CHAPTER XXIII.

BAKER.—DISCOVERY OF THE ALBERT NYANZA.

THE departure from Kamrasi's capital was of such a dramatic and exciting character that it must be quoted entire :

"The day of starting at length arrived ; the chief and guide appeared, and we were led to the Kafoor river, where canoes were in readiness to transport us to the south side. This was to our old quarters on the marsh. The direct course to the lake was west, and I fully expected some deception, as it was impossible to trust Kamrasi. I complained to the guide, and insisted upon his pointing out the direction of the lake, which he did, in its real position, west ; but he explained that we must follow the south bank of the Kafoor River for some days, as there was an impassable morass that precluded a direct course. This did not appear satisfactory, and the whole affair looked suspicious, as we had formerly been deceived by being led across the river in the same spot, and not allowed to return. We were now led along the banks of the Kafoor for about a mile, until we arrived at a cluster of huts ;

THE DEPARTURE FROM M'ROOLI FOR THE LAKE.

here we were to wait for Kamrasi, who had promised to take leave of us. The sun was overpowering, and we dismounted from our oxen, and took shelter in a blacksmith's shed. In about an hour Kamrasi arrived, attended by a considerable number of men, and took his seat in our shed. I felt convinced that his visit was simply intended to peel the last skin from the onion. I had already given him nearly all that I had, but he hoped to extract the whole before I should depart.

" He almost immediately commenced the conversation by asking for a pretty yellow muslin Turkish handerchief fringed with silver drops that Mrs. Baker wore upon her head : one of these had already been given to him, and I explained that this was the last remaining, and that she required it. . . . . He ' must ' have it. . . . . It was given. He then demanded other handkerchiefs. We had literally nothing but a few most ragged towels ; he would accept no excuse, and insisted upon a portmanteau being unpacked, that he might satisfy himself by actual inspection. The luggage, all ready for the journey, had to be unstrapped and examined, and the rags were displayed in succession ; but so wretched and uninviting was the exhibition of the family linen, that he simply returned them, and said ' they did not suit him.' Beads he must have, or I was ' his enemy.' A selection of the best opal beads was immediately given him. I rose from the stone upon which I was sitting, and declared that we must start immediately. ' Don't be in a hurry,' he replied ; ' you have plenty of time ; but you have not given me that watch you promised me.'.... This was my only watch that he had begged for, and had been refused every day during my stay at Mrooli. So pertinacious a beggar I had never seen. I explained to him that, without the watch, my journey would be useless, but that I would give him all that I had except the watch when the exploration should be completed, as I should require nothing on my direct return to Gondokoro. At the same time I repeated to him the arrangement for the journey that he had promised, begging him not to deceive me, as my wife and I should both die if we were compelled to remain another year in this country by losing the annual boats in Gondokoro. The understanding was this : he was to give me porters to the lake, where I was to be furnished with canoes to take me to Magungo, which was situated at the junction of the Somerset. From Magungo he told me that I should see the Nile issuing from the lake close to the spot where the Somerset entered, and that the canoes should take me down the river, and porters should carry my effects from the nearest point to Shooa, and deliver me at my old station without delay. Should he be faithful to this engagement, I trusted to procure porters from Shooa, and to reach Gondokoro in time for the annual boats. I had arranged that a boat should be sent from Khartoum to await me at Gondokoro early in this year, 1864 ; but I felt sure that should I be long delayed, the boat would return without me, as the people would be afraid to remain alone at Gondokoro after the other boats had quitted.

" In our present weak state another year of Central Africa without quinine appeared to warrant death ; it was a race against time, all was untrodden ground before us, and the distance quite uncertain. I trembled for my wife, and weighed the risk of another year in this horrible country should we lose the boats. With the self-sacrificing devotion that she had shown in every trial, she implored me not to think of any risks on her account, but to push forward and discover the lake—that she had determined not to return until she had herself reached the ' M-wootan Nzige.'

" I now requested Kamrasi to allow us to leave, as we had not an hour to lose. In the coolest manner he replied, ' I will send you to the lake and to Shooa, as I have promised ; but, *you must leave your wife with me !*'

" At that moment we were surrounded by a great number of natives, and my suspicions of treachery at having been led across the Kafoor River appeared confirmed by this insolent demand. If this were to be the end of the expedition I resolved that it should also be the end of Kamrasi, and, drawing my revolver quietly, I held it within two feet of his chest, and looking at him with undisguised contempt, I told him that if I touched the trigger, not all his men could save him : and that if he dared to repeat the insult I would shoot him on the spot. At the same time I explained to him that in my country such insolence would entail bloodshed, and that I looked upon him as an ignorant ox who knew no better, and that this excuse alone could save

him. My wife, naturally indignant, had risen from
her seat, and, maddened with the excitement of the
moment, she made him a little speech in Arabic,
(not a word of which he understood,) with a countenance almost as amiable as the head of Medusa.
Altogether the *mise en scène* utterly astonished him ;
the woman, Bacheeta, although savage, had appropriated the insult to her mistress, and she also
fearlessly let fly at Kamrasi, translating as nearly as
she could the complimentary address that ' Medusa'
had just delivered.

Whether this little *coup de théâtre* had so impressed Kamrasi with British female independence
that he wished to be off his bargain, I cannot say,
but with an air of complete astonishment, he said,
' Don't be angry ! I had no intention of offending
you by asking for your wife ; I will give you a wife,
if you want one, and I thought you might have no
objection to give me yours ; it is my custom to give
my visitors pretty wives, and I thought you might
exchange. Don't make a fuss about it ; if you don't
like it, there's an end of it ; I will never mention it
again.' This very practical apology I received very
sternly, and merely insisted upon starting. He
seemed rather confused at having committed himself, and to make amends he called his people and
ordered them to carry our loads. His men ordered
a number of women who had assembled out of curiosity, to shoulder the luggage and carry it to the
next village, where they would be relieved. I assisted my wife upon her ox, and with a very cold

adieu to Kamrasi, I turned my back most gladly on Mrooli."

For three days they travelled westward over a flat, uninteresting country, through swamps and past native villages where it was almost impossible to procure anything, and reached the Kafoor River, where Baker, after all his toils and dangers, was called upon to meet the greatest misfortune of the journey. He says : " The stream was in the centre of a marsh, and although deep, it was so covered with thickly-matted water-grass and other aquatic plants, that a natural floating bridge was established by a carpet of weeds about two feet thick ; upon this waving and unsteady surface the men ran quickly across, sinking merely to the ankles, although beneath the tough vegetation there was deep water. It was equally impossible to ride or to be carried over this treacherous surface ; thus I led the way, and begged Mrs. Baker to follow me on foot as quickly as possible, precisely in my track. The river was about eighty yards wide, and I had scarcely completed a fourth of the distance and looked back to see if my wife followed close to me, when I was horrified to see her standing in one spot, and sinking gradually through the weeds, while her face was distorted and perfectly purple. Almost as soon as I perceived her, she fell, as though shot dead. In an instant I was by her side ; and with the assistance of eight or ten of my men, who were fortunately close to me, I dragged her like a corpse through the yielding vegetation, and up to our waists we scrambled across to the other side, just keeping her head above the water; to have carried her would have been impossible, as we should all have sunk together through the weeds. I laid her under a tree, and bathed her head and face with water, as for the moment I thought she had fainted; but she lay perfectly insensible, as though dead, with teeth and hands firmly clenched, and her eyes open, but fixed. It was a *coup de soleil.*"

Mrs. Baker was carried on, to a miserable native village, where it was impossible to procure anything to eat. She had never stirred since she fell, and merely respired about five times in a minute. "It was impossible to remain; the people would have starved. She was laid gently upon her litter, and we started forward on our funeral course. I was ill and broken-hearted, and I followed by her side through the long day's march over wild park-lands and streams, with thick forest and deep marshy bottoms; over undulating hills, and through valleys of tall papyrus rushes, which, as we brushed through them on our melancholy way, waved over the litter like the black plumes of a hearse. We halted at a village, and again the night was passed in watching. I was wet, and coated with mud from the swampy marsh, and shivered with ague; but the cold within was greater than all. No change had taken place; she had never moved. I had plenty of fat, and I made four balls of about half a pound, each of which would burn for three hours. A piece of a broken water-jar formed a lamp, several pieces of rag serving for wicks. So in solitude the still calm night passed away as I sat by her side and watched.

In the drawn and distorted features that lay before me I could hardly trace the same face that for years had been my comfort through all the difficulties and dangers of my path. Was she to die? Was so terrible a sacrifice to be the result of my selfish exile?

" Again the night passed away. Once more the march. Though weak and ill, and for two nights without a moment's sleep, I felt no fatigue, but mechanically followed by the side of the litter as though in a dream. The same wild country diversifie l with marsh and forest. Again we halted. The night came, and I sat by her side in a miserable hut, with the feeble lamp flickering while she lay as in death. She had never moved a muscle since she fell. My people slept. I was alone, and no sound broke the stillness of the night. The ears ached at the utter silence, till the sudden wild cry of a hyena made me shudder as the horrible thought rushed through my brain, that, should she be buried in this lonely spot, the hyena would . . . disturb her rest.

" The morning was not far distant; it was past four o'clock. I had passed the night in replacing wet cloths upon her head and moistening her lips, as she lay apparently lifeless on her litter. I could do nothing more; in solitude and abject misery in that dark hour, in a country of savage heathens, thousands of miles away from a Christian land, I beseeched an aid above all human, trusting alone to Him.

" The morning broke; my lamp had just burnt out, and, cramped with the night's watching, I rose

from my low seat, and seeing that she lay in the
same unaltered state, I went to the door of the
hut to breathe one gasp of the fresh morning air.
I was watching the first red streak that heralded
the rising sun, when I was startled by the words,
' Thank God,' faintly uttered behind me.   Suddenly
she had awoke from her torpor, and with a heart
overflowing I went to her bedside.   Her eyes were
full of madness!   She spoke; but the brain was
gone!

   "I will not inflict a description of the terrible
trial of seven days of brain fever, with its attend-
ant horrors.   The rain poured in torrents, and day
after day we were forced to travel, for want of provisions, not being able to remain in one position.
Every now and then we shot a few guinea-fowl,
but rarely; there was no game, although the country was most favorable.   In the forests we procured
wild honey, but the deserted villages contained no
supplies, as we were on the frontier of Uganda, and
Mtese's people had plundered the district.   For
seven nights I had not slept, and although as weak
as a reed, I had marched by the side of her litter.
Nature could resist no longer.   We reached a village one evening; she had been in violent convulsions successively—it was all but over.   I laid her
down on her litter within a hut; covered her with
a Scotch plaid; and I fell upon my mat insensible,
worn out with sorrow and fatigue.   My men put
a new handle to the pickaxe that evening, and
sought for a dry spot to dig her grave!

   "The sun had risen when I woke.   I had slept,

and, horrified as the idea flashed upon me that she must be dead, and that I had not been with her, I started up. She lay upon her bed, pale as marble, and with that calm serenity that the features assume when the cares of life no longer act upon the mind, and the body rests in death. The dreadful thought bowed me down ; but as I gazed upon her in fear, her chest gently heaved, not with the convulsive throbs of fever, but naturally. She was asleep ; and when at a sudden noise she opened her eyes, they were calm and clear. She was saved ! When not a ray of hope remained, God alone knows what helped us. The gratitude of that moment I will not attempt to describe.

" Fortunately there were many fowls in this village ; we found several nests of fresh eggs in the straw which littered the hut ; these were most acceptable after our hard fare, and produced a good supply of soup."

Having rested for two days to allow Mrs. Baker time to regain a little strength, they pushed forward and in another day's march reached a larger and more flourishing village than they had seen since leaving Kamrasi's capital. " The name of this village," says Baker, " was Parkani. For several days past our guides had told us that we were very near to the lake, and we were now assured that we should reach it on the morrow. I had noticed a lofty range of mountains at an immense distance west, and I had imagined that the lake lay on the other side of this chain ; but I was now informed that those mountains formed the western frontier of the

M-wootan Nzige, and that the lake was actually within a march of Parkani. I could not believe it possible that we were so near the object of our search. The guide Rabonga now appeared, and declared that if we started early on the following morning we should be able to wash in the lake by noon !

"That night I hardly slept. For years I had striven to reach the 'sources of the Nile.' In my nightly dreams during that arduous voyage I had always failed, but after so much hard work and perseverance the cup was at my very lips, and I was to *drink* at the mysterious fountain before another sun should set—at that great reservoir of Nature that ever since creation had baffled all discovery.

" I had hoped, and prayed, and striven through all kinds of difficulties, in sickness, starvation, and fatigue, to reach that hidden source ; and when it had appeared impossible, we had both determined to die upon the road rather than return defeated. Was it possible that it was so near, and that tomorrow we could say, ' the work is accomplished ?'

" *The* 14*th March.*—The sun had not risen when I was spurring my ox after the guide, who, having been promised a double handful of beads on arrival at the lake, had caught the enthusiasm of the moment. The day broke beautifully clear, and having crossed a deep valley between the hills, we toiled up the opposite slope. I hurried to the summit. The glory of our prize burst suddenly upon me ! There, like a sea of quicksilver, lay far beneath the grand expanse of water,—a boundless sea horizon on the south and southwest, glittering in the noonday sun ; and on the west, at fifty or sixty miles' distance, blue mountains rose from the bosom of the lake to a height of about 7,000 feet above its level.

" It is impossible to describe the triumph of that moment ;—here was the reward for all our labor—for the years of tenacity with which we had toiled through Africa. England had won the sources of the Nile ! Long before I reached this spot, I had arranged to give three cheers with all our men in English style in honor of the discovery, but now that I looked down upon the great inland sea lying nestled in the very heart of Africa, and thought how vainly mankind had sought these sources throughout so many ages, and reflected that I had been the humble instrument permitted to unravel this portion of the great mystery when so many greater than I had failed, I felt too serious to vent my feelings in vain cheers for victory, and I sincerely thanked God for having guided and supported us through all dangers to the good end. I was about 1,500 feet above the lake, and I looked down from the steep granite cliff upon those welcome waters —upon that vast reservoir which nourished Egypt and brought fertility where all was wilderness—upon that great source so long hidden from mankind ; that source of bounty and of blessings to millions of human beings ; and as one of the greatest objects in nature, I determined to honor it with a great name. As an imperishable memorial of one loved and mourned by our gracious Queen and deplored by every Englishman, I called this great lake

' the Albert Nyanza.'   The Victoria and the Albert
lakes are the two Sources of the Nile.

"The zigzag path to descend to the lake was so
steep and dangerous that we were forced to leave
our oxen with a guide, who was to take them to
Magungo and wait for our arrival. We commenced
the descent of the steep pass on foot. I led the
way, grasping a stout bamboo. My wife in extreme
weakness tottered down the pass, supporting herself upon my shoulder, and stopping to rest every
twenty paces. After a toilsome descent of about
two hours, weak with years of fever, but for the
moment strengthened by success, we gained the
level plain below the cliff. A walk of about a mile
through flat sandy meadows of fine turf interspersed
with trees and bush, brought us to the water's
edge. The waves were rolling upon a white pebbly
beach : I rushed into the lake, and thirsty with heat
and fatigue, with a heart full of gratitude, I drank
deeply from the Sources of the Nile. Within a
quarter of a mile of the lake was a fishing village
named Vacovia, in which we now established ourselves."

CHAPTER XXIV.

BAKER.—EXPLORATION OF THE ALBERT NYANZA.

WE continue Baker's narrative : " At sunrise on the following morning I took the compass, and accompanied by the chief of the village, my guide Rabonga, and the woman Bacheeta, I went to the borders of the lake to survey the country. It was beautifully clear, and with a powerful telescope I could distinguish two large waterfalls that cleft the sides of the mountains on the opposite shore. Although the outline of the mountains was distinct upon the bright blue sky, and the dark shades upon their sides denoted deep gorges, I could not distinguish other features than the two great falls, which looked like threads of silver on the dark face of the mountains. No base had been visible, even from an elevation of 1,500 feet above the water-level, on my first view of the lake, but the chain of lofty mountains on the west appeared to rise suddenly from the water. This appearance must have been due to the great distance, the base being below the horizon, as dense columns of smoke were ascending apparently from the surface of the water ; this

must have been produced by the burning of prairies
at the foot of the mountains. The chief assured
me that large canoes had been known to cross over
from the other side, but that it required four days
and nights of hard rowing to accomplish the voyage,
and that many boats had been lost in the attempt.
The canoes of Unyoro were not adapted for so dangerous a journey : but the western shore of the lake
was comprised in the great kingdom of Malegga,
governed by king Kajoro, who possessed large canoes, and traded with Kamrasi from a point opposite to Magungo, where the lake was contracted to
the width of one day's voyage.

"The first *coup d'œil* from the summit of the cliff
1,500 feet above the level had suggested what a
closer examination confirmed. The lake was a vast
depression far below the general level of the country,
surrounded by precipitous cliffs, and bounded on the
west and southwest by great ranges of mountains
from five to seven thousand feet above the level of
its waters—thus it was the one great reservoir into
which everything *must* drain ; and from this vast
rocky cistern the Nile made its exit, a giant in its
birth. It was a grand arrangement of Nature for
the birth of so mighty and important a stream as
the river Nile. The Victoria Nyanza of Speke
formed a reservoir at a high altitude, receiving a
drainage from the west by the Kitangulé River, and
Speke had seen the Mfumbiro Mountain at a great
distance as a peak among other mountains from
which the streams descended, which by uniting
formed the main river Kitangulé, the principal feeder

of the Victoria Lake from the west, in about the 2° S. latitude : thus the same chain of mountains that fed the Victoria on the east must have a water-shed to the west and north that would flow into the Albert Lake. The general drainage of the Nile basin tending from south to north, and the Albert Lake extending much farther north than the Victoria, it receives the river from the latter lake, and thus monopolizes the entire head-waters of the Nile. The Albert is the grand reservoir, while the Victoria is the eastern source ; the parent streams that form these lakes are from the same origin, and the Kitan-gulé sheds its waters to the Victoria to be received *eventually* by the Albert, precisely as the highlands of Mfumbiro and the Blue Mountains pour their northern drainage *direct* into the Albert Lake.

" On the following morning not one of our party could rise from the ground. Thirteen men, the boy Saat, four women, and we ourselves, were all down with fever. The air was hot and close, and the country frightfully unhealthy. The natives assured us that all strangers suffered in a similar manner, and that no one could live at Vacovia without re-peated attacks of fever.

The delay in supplying the boats was most annoy-ing ; every hour was precious ; and the lying natives deceived us in every manner possible, delaying us purposely in the hope of extorting beads.

" The latitude of Vacovia was 1° 15′ N.; longitude 30° 50′ E. My farthest southern point on the road from Mrooli was latitude 1° 13′. We were now to turn our faces towards the north, and every day's journey would bring us nearer home. But where was home? As I looked at the map of the world, and at the little red spot that represented old England, far, far away, and then gazed on the wasted form and haggard face of my wife and at my own attenuated frame, I hardly dared hope for home again. We had now been three years ever toiling onwards, and having completed the exploration of all the Abyssinian affluents of the Nile, in itself an arduous undertaking, we were now actually at the Nile head. We had neither health nor supplies, and the great journey lay all before us.

" Notwithstanding my daily entreaties that boats might be supplied without delay, eight days were passed at Vacovia, during which time the whole party suffered more or less from fever. At length canoes were reported to have arrived, and I was requested to inspect them. They were merely single trees neatly hollowed out, but very inferior in size to the large canoes on the Nile at Mrooli. The largest boat was thirty-two feet long, but I selected for ourselves one of twenty-six feet, but wider and deeper.

" After much bargaining and delay, we started from Vacovia on the broad surface of the Albert Nyanza. The rowers paddled bravely ; and the canoe, although heavily laden, went along at about four miles an hour. There was no excitement in Vacovia, and the chief and two or three attendants were all who came to see us off ; they had a suspicion that bystanders might be invited to assist as

THE GREAT HOOGLY RIVER.

rowers, therefore the entire population of the village had deserted.

" At leaving the shore, the chief had asked for a few beads, which, on receiving, he threw into the lake to propitiate the inhabitants of the deep, that no hippopotami should upset the canoe.

" Our first day's voyage was delightful. The lake was calm, the sky cloudy, and the scenery most lovely. At times the mountains on the west coast were not discernible, and the lake appeared of indefinite width. We coasted within a hundred yards of the east shore ; sometimes we passed flats of sand and bush of perhaps a mile in width from the water to the base of the mountain cliffs ; at other times we passed directly underneath stupendous heights of about 1,500 feet, which ascended abruptly from the deep, so that we fended the canoes off the sides, and assisted our progress by pushing against the rock with bamboos. These precipitous rocks were all primitive, frequently of granite and gneiss, and mixed in many places with red porphyry. In the clefts were beautiful evergreens of every tint, including giant euphorbias ; and wherever a rivulet or spring glittered through the dark foliage of a ravine, it was shaded by the graceful and feathery wild date."

They camped on the shore that night, and next morning the boatmen were gone. Baker and his men then took the navigation of the canoes into their own hands, and proceeded northwards. In crossing the bay eight or ten miles wide they were overtaken by a storm, and narrowly escaped foun-

dering.   Baker's destination was Magungo, the
point where the White Nile was reported to enter
the lake, a distance from Vacovia of less than a
hundred miles, but, owing to the continual delays
in procuring provisions and boatmen, he was thirteen days in making the voyage.

"Day after day passed, the time occupied in
travelling from sunrise to mid-day, at which hour a
strong gale with rain and thunder occurred regularly, and obliged us to haul our canoes ashore.
The country was very thinly inhabited, and the villages were poor and wretched; the people most
inhospitable. At length we arrived at a considerable
town situated in a beautiful bay beneath precipitous
cliffs, the grassy sides of which were covered with
flocks of goats; this was Eppigoya, and the boatmen that we had procured from the last village were
to deliver us in this spot.   The delays in procuring
boatmen were most annoying: it appeared that the
king had sent orders that each village was to supply
the necessary rowers: thus we were paddled from
place to place, at each of which the men were
changed, and no amount of payment would induce
them to continue with us to the end of our voyage.

"After the tenth day from our departure from
Vacovia the scenery increased in beauty.   The lake
had contracted to about thirty miles in width, and
was decreasing rapidly northward; the trees upon
the mountains upon the western shore could be distinguished.   Continuing our voyage north, the western shore projected suddenly, and diminished the
width of the lake to about twenty miles.   It was no

longer the great inland sea that the Vacovia had so impressed me, with the clean pebbly beach that had hitherto formed the shore, but vast banks of reeds growing upon floating vegetation prevented the canoes from landing. These banks were most peculiar, as they appeared to have been formed of decayed vegetation, from which the papyrus rushes took root ; the thickness of the floating mass was about three feet, and so tough and firm that a man could walk upon it, merely sinking above his ankles in the soft ooze. Beneath this raft of vegetation was extremely deep water, and the shore for a width of about half a mile was entirely protected by this extraordinary formation. One day a tremendous gale of wind and heavy sea broke off large portions, and the wind acting upon the rushes like sails, carried floating islands of some acres about the lake to be deposited wherever they might chance to hitch.

" On the thirteenth day we found ourselves at the end of our lake voyage. The lake at this point was between fifteen and twenty miles across, and the appearance of the country to the north was that of a delta. The shores upon either side were choked with vast banks of reeds, and as the canoe skirted the edge of that upon the east coast, we could find no bottom with a bamboo of twenty-five feet in length, although the floating mass appeared like *terra firma.* We were in a perfect wilderness of vegetation. On the west were mountains of about 4,000 feet above the lake level, a continuation of the chain that formed the western shore from the south these mountains decreased in height towards the north, in which direction the lake terminated in a broad valley of reeds.

"After skirting the floating reeds of the shore for about a mile, we turned sharp to the east, and entered a broad channel of water bounded on either side by the everlasting reeds. This we were informed was the embouchure of the Somerset River from the Victoria Nyanza. The same river that we had crossed at Karuma, boiling and tearing along its rocky course, now entered the Albert Nyanza as dead water ! I could not understand this ; there was not the slightest current ; the channel was about half a mile wide, and I could hardly convince myself that this was not an arm of the lake branching to the east. After searching for some time for a landing-place among the wonderful banks of reeds, we discovered a passage that had evidently been used as an approach by canoes, but so narrow that our large canoe could with difficulty be dragged through—all the men walking through the mud and reeds, and towing with their utmost strength. Several hundred paces of this tedious work brought us through the rushes into open water, about eight feet deep, opposite to a clean rocky shore. We had heard voices for some time obscured on the other side of the rushes, and we now found a number of natives, who had arrived to meet us, with the chief of Magungo and our guide Rabonga, whom we had sent in advance with the riding oxen from Vacovia. The water was extremely shallow near the shore, and the natives rushed in and dragged the canoes by sheer force over the mud to the land. We had been so entirely hidden while on the lake on the other side of the reed bank that we had been unable to see the eastern, or Magungo shore ; we now found ourselves in a delightful spot beneath the shade of several enormous trees on firm sandy and rocky ground, while the country rose in a rapid incline to the town of Magungo, about a mile distant, on an elevated ridge.

"The day was beautifully clear. The soil was sandy and poor, therefore the road was clean and hard ; and, after the many days' boating, we enjoyed the walk, and the splendid view that lay before us when we arrived at Magungo, and looked back upon the lake. We were about 250 feet above the water level. There were no longer the abrupt cliffs, descending to the lake, that we had seen in the south, but the general level of the country appeared to be about 500 feet above the water, at a distance of five or six miles, from which point the ground descended in undulations, Magungo being situated on the summit of the nearest incline. The mountains on the Malegga side, with the lake in the foreground, were the most prominent objects, forming the western boundary. A few miles north there appeared to be a gap in the range, and the lake continued to the west, but much contracted, while the mountain range on the north side of the gap continued to the northeast. Due north and northeast the country was a dead flat, and far as the eye could reach was an extent of bright green reeds, marking the course of the Nile as it made its exit from the lake. The sheet of water at Magungo being about seventeen miles in width, ended in a long strip or tail to the north, until it was lost in the flat valley of green rushes. This valley may have been from four to six miles wide, and was bounded upon its west bank by the continuation of the chain of mountains that had formed the western boundary of the lake. The natives told me that canoes could navigate the Nile in its course from the lake to the Madi country, as there were no cataracts for a great distance, but that both the Madi and the Koshi were hostile, and that the current of the river was so strong, that should the canoe descend from the lake, it could not return without many rowers.

" The exit of the Nile from the lake was plain enough, and if the broad channel of dead water were indeed the entrance of the Victoria Nile, (Somerset,) the information obtained by Speke would be remarkably confirmed. Up to the present time all the information that I had received from Kamrasi and his people had been correct. He had told me that I should be about twenty days from Mrooli to the lake; I had been eighteen. He had also told me that the Somerset flowed from Karuma direct to the lake, and that, having joined it, the great Nile issued from the lake almost immediately, and flowed through the Koshi and Madi tribes. I now saw the river issuing from the lake within eighteen miles of Magungo; and the Koshi and the Madi countries appeared close to me, bordering it on the west and east.

" I had a bad attack of fever that evening, and missed my star for the latitude ; but on the following morning before daybreak I obtained a good observation of Vega, and determined the latitude of Magungo 2° 16' due west from Atada or Karuma Falls. This was a strong confirmation that the river beneath my feet was the Somerset, that I had crossed in the same latitude at Atada, where the river was running due west, and where the natives had pointed in that direction as its course to the lake. Nevertheless, I was determined to verify it, although by this circuitous route I might lose the boats from Gondokoro and become a prisoner in Central Africa, ill, and without quinine, for another year. I proposed it to my wife, who not only voted in her state of abject weakness to complete the river to Karuma, but wished, if possible, to return and follow the Nile from the lake down to Gondokoro !"

Starting immediately in canoes, Baker made ten miles up the Nile the first day, finding a channel about 500 yards in breadth, but no perceptible current. The second day the channel contracted to 250 yards, and after advancing eight miles further, the water gave indications of a very slight movement towards the west. He was now convinced that the accounts of the natives were correct, and this was really the same stream which Speke had found issuing from the Victoria Nyanza at Ripon Falls— the main stream of the Nile. The end of Baker's voyage and of his discoveries is thus described :

" The woman Bacheeta knew the country, as she had formerly been to Magungo when in the service of Sali, who had been subsequently murdered by Kamrasi; she now informed me that we should terminate our canoe voyage on that day, as we should arrive at the great waterfall of which she had often spoken. As we proceeded the river gradually narrowed to about 180 yards, and when the paddles ceased working we could distinctly hear the roar of water. I had heard this on waking in the morning, but at the time I had imagined it to proceed from distant thunder. By ten o'clock the current had so increased as we proceeded, that it was distinctly perceptible, although weak. The roar of the waterfall was extremely loud, and after sharp pulling for a couple of hours, during which time the stream increased, we arrived at a few deserted fishing huts, at a point where the river made a slight turn. I never saw such an extraordinary show of crocodiles as were exposed on every sandbank on the sides of the river; they lay like logs of timber close together, and upon one bank we counted twenty-seven, of large size; every basking place was crowded in a similar manner. From the time we had fairly entered the river, it had been confined by heights somewhat precipitous on either side, rising to about 180 feet. At this point the cliffs were still higher, and exceedingly abrupt. From the roar of the water, I was sure that the fall would be in sight if we turned the corner at the bend of the river; accordingly I ordered the boatmen to row as far as they could; to this they at first objected, as they wished to stop at the deserted fishing village,

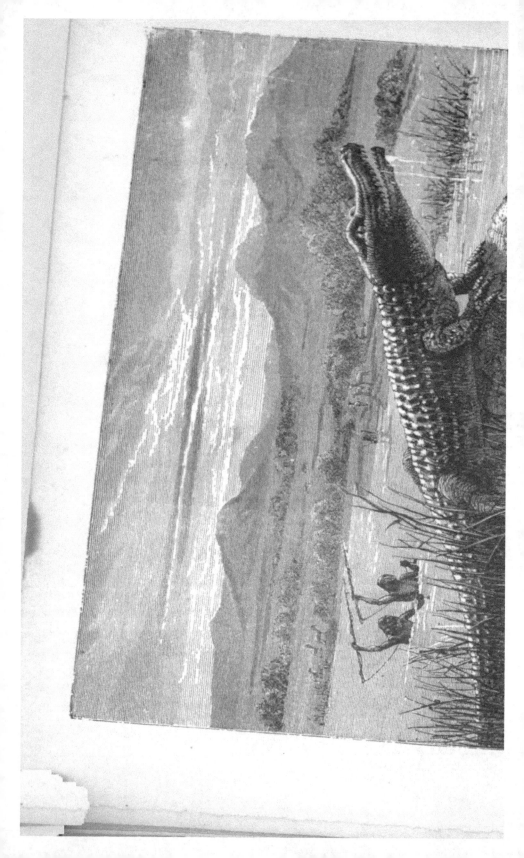

which they explained was to be the limit of the journey, farther progress being impossible.

" However, I explained that I merely wished to see the fall, and they rowed immediately up the stream, which was now strong against us. Upon rounding the corner, a magnificent sight burst suddenly upon us. On either side the river were beautifully wooded cliffs rising abruptly to a height of about 300 feet ; rocks were jutting out from the intensely green foliage ; and rushing through a gap that cleft the rock exactly before us, the river, contracted from a grand stream, was pent up in a narrow gorge of scarcely fifty yards in width ; roaring furiously through the rock-bound pass, it plunged in one leap of about 120 feet perpendicular into a dark abyss below.

" The fall of water was snow-white, which had a superb effect as it contrasted with the dark cliffs that walled the river, while the graceful palms of the tropics and wild plantains perfected the beauty of the view. This was the greatest waterfall of the Nile, and, in honor of the distinguished President of the Royal Geographical Society, I named it the Murchison Falls, as the most important object throughout the entire course of the river."

CHAPTER XXV.

BAKER'S object was now accomplished. He had followed the banks of the Nile eastward for two days, to within a few miles of the point where he had first struck it on his journey southward : he had ascertained that the "Nzige" of Speke was not a mere marsh or back-water of the river, but a great, magnificent lake, probably equal in size to the Victoria Nyanza; and thus the truth of the old Ptolemaic map was fully established. It was now the beginning of April, and very near the time when the boats of the Egyptian traders always quitted Gondokoro, to descend the White Nile to Khartoum. It was absolutely necessary to proceed directly to Shooa, in order to avoid a detention of another year, and Baker offered the natives all his beads, fifty pounds, if they would set him across the river and take him thither at once. They promised to do this, but he discovered in season that they meant to take his beads and leave him alone .in the unin-habited wilderness on the northern bank. Had he been well and strong , he might nevertheless have

MURCHISON FALLS.

made his way; but himself and wife could not walk a quarter of a mile without fainting; the whole country was overgrown with grass eight feet high, and the prospect of venturing forward alone was certain death.

He finally took possession of a hut on the southern shore. It was the height of the rainy season; the animals were nearly all dead, and the few wild vegetables, and the bitter, mouldy meal of the country were scarcely sufficient to support life. Thus, for two months, consumed by fever, the explorer and his wife languished, expecting every day to be their last. Finally, in his desperation, Baker sent his vakeel, or agent, to Kamrasi, requesting fifty porters to convey him and his party to that monarch's camp.

"After a few days a messenger arrived with the leaf of a book, as a token that he came from Kamrasi. He was followed by a guide and porters, and a lean ox, which was immediately slaughtered to feed the starving party. After five days of . slow marching in a southwesterly direction, Baker and his wife being carried on litters, they reached a village called Kisoona, where they found a party of Kamrasi's army and some of Ibrahim's men. This was a welcome meeting: "An immense amount of news had to be exchanged between my men and those of Ibrahim; they had quite given us up for lost, until they heard that we were at Shooa Moru. A report had reached them that my wife was dead, and that I had died a few days later. A great amount of kissing and embracing took place, Arab

fashion, between the two parties; and they all came
to kiss my hand and that of my wife, with the exclamation, that 'By Allah, no woman in the world
had a heart so tough as to dare to face what she
had gone through.' 'El hamd el Illah! El hamd
el Illah bel salaam!' ('Thank God—be grateful to
God,') was exclaimed on all sides by the swarthy
throng of brigands who pressed round us, really
glad to welcome us back again; and I could not
help thinking of the difference in their manner now
and fourteen months ago, when they had attempted
to drive us back from Gondokoro."

Here Baker discovered, to his great surprise, that
the person to whom he had been presented as
Kamrasi, and who assumed the latter's name and
office, was in reality M'Gambi, a younger brother of
the king. In his irritation at the trick which had
been played upon him, he at first refused to see
the real Kamrasi, but his dependent position finally
obliged him to accede to an interview, which he describes as follows:

"At the hour appointed M'Gambi appeared, with
a great crowd of natives. My clothes were in rags,
—and as personal appearance has a certain effect,
even in Central Africa, I determined to present myself to the king in as favorable a light as possible.
I happened to possess a full-dress Highland suit
that I had worn when I lived in Perthshire many
years ago; this I had treasured as serviceable upon
an occasion like the present;—accordingly I was
quickly attired in kilt, sporran and Glengarry bon-
net, and to the utter amazement of the crowd, the

ragged-looking object that had arrived at Kisoona now issued from the obscure hut, with plaid and kilt of Athole tartan. A general shout of exclamation arose from the assembled crowd ; and taking my seat upon an angarep, I was immediately shouldered by a number of men, and attended by ten of my people as escort, I was carried towards the camp of the great Kamrasi.

" In about half an hour we arrived. The camp, composed of grass huts, extended over a large extent of ground, and the approach was perfectly black with the throng that crowded to meet me. Women, children, dogs and men all thronged at the entrance of the street that led to Kamrasi's residence. Pushing our way through this inquisitive multitude, we continued through the camp until at length we reached the dwelling of the king. Halting for the moment, a message was immediately received that we should proceed ; we accordingly entered through a narrow passage between high reed fences, and I found myself in the presence of the actual king of Unyoro, Kamrasi. He was sitting in a kind of porch in front of a hut, and upon seeing me he hardly condescended to look at me for more than a moment ; he then turned to his attendants and made some remark that appeared to amuse them, as they all grinned as little men are wont to do when a great man makes a bad joke.

" I had ordered one of my men to carry my stool ; I was determined not to sit upon the earth, as the king would glory in my humiliation. M'Gambi, his brother, who had formerly played the part of king, now sat upon the ground a few feet from Kamrasi, who was seated upon the same stool of copper that M'Gambi had used when I first saw him at Mrooli. Several of his chiefs also sat upon the straw with which the porch was littered. I made a 'salaam,' and took my seat upon my stool. Not a word passed between us for about five minutes, during which time the king eyed me most attentively, and made various remarks to the chiefs who were present; at length he asked me why I had not been to see him before? I replied, ' Because I had been starved in his country, and I was too weak to walk.' He said —I should soon be strong, as he would now give me a good supply of food, but that he could not send provisions to Shooa Moru, as Fowooka held that country. Without replying to this wretched excuse for his neglect, I merely told him that I was happy to have seen him before my departure, as I was not aware until recently that I had been duped by M'Gambi. He answered me very coolly, saying that although I had not seen him he had nevertheless seen me, as he was among the crowd of native escort on the day that we left Mrooli. Thus he had watched our start at the very place where his brother M'Gambi had impersonated the king."

After this interview Baker was supplied with a cow, and a sufficient supply of plantains and flour. His health and his wife's improved with a better diet, but he was obliged to remain in the country until Ibrahim's return. The summer passed away with wars and rumors of wars; the camp at Kisoona was abandoned on account of the approach of a

THE WELCOME OF BARROW

hostile force from Uganda, and Baker made a forced march with his party to a village near the Karuma Falls of the Nile. Here he again settled, and employed his time in distilling a kind of brandy from sweet potatoes. Singularly enough, the use of the liquor soon cured all the cases of fever and restored every one to complete health.

On the 20th of September Ibrahim arrived, bringing letters and newspapers which had reached Gondokoro. Two months more were spent in collecting the ivory which the Turks had procured in Unyoro, and engaging 700 porters to transport it to the camp at Shooa. On the 17th November they all finally commenced the return journey together, and in five days reached their old quarters at Shooa, where the natives performed a dance of welcome for Baker and his wife. Here they remained more than two months, on account of the greater salubrity of the climate, since the trading vessels could not have reached Gondokoro. The alliance with Ibrahim had turned out most advantageously for the latter, and the two parties were on the best of terms.

"The hour of deliverance from our long sojourn in Central Africa was at hand," Baker writes; "it was the month of February, and the boats would be at Gondokoro. The Turks had packed their ivory; the large tusks were fastened to poles to be carried by two men, and the camp was a perfect mass of this valuable material. I counted 609 loads of upwards of 50 lbs. each; thirty-one loads were lying at an out-station : therefore the total results of the ivory campaign during the last twelve months were about 32,000 lbs., equal to about £9,630 when delivered in Egypt. This was a perfect fortune for Koorshid.

"We were ready to start. My baggage was so unimportant that I was prepared to forsake everything, and to march straight for Gondokoro independently with my own men; but this the Turks assured me was impracticable, as the country was so hostile in advance that we must of necessity have some fighting on the road; the Bari tribe would dispute our right to pass through their territory."

A few days more, and the march commenced. The route was almost identical with that followed by Speke and Grant. Baker also found Miani's tree, at which point he saw the Nile again, crossed the Asua River near its mouth, and pressed on through the Bari country, the caravan being constantly harassed by attacks of the natives. The force, however, was safe in its numbers, and lost only one man by the way. On the 22nd of March, 1865, they saw the mountains of Regiaf, near Gondokoro, and the blue peaks of Ellyria in the east. This is Baker's description of the last day of his most adventurous journey :

"We started ;—the English flag had been mounted on a fine straight bamboo with a new lance-head specially arranged for the arrival at Gondokoro. My men felt proud, as they would march in as conquerors ;—according to White Nile ideas such a journey could not have been accomplished with so small a party. Long before Ibrahim's men were ready to start, our oxen were saddled and we were off, longing to hasten into Gondokoro and to find a comfortable vessel with a few luxuries and the post from England. Never had the oxen travelled so fast as on that morning ;—the flag led the way, and the men in excellent spirits followed at double quick pace. ' I see the masts of the vessels !' exclaimed the boy Saat. ' El hambd el Illah !' (Thank God !) shouted the men. ' Hurrah !' said I—' Three cheers for Old England and the Sources of the Nile ! Hurrah !' and my men joined me in the wild, and to their ears savage, English yell. ' Now for a salute ! Fire away all your powder, if you like, my lads, and let the people know that we're alive !' This was all that was required to complete the happiness of my people, and loading and firing as fast as possible, we approached near to Gondokoro. Presently we saw the Turkish flag emerge from Gondokoro at about a quarter of a mile distant, followed by a number of the traders' people, who waited to receive us. On our arrival, they immediately approached and fired salutes with ball cartridge; as usual advancing close to us and discharging their guns into the ground at our feet. One of my servants, Mahomet, was riding an ox, and an old friend of his in the crowd happening to recognize him, immediately advanced, and saluted him by firing his gun into the earth directly beneath the belly of the ox he was riding ;—the effect produced made the crowd and ourselves explode with laughter. The nervous ox, terrified at the sudden discharge between his legs, gave a tremendous kick, and continued madly kicking and plunging, until Mahomet was pitched over his head and lay sprawling on the ground ;—this scene terminated the expedition.

" Dismounting from our tired oxen, our first inquiry was concerning boats and letters. What was the reply ? Neither boats, letters, supplies, nor any intelligence of friends or the civilized world ! We had long since been given up as dead by the inhabitants of Khartoum, and by all those who understood the difficulties and dangers of the country. We were told that some people had suggested that we might possibly have gone to Zanzibar, but the general opinion was that we had all been killed. At this cold and barren reply, I felt almost choked. We had looked forward to arriving at Gondokoro as to a home ; we had expected that a boat would have been sent on the chance of finding us, as I had left money in the hands of an agent in Khartoum—but there was literally nothing to receive us, and we were helpless to return. We had worked for years in misery, such as I have but faintly described, to overcome the difficulties of this hitherto unconquerable exploration ; we had succeeded—and what was the result ? Not even a letter from home to welcome us if alive ! As I sat beneath a tree and looked down upon the glorious Nile that flowed a few yards beneath my feet, I pondered upon the value of my toil. I had traced the river to its great Albert source, and as the mighty stream glided before me, the mystery that had ever shrouded its origin was dissolved. I no longer looked upon its waters with a feeling approaching to awe, for

I knew its home, and had visited its cradle. Had
I overrated the importance of the discovery? and
had I wasted some of the best years of my life to
obtain a shadow? I recalled to recollection the
practical question of Commoro, the chief of Latooka—'Suppose you get to the great lake, what
will you do with it? What will be the good of
it? If you find that the large river does flow from
it, what then?'"

During Baker's voyage down the White Nile,
the plague broke out on board his vessel, and his
faithful boy Saat fell a victim to it a few days
before reaching Khartoum. Arriving there on the
5th of May, he remained until July 1st, and then
set out with Mrs. Baker, and his servant Richarn,
for Berber. They had a narrow escape from ship-
wreck on the rapids of the Nile, and from an Arab
attack in the desert between Berber and the port of
Sowakin, on the Red Sea. But all dangers and difficulties were finally surmounted; after a fortnight's
delay at Sowakin, an Egyptian frigate took them to
Suez, whence Europe was but four days' journey
distant.

Baker not only received the gold medal of the
Royal Geographical Society for his discovery of the
Albert Nyanza, but also the honor of knighthood,
which would have been conferred on Speke, but for
his untimely death. For four years after his arrival

in England, he devoted himself to the narration of his adventures in the Atbara region, Abyssinia, and Ceylon. In the year 1869, the Viceroy of Egypt appointed him to the command of an expedition, the object of which was to reach the Albert Nyanza, navigate it with a small steamer, and open as much as possible of Central Africa to commerce with Egypt.

With the rank of Pasha, a force of 1,600 soldiers, a small iron steamer in compartments, a company of engineers and scientific men, and all requisite supplies, Sir Samuel and Lady Baker left Cairo in 1870, expecting to reach the Albert Nyanza by the close of the following year. After their departure nothing was heard of the expedition for a long time, but intelligence finally came that nearly a year had been consumed in getting the vessels and supplies to Gondokoro. Baker had been obliged to encamp for some months near the mouth of the Sobat, and had only succeeded in getting his steamer through the shallow, marshy regions of the White Nile by cutting a channel which required the labor of three months.

The latest reports, [June, 1872,] not entirely trustworthy, state that the Baris refused to furnish him with porters and provisions; that he had attacked them and was repulsed; that his Egyptian troops had been diminished, by sickness and desertion, to 800, but that the Europeans of the party, encamped near Gondokoro, enjoyed excellent health; and finally, that the further progress of the expedition was not yet assured. But whatever energy and courage can accomplish, under the circumstances, will most certainly be exemplified by Baker and his heroic wife.

THE END.